Essays in Later Medieval History

To Stephan Kuttner

E F Jacob

Essays in Later Medieval History

Manchester University Press

Barnes & Noble Inc., New York

Manchester University Press
316–324 Oxford Road
Manchester 13
England

GB SBN 7190 0304 0

USA Barnes & Noble, Inc.
105 Fifth Avenue
New York

Printed in Great Britain by
Butler & Tanner Ltd
Frome and London

Contents

Preface

Unlike *Essays in the Conciliar Epoch* (1963), this book is not a series of strictly Conciliar studies. There are, indeed, two central chapters on the General Councils of the fifteenth century, but, with two exceptions, the others deal with the life and personalities of the fifteenth century, beginning with a very unorthodox prelate, silenced for his philosophical views, and a very orthodox one, occupied with the administration of justice in Church and State. Working relations with the Roman Curia are illustrated by two studies in which the main subject is William Swan, the English Proctor at Rome. After the two Conciliar chapters (one of them looking at the Council of Constance from an east European angle), the rest of the book is concerned with the thought and institutions of the later medieval period. These are approached through a critique of Huizinga with his thesis of beauty, violence and decline, balanced, I hope, by some reflections on the founders and the corporate foundations of the period, which represent the steady, permanent aspect of the epoch. And lest people should think that medieval England could not be merry, a Rylands lecture on the Book of St Albans has found its way in here.

This lecture, as well as the chapters on recent Conciliar study and on the alchemist John of Roquetaillade, are reproduced from the Bulletin of the John Rylands Library (1944, 1956, 1958), by kind permission of the Librarian and Governors of the Library. I thank the British Academy for permission to reprint the Ralegh Lecture of 1951 on Reynold Pecock; the Council of the Royal Historical Society for permission to reprint 'Archbishop John Stafford' from their Transactions (5th series, 1962); the Committee of the Institute of Historical Research, University of London, for allowing me to reproduce the chapter on 'Founders and Foundations in the later Middle Ages' from the *Bulletin of the Institute of Historical Research*, Volume XXXV; The Committee of the Ecclesiastical History Society for letting me reprint from the first volume of *Studies in Church History*, the article 'Reflections upon the study of the General Councils of the 15th Century' under a slightly different title; and the editors of the *Studies in French Language and Medieval Literature presented to Professor M. K. Pope* (Manchester University Press, 1939), and of *Medieval Studies presented to Dr. Rose Graham* (Oxford University Press, 1950), for Chapters 3 and 5 respectively. I also thank the Warden and Fellows of All Souls College for permission to study and photograph (p. 178) their MS. 81.

The following abbreviations are used:

C.P.L., Calendar of Papal Letters.

C.P.R., Calendar of Patent Rolls.

E.H.R., English Historical Review.

P.R.O., Public Record Office.

Rot. Parl., Rotuli Parliamentorum.

Reg. Chichele, Registrum Henrici Chichele (4 vols. Cant. and York Soc., 1938–47).

V.C.H., Victoria County History.

Chapter I
Reynold Pecock, Bishop of Chichester

Fatuus est enim homo qui sagittat ut destruat solem. Thus Thomas Gascoigne described the man who presumptuously traduced the holy doctors of the Church.[1] To Gascoigne, the bishop who finally ate his own words and abjured all his positions was an example of the nemesis wrought by conceit and impertinence: and Gascoigne further looked upon him as a symptom of the Church's decline in the current age. To a critic early in the present century his fall illustrated the intellectual deadness of his country, its extreme insignificance in the history of intellectual development in Europe.

Truth of proportion [wrote Professor J. L. Morison in 1909] comes only when we set beside England and its sturdy, stupid standards the intellectual illumination of contemporary Florence with some man of action like Machiavelli to serve as prophet and summarize a century's gains and losses. . . . The Lancastrian Englishman, true to the national principle that God works while the farmer sleeps, preferred to leave to Providence ideas wherein no surface cleverness could, in his eyes, atone for possible error, and was satisfied to know that means and end were adjusted to the next day's work without looking for ulterior ideal justification. His land knew nothing of the life lived intellectually for the mere sake of intellect; his rulers were warriors of antique mould, local potentates immersed in hunting and parochial self-assertion.[2]

This, according to Professor Morrison, was the materialist world that Pecock had to face; he is 'the one man of the country who may be classed with the Italians'.

Since this was written, views of Lancastrian England have undergone much change, particularly where the 'sturdy, stupid standards' are concerned: nor does the intellectualist assessment of the Italian Renaissance pass unchallenged. True, this country has never lacked, throughout its history, the type of person for whom

> each good day of sport (and thatt
> the dog knoweth and enjoyeth with his master as well)
> is a thing in itself, whole even as life is one.[3]

---

[1] *Loci e libro veritatum*, ed. Thorold Rogers (1881), p. 217.
[2] *The Book of Faith by Reginald Pecock, Bishop of Chichester* (1909), Introductory Essay, p. 27.
[3] Robert Bridges, *The Testament of Beauty*, book iii, ll. 123–5.

But in the fifteenth century he was in the minority, and the bulk of the upper and middle classes were using their wits in ceaseless and ambitious competition to other ends. It is also tempting to exaggerate the isolation of anyone who opposed conventional orthodoxy and to represent him as a persecuted intellectual, lamentably misunderstood. But this liberal view ignores Pecock's numerous disciples and admirers, and tends to emphasize purely personal factors to the neglect of the larger issues which were slowly being decided in England during this critical period and affected Pecock's life. The political issue was whether a great family which had come by usurpation to the throne could maintain itself in a period of social and economic change against a powerful legitimist reaction by creating a faction, a party, through the use of patronage and the systematic exclusion of its opponents from office and appointment. The religious issue which cut across these party divisions was more complex. There was the problem of how to deal with the forces liberated by the Wycliffite movement; forces encouraged by the naturally satirical and dramatizing temper of a rising middle class, individualist and not infrequently anti-clerical, but in no way anti-religious. The clash between institutional religion and the lay spirit was no new thing: but it was exacerbated by advances in lay education, by the thirst for reading and the corresponding growth of the trades engaged in book-production, by the prominence in the community of the sharp-witted and secularly-minded merchant, and by many other factors. Lollardy, the extreme wing of this movement, had passed through its violent stage by 1417, the year when Sir John Oldcastle was captured and put to death; but the spirit underlying it had worked, if locally and selectively, none the less deeply upon the English countryside and, even more, upon the English town.[1] Measures taken by the royal jurisdiction in co-operation with the courts Christian might well drive it underground, but they could not suppress the groups formed for Bible reading or the unorthodox preaching, as the trials before the Convocation of Canterbury during the pontificates of Arundel and Chichele abundantly show.

The other and more complicated part of the religious issue arose from the situation in the universities, Oxford in particular. At Oxford it was the *De Eucharistia*, Wyclif's lectures delivered at the end of 1380 or the beginning of 1381, that had made it plain

[1] See especially J. A. R. Thomson, *The Later Lollards* (Oxford, 1966).

how far ultra-realist metaphysics were carrying their supporters;[1] yet this *dénouement* did not prevent many of the younger regents from regarding Wyclif's views as *probabiles*, i.e. as capable of being argued in academic disputations, or from remembering the time when his determinations were quoted, just as one might quote Henry of Ghent or FitzRalph of Armagh, as a venerated authority.[2] It is difficult to grasp the situation in the university without being aware that the *actus scholastici* of the leading teachers did not invariably reflect any preponderating system of thought but rather represented the dialectic of skilled demonstrators of method who knew their classic masters and cited them with ease and effect, even when those masters were far removed from the positions which they were themselves expounding. This was the situation which Archbishop Arundel, with his literal and more external view of university disputations, found it difficult to understand. If this was the case with the seculars, recent study has also emphasized how varied were the currents of opinion among the religious at Oxford. *Possessionati* like the Benedictines and Cistercians opposed the new doctrines, but the Mendicants were divided, some of them upholding the Augustinian theory of lordship and grace which Wyclif preached, or on other grounds supporting him against the English hierarchy; others, like William Woodford the Franciscan, or the Carmelites, scenting the danger of Wyclif's position from the start. All these hesitations and divisions still combined to create, in the first two decades of the fifteenth century, a situation of tension and complexity, even though Wyclif was dead and many of his tenets had been declared heretical.

Such was the stimulating scene upon which Pecock made his appearance. Among recent modern works he has been the subject of a London University thesis by Mrs Buckland; of a thoughtful biography by Mr V. H. Green,[3] which corrects many of the statements of Lewis and Babington (the editor of the *Repressor*); and of a close examination both of his life and of the sequence of his

[1] A. Gwynn, *The English Austin Friars* (1940), p. 258.

[2] S. L. Forte, 'A Study of some Oxford Schoolmen of the Middle of the Fourteenth Century, with special reference to Worcester Cathedral MS. F. 65' (Oxford University B.Litt. dissertation, 1948), pp. 110–11. Gwynn, op. cit., p. 229.

[3] *Bishop Reginald Pecock: a Study in Ecclesiastical History and Thought* (The Thirlwall Prize, 1941), Cambridge, 1945.

works by Mr Thomas Kelly, as yet unprinted.[1] The difficulty about
Pecock's career is that he is mainly known from the testimony
and invectives of his opponents, particularly Thomas Gascoigne,
Chancellor of Oxford in 1434, 1442-3, and 1445, the author of
the *Dictionarium Theologicum*; and the equally celebrated John
Whethamstede, twice abbot of St Albans, a personality and a
stylist. Neither Gascoigne nor Whethamstede had any love for
Pecock whom they regarded as a pushing ecclesiastic, given up
to doubtful philosophy when he should have been performing his
duties as a diocesan. The Oxford Chancellor, whose accuracy is
often at the mercy of his emotions, shows himself particularly
bitter and prejudiced.[2] Nor are contemporary chroniclers more
favourable. *The Brief Latin Chronicle*, which James Gairdner
edited as one of his fifteenth-century collection, is most of all
impressed by Pecock's attitude towards Scripture and even charges
him with heretical opinions on the Eucharist; and the *English
Chronicle* published by J. S. Davies for the Camden Society (1856)
shares the popular belief in Pecock's exaltation of reason over any
and every authority. It is not surprising, therefore, that later
biographers in the reforming tradition should have laid stress on
him as a fore-runner of doctrinal change. If only Henry Wharton,
prodigy among manuscript scholars, had had the time to digest
the material he had collected on Pecock, much mistaken emphasis
would have been avoided at a later date. Not that John Lewis
of Margate (whom Hearne detested)[3] and, to a greater extent,
Churchill Babington, Pecock's editor in the Rolls Series, did not
make excellent contributions to their subject; they wrote, how-

---

[1] M.A. dissertation, University of Manchester, 1945, to which I am
generously permitted to refer. For earlier bibliographical notices see
E. V. Hitchcock, *The Folewer to the Donet* (E.E.T.S. 164, 1924), Introduction, pp. xviii–xxiv; and Green, op. cit., pp. 1–7.

[2] I question Mrs Maxwell's statement that while 'admittedly Pecock
was Gascoigne's *bête noire* . . . Gascoigne's interest in him was much less
than has been supposed. . . . He treats the sermon of 1445 as if it were the
central feature of Pecock's work, whereas for Pecock the doctrine that
bishops *qua* bishops were not bound to preach was but a piece of equivo-
cation, as he later confesses', W. A. Pronger (Mrs Maxwell), 'Thomas
Gascoigne', *Eng. Hist. Rev.* liv (1939), 30. It was not only Pecock's views
on preaching, which he modified, but did not basically repudiate, that
shocked Gascoigne, but also (and here again I differ from her) Pecock's
attitude to the doctors of the church, discussed below.

[3] 'That vile, pragmatical, silly Pimp, J. Lewis, a man that is abho-
minated by all orthodox honest men': *Hearne's Collections*, x. 128.

ever, before most of the existing texts of his writings had been studied in a critical way, and before the academic thought of his age had begun to be seriously analysed. Even now there is a particular need for prolonged examination of Pecock's philosophical position. The biographer has also to face the problem of gaps. There are periods of years in Pecock's life at Whittington College, St Asaph, and Chichester, when, in the absence of registers, we know nothing whatever about him apart from his literary works, many of which have perished and are merely alluded to in his extant writings. At certain moments he emerges as a figure of controversy, then sinks back into obscurity.

Reynold Pecock was born in Wales somewhere between 1392 and 1395. The bull of provision issued to him by Eugenius IV for the see of St Asaph terms him priest of the diocese of St Davids;[1] and tradition asserts his connexion with Laugharne in Carmarthenshire.[2] The chronology of his early years is by no means easy: it appears that he entered Oxford University in 1409, graduated B.A. in 1413, and the next year was elected to a fellowship at Oriel College. In 1414 four fellowships were vacant, the first vacancy since 1411, and a note of expenses in the college accounts under the week of the Conception of the Blessed Mary (8 December) indicates that Pecock was a fellow by that date.[3] The termination of his fellowship can now, as Mr A. B. Emden has shown, be placed some time before 25 October 1424, on which day he was instituted to the rectory of St Michael's, Gloucester.[4] In the meantime he had passed through his preliminary orders: he was ordained acolyte and sub-deacon on 21 December 1420 by Bishop Richard Fleming; deacon on 15 February 1421, and priest, probably at Spalding, on 8 March that year.[5] John Carpenter, his Oriel colleague who was to become Bishop of Worcester, was

[1] C[alendar of] P[apal] L[etters], ix. 433.

[2] E. Laws and E. H. Edwards, 'Monumental Effigies in Pembrokeshire', *Archaeologia Cambrensis*, 6th ser., xii (1912), 11, in describing the effigy of Thomas White (d. 1482) in St Mary's Church, Tenby, refer to his mother as the daughter and heiress of John or Jenkin Peacock of Laugharne.

[3] 'In jornall [the day-book] pro preposito et pecok xi d.', G. C. Richards and C. L. Shadwell, *The Provosts and Fellows of Oriel College* (1922), p. 26: the date is given in Dr Shadwell's transcript of Oriel College accounts, fo. 199, a reference I owe to Mr T. Kelly.

[4] *Times Literary Sup.*, 13 October 1945, from Reg. Polton, fo. 92v.

[5] Richards and Shadwell, op. cit., p. 26, from Reg. Fleming (fos. 172–5).

ordained on the same occasions;[1] and William Waynflete, later
Bishop of Winchester, was made deacon when Pecock received
his priest's orders.[2] At Oxford, therefore, during at least ten of his
student years he was a member of a small community consisting
of a provost and ten fellows, all engaged in the study of theology
or the civil or canon law, or in the preparatory courses in the
Faculty of Arts. Oriel was a nursery of Lancastrian bishops: apart
from Carpenter and Pecock himself, Richard Praty, who became
a fellow and resigned about the same time as Pecock, became one
of his predecessors in the see of Chichester (1438–40); and Walter
Lyhert, later Bishop of Norwich and, according to Gascoigne,
Pecock's patron, was one of those elected in 1425, the year after
his resignation from Oriel.[3] It was a society of able men just
emerging, when Pecock graduated, from a domestic struggle
between the supporters and the opponents of Archbishop Arundel
arising from the crisis provoked by the Archbishop's determination to include the university in his metropolital visitation of the see
of Lincoln.[4] Pecock was not unworthy of the company; for the *Brief
Latin Chronicle* describes him as 'ingenio quidem et scientia satis
clarus, et in primeva etate reputatus boni regiminis et honeste fame',[5]
and even Gascoigne calls him 'famoso quondam gradu et scientia'.[6]

For nearly seven years Pecock held the Gloucester rectory. It
is not known if he resided. His next move was to accept, from the
prior and convent of Christ Church Canterbury, the mastership
of Whittington College and the rectory of St Michael Royal. The
presentation is dated 19 July 1431.[7] St Michael in Riola (Royal
Street in Vintry Ward, so called because the wine merchants from

[1] Richards and Shadwell, op. cit., pp. 24–6.

[2] R. Chandler, *Life of William Waynflete* ii (1811), 84 n.

[3] For Praty cf. Richards and Shadwell, op. cit., p. 23 and A. B. Emden,
A Biographical Register of the University of Oxford to A.D. 1500, iii (1959),
1514; *Reg. Praty*, ed. C. Deedes (Sussex Rec. Soc., vol. 4, 1905); *Epistolae
Academicae*, ed. Anstey, I. i. 237; *Reg. Chichele*, I. ix; iii. 242 (as Chancellor of Salisbury). For Lyhert, the Cornishman, later provost, Richards
and Shadwell, pp. 27–8; *Reg. Chichele*, i. 344 (certificate by the President
of Oriel of the archbishop's licence to admit Lyhert as fellow, without
probationary year, 16 July 1425); *Dict. Nat. Biog.* xxxiv. 285; *Loci e
libro veritatum*, p. 40.

[4] *Snappe's Formulary*, ed. H. E. Salter (Ox. Hist. Soc.), pp. 197–205.

[5] *Three Fifteenth-Century Chronicles*, p. 167.

[6] *Loci*, p. 18.

[7] Henry Wharton, *Historia de Episcopis et Decanis Londiniensibus et
Assavensibus* (1695), p. 349, gives the date of the presentation as 19 July

La Réole had made their abode there), was one of the thirteen peculiars of the Archbishop of Canterbury in the City of London. The building was a new one, provided by Richard Whittington, and the new church contained a college founded there in December 1424 in honour of the Holy Spirit, the Blessed Virgin, and the archangel Michael.[1] It was a college of five secular chaplains one of whom was master, two clerks, and four choristers, maintaining an almshouse for thirteen poor persons, and with an income of about £63 a year; the master received a fee of 10 marks, but he was also rector. The appointment of the master lay with the Mercers, and Whittington's executors had arranged with the prior and chapter of Canterbury that the person appointed should also be presented to the rectory. The sole surviving executor was John Carpenter, Provost of Oriel in 1428, and his influence in the appointment of the Oriel graduate may be surmised.[2]

Pecock was master of Whittington College from July 1431 to his appointment in 1444 to the bishopric of St Asaph. The benefice brought him into contact with the city merchant and the

---

1431, citing 'Reg. Eccles. Cant.' (i.e. a Christ Church register). Tanner, *Bibliotheca Britannico-Hibernica*, p. 584, cites Wharton's note from the same source.

[1] The licence of foundation to Whittington's executors is in *Reg. Chichele*, i. 244–5. It was printed in Dugdale, *Monasticon Angl.*, vi. 738–9 from the royal confirmation, C[*alendar of*] P[*atent*] R[*olls*], 1429–36, p. 215.

[2] Kelly, op. cit., p. 24. Mr Kelly points out that another John Carpenter, generally known as John Carpenter, junior (his will is printed by T. Brewer, *Life of John Carpenter*, 2nd ed., 1850, p. 136), was Common Clerk of London and the chief executor of Whittington's will; and that while the relationship between the two Carpenters is obscure, the will of the London citizen makes it clear that the Oriel Carpenter was a close friend, and that he may have suggested Pecock's appointment to his namesake. There is no evidence that it was due to Humphrey, Duke of Gloucester, as Mr Green (op. cit., p. 17) supposes. In 1928 there came to light, on the back of the Broke brass in St Margaret's Parish Church, Barking, an inscription plate and effigies commemorating John Pecock, citizen and vintner of London, who died 4 August 1442, and Lucy his wife. (I owe this to the Rev. Percival Chadwick, some time Vicar of Barking.) This may be the John Pecock who, with others, witnessed (30 August 1429) to the property held at the time of his decease by John Coventry, Alderman of Aldgate Ward and Mayor 1425–6, in the parish of St Mary-le-Bow (*Calendar of Letter Books of the City of London*, ed. Sharpe, *Letter-Book K*, p. 105). A Robert Pecock is also described as citizen and grocer of London, *C.P.R.*, *1452–61*, p. 316. Reynold Pecock may therefore have had relatives in the City.

city rector and he is found taking part in transactions affecting both classes. It was during this time that he plunged into the main work of his life: the attempt, by his writings in English and in Latin, to win back the Lollards to the orthodox faith. While Pecock detested Lollardy and all its works, and in one of his later writings justifies the condemnation of 'the now late brenned men in Ynglond',[1] the positive task of conversion was above all necessary. The clergy ought to labour

for to bi cleer witt drawe men into consente of trewe feith otherwise than bi fier and swerd or hangement; thouӡ y wole not seie that the bothe now seid meenys ben good, so that the former meene be parfitli exercisid, eer it schal be come into the ii[e].[2]

'Cleer witt' meant for him the employment of syllogistic logic: such logic, Pecock thought, could not be gainsaid.

If the Cristen clergie were well avisid of the evydencis whiche myghten prove her bileeve of ech article, and if the seid Cristen clergie wolden gadere the evydencis togidere, ordynatli and formabli, in forme of silogismes, for to have redili and currauntli at honde and at mouthe, whanne ever nede were to make by hem eny profis, and if herwith the Iewis and the Sarracenes wolden ӡeve audience, for to hccre the now seid evydencis to be mynystred to hem in the seid foorme and by sufficient leiser at dyvers tymes, the Cristen clergie schulde convicte, and in maner constreyne, or ellis nede the undirstonding, both of alle Iewis and of alle Sarracenes, to bileeve aftir Cristen feith, and to be convertid therto, where thei wolden or nolden. . . .[3]

It is interesting that such a passage can occur in a work written well on in his literary career: it might have been expected in the early days of optimism, but belief in the deductive method was of Pecock's essence, and he never wavered in upholding it. The disciple whom, in the Book of Faith, he purports to be instructing, reminds him that he had said the same in former works: he had maintained that

resoun which is a sillogisme wel reulid aftir the craft taught in logik, and having ii premyssis, openli trewe and to be graunted, is so strong and so myӡti in all kindis of maters, that thouӡ al the aungels of hevene wolden seie that his conclusion were not trewe, ӡitt we schulde leeve

---

[1] *Book of Faith*, p. 192. The texts cited here are given as found in the printed editions.

[2] *Book of Faith*, p. 139.

[3] Ibid., p. 130.

the aungels seiying, and we schulden truste more to the proof of thilk sillogisme than to the contrarie seiyng of alle the aungels in hevene, for alle Goddis creaturis musten needis obeie to doom of resoun.[1]

It was worthy of James Mill.

In this confident spirit Pecock planned a series of expository works to confute the Lollards and to give the laity a reasoned basis for their belief and the clergy the right replies to the attacks of the 'Bible men'. It was the method rather than the content that was original. Statements of the orthodox faith were not lacking: only recently heretical pressure had evoked the copious *Doctrinale* of Thomas Netter; verbal exposition of church teaching in the vernacular had long been recognized as part of the duty of a parish priest, and had its place in Arundel's constitutions of 1409;[2] and devotional treatises, like the literature that grew up round Richard Rolle, were also multiplying.[3] But Pecock's teaching was meant to be of an analytical kind: he was to argue, not merely to assert. As he observed in his prologue to the *Book of Faith*: it is no good merely setting the authority of the Church over against Lollardy. The Lollards did not accept that authority.

The series of works to be issued he expounded in a kind of prospectus, the *Afore Crier*. Much of the scheme was put into operation while he was master of Whittington. He began with what was to be the key work of the whole series, the *Book* or *Reule*

---

[1] Ibid., p. 174. The disciple refers to *Repressor of over much blaming of the Clergy* (ed. Babington, Rolls Ser., 1860), i. 8: 'Wherefore certis if eny man can be sikir for eny time that there ij premyssis be trewe, he mai be sikir that the conclusioun is trewe; thou3 alle the aungelis in heven wolden sere and holde that thilk conclusioun were not trewe.' Peacock goes on to demonstrate the advantage to the generality 'if a schort compendiose logik were deuysid for al the comoun peple in her modiris langage; and certis to men of court, leernyng the Kingis lawe of Ynglond in these daies, thilk now seid schort compendiose logik were ful preciose' (p. 9).

[2] Wilkins *Concilia*, iii. 215, the first clause of which enjoined the observances of Archbishop Pecham's constitution *Ignorantia sacerdotum*. On the handbooks and collections of instructions on preaching compiled for the clergy cf. G. R. Owst, *Preaching in Medieval England* (1926), pt. iii, and articles 'Sermon' in *Chambers's Encyclopaedia*, xii (1950), and 'Preaching', *Dictionary of Church History*, 3rd ed. by Ollard, Crosse, and Bond (1948), pp. 488–9.

[3] Hope Emily Allen, *Writings ascribed to Richard Rolle, hermit of Hampole* (1927), ch. x–xiii. On the 'classic Middle English tradition' of devotional mysticism cf. Miss Allen's Prefatory Note to *The Book of Margery Kempe*, ed. Meech and Allen, i (1940), p. liv.

B

of Crysten Religioun. Soon afterwards came the *Donet*, a summary
of the *Reule*, probably *The Just Apprising of Holy Scriptures*, two
books of devotion (the *Book of Divine Office* and the *Enchiridion*)
and the *Book of Worshipping* or *of Signs*. A start was also made on
his main apology for the living agents, the *Repressor of over much
blaming of the Clergy*. A number were begun and left half finished.
The most difficult to date in the whole series of Pecock's works is
the *New English Creed*, since it was this book that did much eventually to discredit him. Babington's suggestion that the *New Creed*
was part of the *Book of Faith* is based on a statement by Pecock in
the *Donet* to the effect that the question whether the Apostles
made the creed or not would not be discussed there, but would
be treated in the *Book of Faith*. I am inclined to agree with Mr
Kelly that the *New English Creed* was a separate work, containing
a complete restatement of the articles of the creed based on the
teaching of the New Testament, along with some discussion of
Pecock's reasons for the restatement.[1] I also concur in thinking
that the *Creed* was a late rather than an early work, and one written
after he became a bishop. But a feature that complicates all
attempts to give an exact date to many of his works is the fact that
he did not write his books one after the other: it was his custom,
he says, to work on several books at a time, so that the series
of his writings grew like a fifteenth-century house, bit by bit
around the central hall. This was in fact his metaphor:

Y kepte þis reule þat the former bookis hadden not her fullist and par-
fitist filling and eending eer þan þe latter bigunne bokis were al moost
eendid. And aftir þat y hadde eended the foormer book, y eftsoone ouer
ranne it after the making of þe latir book, ther by y filled ofte aȝen into
gretter plente þe former, so þat y maad my cours fro book to book þat
each of hem my ȝte helpe the oþer to be maad, and þat ech schulde
accorde wiþ oþer and leene to oþer and be joyned and knytt to oþer,
right as chaumbris, parloiris, and manye housis of officis answeren and
cleeven to þe cheef halle for to make of all hem so togidere placid and
knytt oon formal, oon semely, beuteful, esiful and confortable habita-
cioun.[2]

Pecock put copies of the books, when completed, into private
circulation among his friends for their instruction and probably
for their criticism. His friends liked what they read, and had the

[1] Op. cit., pp. 120–2.
[2] *Reule of Crysten Religioun*, ed. W. C. Greet (E.E.T.S. 171, 1927),
p. 22.

books copied, in some cases prematurely, before doubtful passages
had been castigated, so that, as he complains, the 'uncourtesie
undiscrecioun of freends' were responsible for versions which he
was anxious to disclaim. The problem for the bibliographer is to
put these works, only six of which survive today, into the correct
order. It has been suggested that Pecock composed close upon
fifty books and pamphlets, fourteen of which were in circulation
at the time of his trial:[1] though some, it may be suspected, existed
only in very rudimentary form, perhaps as notes or as outlines. At
all events by the time he left Whittington College, in 1444, a
number of his most important English works were complete.

In April of that year he was appointed to the see of St Asaph.
He had attached himself to the party of the Earl of Suffolk, the
anti-war party, and in the *Repressor* he expresses very definite
opposition to the continuance of the struggle with France:

Wolde God that the King of Ynglond wolde sett so myche bisynes
forto conquere and reforme his lond of Ynglond fro this wickid scole
[the Lollards] and fro othere defautis as muche as he doeth about the
conquest of his lond of Normandi and of Fraunce.[2]

It is not clear, however, exactly when this passage was written:
probably at the end of his Whittington period. Gascoigne says
of him rather ambiguously that he was promoted to the bishopric
at the instance of secular lords.[3] It was not a lucrative promotion.
The cathedral church of St Asaph, the palace and manors of the
bishop had been destroyed in 1402 by Owen Glyndwr, doubtless
in retaliation for the part played by Bishop Trevor (1395–1404) in
the deposition of Richard II.[4] In May 1445 Pecock had to petition
the king and secure exemption from all tenths and fifteenths paid
by the clergy.[5] From the diocese Pecock was persistently absent.
Gascoigne says of him that he never visited his bishopric at all,
but lived in London.[6] He was going on with his writing. Shortly
after his appointment he received the doctorate of divinity from
Oxford: Gascoigne who, as Mr Gibson infers, was the source of

[1] By Mr Kelly, op. cit., p. 93.
[2] i. 90.
[3] *Loci*, p. 18.
[4] D. R. Thomas, *The History of the Diocese of St Asaph*, new ed., i
(1906), 66–7. The bishop's houses so destroyed were at Meliden, Bodi-
dris and St Martin's. Trevor later went over to Glyndwr.
[5] *C.P.R., 1441–6*, p. 348.
[6] *Loci*, p. 18.

more stringent regulations for the D.D., remarks that it was granted *per gratiam absentandi* (Thorold Rogers misread this as *per gratiam absurdam*), and that he responded to no doctor to complete his form, nor afterwards lectured as the regulations required.[1] The grace must have been a substantial one.

Yet he could not remain a purely literary bishop. The Suffolk party was bent on creating for itself an influential following in the Church, and before long Pecock found himself one of a group of court bishops, closely connected with the household of the king or the queen, in which they held positions of a more or less minor sort: men like William Ayscough, Bishop of Salisbury since 1438, confessor to the king, the bishop who married Henry and Margaret of Anjou in 1445; Marmaduke Lumley, Bishop of Carlisle since 1430, treasurer in 1446, long a supporter of Beaufort against Gloucester; and more important still, Adam Moleyns, the former clerk to the Council, keeper of the privy seal in 1444 and Bishop of Chichester in 1446. Moleyns, with his literary sense, his culture, and his diplomatic experience must have been particularly attractive to Pecock. Two bishops holding office in the queen's household were her chancellor, William Booth, appointed to Lichfield in July 1447 and later, on Kemp's promotion, to York (1452), whom Gascoigne criticized for his lack of learning and his legalistic bent—'nor is he a good scholar nor a man of learning, nor considered to be virtuous, nor a graduate, but a common lawyer who confers benefices culpably on boys and comparative youngsters';[2] the other, the Oriel prelate alluded to, Walter Lyhert, Margaret's confessor. Lyhert had been provost of Oriel 1435–6; early attached to the Beaufort party, he owed his first benefice of Lamarsh to Margaret Beaufort, daughter of Edward Duke of Somerset. Later, Lyhert became chaplain to Suffolk himself, by whose favour he was promoted in 1446 to the bishopric of Norwich. It was a circle of almost Caroline selectivity.

As a member of this court group, Pecock was exposed to criticism on a number of counts, such as absenteeism and neglect of

---

[1] *Statuta Antiqua Universitatis Oxoniensis*, ed. S. Gibson, pp. xix, 224–5. The inceptor had to be vouched for, both in character and in knowledge, by all the doctors of theology present when the candidate was presented.

[2] *Loci*, p. 52. 'His [Booth's] clerical staff at any rate were above reproach, and, from the formal point of view his Register, covering only twelve years, is a model book', A. Hamilton Thompson, 'The Registers of the Archbishops of York', *Yorks. Arch. Journal*, xxxii (1935), 256.

preaching. These charges irritated him exceedingly and he set himself to repel the accusations. In sermons preached at St Paul's Cross, with the utmost publicity, he denounced his critics and justified his own conduct like that of his colleagues. Both he and Gascoigne have left accounts of the famous intervention on the subject of episcopal preaching, but the latter's dates are very confused. The evidence indicates that there were at least two sermons, in 1447 and 1449, and a possible third, either between those dates or after 1449.[1] The argument, however, was substantially the same: a bishop as such is not bound to preach in person to the people of his diocese. He may, when necessary, assume the duty of preaching to the people, just as he may assume any of the duties of the inferior clergy. Furthermore, bishops may have various adequate reasons for absenting themselves from their dioceses; and there are more important things for the salvation of souls than preaching.[2] If, as Gascoigne states, the bishops approved of this defence, Pecock's thesis none the less aroused great popular indignation. The people, he laments, behaved to him 'in many kyndis vnmanli, vncurteisli, and untrewli'.[3] A good deal of academic opinion, voiced by 'high degreed men in dyuynyte'[4] was gathered against him. His critics were some of the leading scholars, people like Gilbert Worthington, rector of St Andrew's, Holborn; William Lichfield, rector of All Hallows the Great, London, an indefatigable preacher, said by Stowe to have left 3,803 manuscript sermons at his death; Peter Beverley, formerly Bedford's confessor; Thomas Eborall, Pecock's successor at Whittington

---

[1] For Gascoigne's account see *Loci*, pp. 15, 26, 28, 31, 38, 39, 41, 48. The London Chronicle printed in Ralph Flenley, *Six Town Chronicles of England*, p. 121, gives Sunday the 15th day of May (obviously for Sunday, 14 May) 1447. The date 1449, whatever he may have written elsewhere, is vouched for by Gascoigne, *loci*, p. 15, 'haec scribo in veritate anno Domini M^{mo}CCCC^{mo}XLIX°'. He makes one vague reference to 1445, but all the remaining testimony is to 1447 and 1449.

[2] 'Abbreviatio Reginaldi Pecock', in *Repressor*, ii. 615–19. He published his seven conclusions in English and sent copies to Moleyns, Lyhert, and the papal subdeacon, Dr Vincent Clement, the anglicized Spaniard whom Gascoigne called *Doctor insolens*. On Clement, who had represented both Henry VI and Gloucester at Rome and was an influential and wealthy pluralist, cf. R. Weiss, *Humanism in England during the Fifteenth Century* (2nd ed.) 1957, pp. 76–7.

[3] *The Folewer to the Donet*, ed. E. V. Hitchcock (E.E.T.S. 164), p. 105.

[4] Ibid., p. 108. It is a great pity, he notes, to find 'so greet clubbisshenes in so greet graduated dyuynys'.

College; and, above all, Gascoigne of Oxford, whose passionate outpourings under the headings of *praedicare, praedicatio* in the *Dictionarium Theologicum* appear as witness to the shock he received. Apart from Eborall and Gascoigne, it was an attack by a group of progressive Cambridge graduates, incumbents of city livings.[1] In reply to these strictures, Pecock modified his position a little, maintaining that bishops were bound to preach, but not in their capacity as bishops. Throughout the controversy aroused between 1447 and 1450, the people, we are told, complained loudly, crying *Vae episcopis*; and William Millington, the former Provost of King's College, Cambridge, preaching at St Paul's Cross soon after Pecock, declared that the kingdom of England would never prosper till those who favoured Pecock's views on preaching were properly corrected.[2] It should be remembered that this is Gascoigne's account of the matter, and the silence of Oxford need not be attributed to 'fear of displeasing the bishops'. That was scarcely an Oxford characteristic.

Pecock was appointed to the see of Chichester in 1450 after the death, at the hands of the mob, of Bishop Adam Moleyns at Portsmouth. It was the fateful year of the Cade rebellion, the death of Suffolk and the brutal murder of Bishop Ayscough by the people of his diocese. Booth and Lyhert were both subjected to attack, and, as Gascoigne declares, four bishops in the service of the king and queen had to flee for their lives.[3] These disasters, he thought, were probably due to the evil condition of the Church and above all to Pecock's preaching in defence of ecclesiastical abuses. With his mind obsessed with the need for reform, Gascoigne underestimated the strength of purely political factors: the unwise concentration of power in disputed hands, the lost initiative of the Commons, the uncompromising influence of the queen in the government, the use made of the forms of law to cover private rapacity, and much besides. Pecock himself was taking no promi-

---

[1] Worthington, Lichfield, and Millington (below), were Cambridge D.D.s. The two former had been associated with William Byngham in his plan for the enlargement of the original foundation of God's house, and also with plans for establishing schools in the City of London, A. H. Lloyd, *The Early History of Christ's College*, pp. 75, 83. Dr Lloyd gives biographies of Lichfield and Worthington (ibid., pp. 397–9) supplementing the material in *Alumni Cantabrigienses*. See also, Emden, *Biographical Reg. Univ. of Cambridge to 1500*, 368, 417, 652.

[2] *Loci*, pp. 44–5.

[3] Ibid, p. 174.

nent part in politics. His diocesan register has not survived, and very little, apart from routine entries, can be gathered from other sources about his administration.[1] Twice, on 10 November and 11 December 1455, he is found witnessing minutes of the Council; but he never appears, like Lyhert, in the small inner Council which transacted ordinary business.[2] Like many other lords, he absented himself from the second session of the parliament opened by the Duke of York in November 1455.

He was writing hard, and some of his best-known works belong to this period. The *Folewer*, a sequel to the *Donet*, written in 1453; the *Book of Faith*, completed in 1455–6, a supplement to the *Repressor*, which may be closely linked to the series of Latin works on the sacraments which he had composed when he was Bishop of St Asaph; and probably in Latin, the *Book of Matrimony*, the *Book of Baptism*, the *Book of Eucharist*, the *Book of Penance*, and the *Book of Priests*. All these were published, in the sense of being sent to patrons who would do what they could to make them known. By this time, criticism of his works was growing, though there seems no evidence to support Gascoigne's contention that he was summoned before Archbishop Kemp for examination some time between 1452–4. In the prologue to the *Donet* he guards himself elaborately against 'over hasty and vndiscreet awaiters and bacbiters' by asking that in criticizing his works only the meaning of the author and not the mere words employed should be considered;[3] and in the *Folewer* he observes that the malice of some clerks was so great against him that what he had written was little enough defence.[4] In any case he realized that he was running the gauntlet by writing theological argument in English, and warned his readers among the laity that it was not his intention to make theology too easy, for, as it was, they would

[1] From *C.P.R.*, *1452–61*, 323, 343, 346, it appears that he was due to forfeit (25 September 1456) £100 for the escape of Nicholas Brian, a convicted clerk committed to his keeping, from his prison at Chichester, but that some doubt about the circumstances had arisen, and the sheriff of Sussex and others were twice commissioned to inquire about the facts. The outcome is not stated. The other Patent Rolls entries (*1446–52*, 527; *1452–61*, 162, 195, 216, 434) are only concerned with matters of routine.

[2] *Proceedings and Ordinances of the Privy Council*, ed. Harris Nicolas, vi. 262, 275. He appears in summonses to a Great Council in 1454, ibid., pp. 185, 215; as a commissioner (with others) to raise money for the defence of Calais, 1455, ibid., p. 240.

[3] *Pecock's Donet*, ed. Hitchcock (E.E.T.S. 156), p. 4.

[4] *Folewer*, pp. 226–7.

respect the superior learning of clerks.[1] It was never Pecock's plan to write down to his public: there are passages where, in an English work, he deliberately goes into Latin, because the matters discussed are of so high and theological a character that they cannot be expressed in the vernacular. He was too much in earnest to think of vulgarizing his material: he would wrestle painfully with words, and wind prosaically on till his meaning was clear. He had at least the courage to be tedious.

In 1457, at the time of his trial Pecock declared that he would be responsible only for books issued within the last three years. This looks as if criticism had been coming to a head, for if in 1447 it was his preaching that drew attack, and in 1450 his sympathy with the Suffolk party, from 1452 onwards it was the works themselves. Doubt of his orthodoxy now led to a prosecution and trial which, from the four main surviving accounts, is not easy to reconstruct in detail, yet in its main outline is sufficiently clear. It started, according to Gascoigne, owing to a letter sent by Pecock in 1456 to the mayor of London, Thomas Canyng, which Gascoigne calls *valde suspiciosa perturbationis fidei et insurreccionis in regno Anglie.*[2] The mayor sent the letter on to Henry VI, and in another place Gascoigne says that there were to be found in it evidences or 'likely persuasions' to change the *fides* in the kingdom of England and greatly to disturb the people in the realm. The word *fides* certainly refers to the faith rather than to political loyalty to the existing dynasty, as used to be thought, though in that highly charged atmosphere unorthodoxy might be suspected as lying very near rebellion. That people suspected the faith to be in danger from Pecock appears from a letter sent to Henry by John, 1st Viscount Beaumont of Folkingham in Lincolnshire, successively constable and chamberlain of England, a kinsman of the king and a strong Lancastrian, who was later killed at Northampton. That a former supporter of Suffolk should prefer the complaint shows that the charges had little political animus behind them. Beaumont asked for an examination of Pecock's teaching by the archbishop and prelates, and for his punishment, if his errors were established.[3] This was brought before the Council at

---

[1] *Folewer*, p. 7.

[2] *Loci*, pp. 212, 213.

[3] Register of Abbot Richard Asshton, fo. 43, MSS. of Dean and Chapter of Peterborough, printed in *Hist. MSS. Commission, 12th Rep.*, App. ix, 584-5. The date is 24 June (1457).

one of its ordinary meetings, probably at the beginning of October 1457. The Council arranged with Archbishop Bourgchier that an examination of Pecock's works should be made by a special tribunal which was to hear and consider the opinion of a number of expert examiners, question Pecock himself, and report back. In other words, the Council controlled the proceedings, though the verdict of heresy, if it was to be given, lay with the authorities of the Church. This was unprecedented, for an English bishop had not previously been convened for heresy, and, 1554 apart, was not again to be examined until 1890, when Archbishop Benson appointed special assessors (including Bishop Stubbs) to hear at Lambeth the charges made against Bishop King of Lincoln for alleged irregularities in the administration of the Eucharist. But this was a purely ecclesiastical trial, without secular intervention.

On 22 October, therefore, Bourgchier issued his mandate for Pecock's accusers to appear,[1] and the case was handed to the assessors who were due to report on 11 November (Gascoigne's *circa festum Sancti Martini*[2]). A note upon the title of the Cambridge manuscript of the *Repressor* states that on this day the book was 'displayed before the Lord Archbishop in his chapel at Lambeth'.[3] The twenty-four assessors included both seculars and religious: one of them was evidently John Bury, Provincial of the Austin friars, who was apparently commissioned by Bourgchier to examine the *Repressor* and subsequently recorded his conclusions in the *Gladius Salamonis*.[4] Pecock objected to the assessors, asking to be judged not by these doctors but by his peers: not by bishops like John Lowe of Rochester, Chedworth of Lincoln, or Waynflete of Winchester, but by his equals in scholastic disputation.[5] His protest was rejected. The process accordingly had its beginning on 11 November; by the 21st, the opening of the second week, a number of points had been established against him to the satisfaction of the judges, and he agreed, in conformity

---

[1] Printed by J. Foxe, *Acts and Monuments*, ed. J. Pratt (1870), iii. 732.

[2] *Loci*, p. 210. Mr Kelly, in my view correctly, suspects (pp. 197 f.) that Gascoigne has telescoped the account of the trial which lasted from 11 November (the report of the assessors) to 28 November (the meeting of the Great Council).

[3] Babington, *Repressor*, i. lxii.

[4] Excerpts are ibid. ii. 567–624. For the assessors cf. Green, op. cit., pp. 52–3.

[5] *Loci*, p. 212.

with their findings, to revoke certain of his conclusions. The full
indictment against Pecock was thereupon sent to the Council
which met at Westminster on 28 November. This was a gathering,
Whethamstede says, 'with many magnates from various parts of
the kingdom present'.[1] Evidently it was a Great Council, not an
ordinary meeting of the routine or 'continual' Council. In it the
archbishop gave Pecock the formidable choice of abjuration or of
degradation and delivery to the secular arm for burning. In this
cruel dilemma, Pecock, as a true son of the Church, elected to
abjure. Writers have spoken of his choice as a mean recantation
or as 'miserable cowardice', but Pecock had never contended that
the individual could successfully challenge the Church's authority.[2] When sending his works to be examined, he had specifically
stated that 'if any things were contained there contrary to the
Catholic Faith, he did not wish to hold them'. He had considered
himself free to speculate within the general framework of the
Church's teaching, and he had undoubtedly carried speculation
to daring limits; but the Church had given its decision against
him, and he was prepared to obey. His abjuration was in two
phases: at Lambeth on Saturday, 3 December, he repudiated six
points in Latin,[3] which were deductions from his work on the
Creed, where for *belief in* he had substituted *belief in the existence
of*: e.g. he was charged with holding that it is not necessary to
believe in the Holy Spirit; or to believe in the Holy Catholic
Church.[4] One of his tenets, that it is not necessary to salvation to
believe that Our Lord Jesus Christ after death descended into

---

[1] There is a conflict between Gascoigne (p. 214), who describes a meeting at Lambeth on Monday, 28 November, at which there were present
the archbishop, bishops and doctors, Lord Thomas Stanley, Lord Scales,
and many knights, and Whethamstede, who says that it took place at
Westminster in the presence of the king, the archbishop, and many
magnates from various parts of the kingdom (*Reg. Abbat. Jo. Whethamstede*, i. 281–4). The available evidence points to a meeting of the Great
Council at Westminster on that day.

[2] 'His recantation was in accordance with the views which he had put
forward time and time again', Green, p. 56.

[3] Printed in J. Lewis, *Life of Reynold Pecocke* (1820), p. 160, note e.
Evidently Babington refers to the same document in *Repressor*, i. p. xlvi,
n. 2.

[4] E.g. *Book of Faith*, pp. 283–4. On the article of the Creed, *I believe in
the Holy Catholic Church*, he says: 'We ben not tauȝt as bi strenghte of
thilke wordis for to bileeve other than this, that oon hole universal chirche
is, and what folowith thereof.'

Hell, came from the *Book of Faith*.[1] The Latin points were included within the formal abjuration made the next day, Sunday, 4 December, at St Paul's Cross, which had an English prologue and an English termination,[2] and at this ceremony three large books and nine sets of quires were thrown into a large bonfire lit near by; a similar holocaust (the number of books unspecified) took place at Carfax on 17 December.

Pecock had written to uphold the Christian religion and to show that belief in the institutions prescribed by the Church was reasonable even before it was commanded. The English part of the recantation at St Paul's makes the source of his errors clearer. He was made to confess and acknowledge that 'here before this tyme, presuming of mine natural wit and preferring mine judgement and natural reason before the New and the Old Testament and the auctorite and determinacioun of our Mudder Holie Church', he had written and taught otherwise than the Roman and Universal Church taught. At the end of the English statement Pecock, as was customary, submitted to the correction of the Church and the archbishop. Although suspended and, for the time being in the archbishop's custody, he was not deprived of his bishopric as the result of the trial. This is clear from the royal and other letters copied by a contemporary hand into the Ashmole Letter-book (MS. Ashmole 789) from which Foxe, Wharton, Baker, and others drew their material for the events after the trial, and from it the narrative of Pecock's fate can be constructed. If Archbishop Bourgchier took all possible measures to extirpate Pecock's heretical ideas, there was, since the bishop had submitted, no reason to deprive him, provided that he made his peace with Rome. Pecock took steps to secure absolution and reinstatement, and at Pope Calixtus III's direction, John Stokes, Bishop

---

[1] Ibid., p. 304. Cf. *Whethamstede Reg.* i. 280. The remarks of Green (pp. 174–81) on the Descent are valuable.

[2] The public recantation exists in a number of forms. The most authentic is in Bodl. Lib., MS. Ashmole 789, fo. 303v (old foliation, 138). From this both Wharton and Baker copied it and Babington drew upon Wharton's text in Wharton MS. (Lambeth Lib.) 577, to insert it in *Repressor*, Introd., i, pp. xlvii–xlix. With this version *C.P.L.* ix. 77–8 is in conformity. The *English Chronicle* gives only four of the six points, and is followed by Stowe, *Annals* (1507), p. 402 and by Holinshed (1577), ed. H. Ellis (1807–8), iii. 245–6. *Whethamstede Reg.* i. 285–7, gives a Latin version, with a seventh point, on the interpretation of Scripture, which seems apocryphal.

of Ely, as the archbishop's commissary, absolved him of all sentences of punishment and excommunication.[1] Pecock's enemies, however, while gloating over his deplumation (*sic deplumatus pavo fuit*, wrote the Abbot of St Albans) were not satisfied with his limited disgrace. Critical of the papal commission to Bourgchier to absolve Pecock and restore him to his good fame, they attempted, when Pius II succeeded to the tiara in 1458, to secure a reversal of the decisions of his predecessor. They represented to Henry VI that Pecock had infringed the 'laws and statutes provisours' by surreptitiously purchasing from the Pope for his 'declaracioun and restitution' contrary to the royal prerogative.[2] It seems that Pecock had recovered his breath somewhat, for the Papal commission emphasized his good intentions in circulating his carefully corrected tractates, and the wording of the bull normally follows the actual tenor of the petition. Henry thereupon ordered Thomas Bird, Bishop of St Asaph, and Dr Robert Stillington, Archdeacon of Taunton and keeper of the privy seal, to acquaint themselves with the 'effect and content' of the Papal letters, to consult on the matter 'as many of the moost famous doctours in Theologie and Lawe as ye shal thinke moost necessarie', and to report before Christmas 1458 to the Council. To catch Pecock out in an offence against the Provisors legislation (clearly the Great Statute of *Praemunire* was the enactment they had in mind) was a clever move, and from the famous doctors in law as much as in theology his opponents got the answer they wanted. It was that 'Reynold distrueth not oonly the pouair and iurisdiction of Regalite and Presthode and so seemingly subuertethe all order and direction of the lawe positive and polletique governauncis among cristen pouple aswel in spiritualite and temporalite, but also dispiseth and anulleth thauctorite of al holy scripture . . .' Henry, the report continues, should acquaint the Pope with the facts and ask for Pecock's deprivation, on the ground that it is dangerous to have 'such an ungracious and corrupted person to stonde in the state of prelacie'. For Pecock has already been proved a heretic, and it is thought by us all that by canon law the Church of Chichester is already *ipso facto* vacant. The report ends by recommending the king to seize the temporalities of the see. The document, un-

---

[1] *C.P.L.* ix. 77–8, 178. This implies that he had been suspended. His resignation is assigned '*post* 4 Dec., in 1957' in *Handbook of British Chronology*, 2nd ed., p. 217. But cf. below.

[2] MS. Ashmole 789, fo. 322.

dated in the formulary, was subscribed by Bird, Stillington, and the twenty doctors consulted.[1]

Henry thanked his commissioners for their pains, and sent two emissaries, the prothonotary Dr John Derby, and his chaplain, Gilbert Haydock, to Pecock, suggesting resignation, with a promise of a competent pension, but adding that if the king was forced to report on him to the Pope, the latter would ask for the utmost rigour of the law to be inflicted.[2] It was then that in all probability Pecock resigned. The actual date must have been somewhere in the autumn of 1458, for he figures in the Patent Rolls on 8 August that year,[3] and the king's commission to Bird and Stillington, alluded to above, is dated St Albans, 17 September (1458). Pecock's position during the summer is revealed by an entry in Archbishop Bourgchier's register. On 27 July Bourgchier collated the prebends of Highley and Wisborough to two Chichester canons who were making an exchange, Wisborough being said to belong 'ad nostram collacionem premissorum occasione hac vice'. In notifying the dean and chapter, Bourgchier expounded his right to collate:

Thomas . . . ad quem omnis et omnimoda iurisdiccio . . . quas episcopus Cicestrensis suffraganeus noster pro tempore existens solebat exercere, confratre nostro domino Reginaldo Cicestrensi episcopo ab huiusmodi administratione et exercicio iurisdiccionis predicte ex certis causis iam cessante, tam de iure quam de prerogativa ecclesie nostre Cantuariensis eciam de consensu dicti confratris nostri notorie dinoscuntur pertinere, dilectis in Christo filiis . . .[4]

Pecock, for the reasons we know, was not functioning as a diocesan and had 'consented' to the archbishop exercising the jurisdiction and administration where the bishop would normally act, just as if the see was vacant. His successor, John Arundel, Archdeacon of Richmond, was provided by Pius II on 8 January 1459,[5] but the

[1] Ibid, fos. 322v, 323.

[2] Ibid., fo. 323v. Derby, LL.D., was Rector of Marston Moretaine, dioc. Lincoln, and of Cranfield (C.P.L. xi. 591); for his chancery appointment cf. Cal. Close Rolls, 1454-61, pp. 49-50, 205. Haydock, S.T.M., described as serviens regis and in receipt of a livery therefrom, was to benefit by the measures taken against Pecock's adherents, C.P.R., 1452-1461, 465. He was prebendary of St Asaph (ibid., p. 462) St Stephen's Westminster (ibid., p. 510), and Tamworth (ibid.).

[3] Ibid., p. 434.

[4] Reg. Bourgchier, ed. Du Boulay (Cant. & York Soc.), p. 244.

[5] C.P.L. xi. 377.

bull of provision had not arrived by 4 February, when Bourgchier in instituting to the vicarage of Chidham, described the see as 'then vacant by the free resignation of lord Reginald'.[1] This disposes of the story that Pecock was deprived.

Yet his resignation was not sufficient for his opponents. It was alleged that he still retained certain heretical works in English and in Latin which had not been published at the time of his examination and had been deliberately concealed. On this ground representations were addressed to the Pope for another inquiry, and Archbishop Bourgchier, Bishop Thomas Kemp of London, and Bishop Waynflete of Winchester were commissioned to investigate the alleged concealment and to ascertain whether Pecock was properly penitent or not, the remaining books to be destroyed.[2] As far as we know, no action was taken on the mandate so issued. At some date in 1459 Bourgchier gave instructions to the Abbot of Thorney near Peterborough concerning the treatment of Reynold Pecock who was being placed in his charge. He was to be provided with a secret closed chamber with a chimney (fire-place) and a house of easement, within the abbey. He was to have a servant to make his bed and his fire, as should be necessary. He was to be made as physically comfortable as the circumstances of close confinement might permit, but he was to have no books to read except a breviary, a mass book, a psalter, a legend, and a bible, and he was to have 'no thing to write with, ne stuff to write upon'.[3] And there, at Thorney, probably in his sixty-sixth year, he died.

It is not difficult to understand why Pecock's writings both attracted and repelled. It was impossible to ignore a man who had the courage to use an English philosophical vocabulary which he had to create for himself in the dialect of the East Midlands, and to do so when the sounds and the spellings of English were continually changing, when, in his own words, the 'seid langagis ben not stabili and foundamentali written':[4] one not afraid to write in the plain style, as Wyclif had done,[5] and to make use of

[1] *Reg. Bourgchier*, pp. 249–50.

[2] *C.P.L.* xi. 529.

[3] MS. Ashmole 789, fo. 326. Hearne, who was interested in the method of Pecock's so-called deprivation, inserted in his diary (*Hearne's Collections*, x. 388) a copy made by Baker who sent it to him on 14 February 1731. He was unable to consult the Ashmole formulary (ibid., p. 418).

[4] *Book of Faith*, p. 251.

[5] E. V. Hitchcock, *Folewer*, Introd., p. lvii.

a wealth of pertinent illustrations to his points. Contemporaries would observe with interest his reference to 'hem whiche maken long parliament spechis'; to the lawyers of the Inns of Court laboriously discussing the statutes of the realm during vacation; to the apprentices of city magnates who do much better by serving in the shop than by escorting their masters through the streets of London; or to 'the oolde symple widowe or oolde symple husbonde man' living 'in a large wyde parishe, vp londe'. The more imaginative would note in the *Reule* the passage where he sees 'a multitude of persoonys ful comely and faire, as it were out from derkenes or a desolate cloude forþ going', the ladies (had they *intelletto d'amore?*) representing the long-exiled truths of philosophy, who offered themselves to clerks, but the clerks had turned away;[1] or the place where he discusses the pleasures of the saved, enjoying 'famyliarite had with worþier persoonys, and with her lovid persoonys, as to talke wiþ hem, to handle and fele þem, to se þem, here hem and be nyȝ to hem';[2] and some might appreciate the common sense of a man ready to maintain that 'perauenture more perel schal befalle in ouer greet pouerte than in ouer grete richessis'.[3] On the other hand, if he did not deter some readers by his prolixity and his persistence, he clearly did so by his vanity and by the blatant way in which he recommended and advertised his own writings on all convenient occasions (*iactantia et laus suorum opusculorum*, Bury called this). His arguments, he says, are so strong that they will convert all Jews and heathens as well as Christians: they are unconverted because they have not had the arguments put to them convincingly: 'god amende alle defautis and among alle oþer þes defautis þat clerkis han not laborid to fourme out cleerli such now seid arguments'. One of the reasons, he says, why he was writing his books in English and in Latin was to instruct religious orders in what the founders of those orders, notably 'St Benet and St Austyn', intended that they should learn or teach. Reading these books should, for the monks,

---

[1] *Reule*, ed. Greet, p. 32: cf. p. 36: 'whilis y was with þis cumpanye y-visited so hevenly and after y ȝaf graunt to receive and suffre alle her owne benevolent demeenyng attrettly, in an vndeclarable cherisching and chast maner ech of hem oon aftir an oþer me beclipped and in me embreþid, and whilis wiþ ech of hem y was in hondis so occupied and demeened a special trouþe y receivid.'

[2] Ibid., p. 146.

[3] *Repressor*, ii. 304.

be as 'vnlakable and an vnleuable daily obseruaunce'.[1] One can imagine how this would be received by the religious, particularly by the assessors to whom Bourgchier submitted the works.

To his critics the rock of offence was the place assigned in his system to reason, as opposed to the authority of the Bible, the Fathers and the Church. The *Brief Latin Chronicle* sums up the views of his opponents. 'In many points despising the catholic faith, holding cheap the sanctions and sayings of the holy doctors and the fathers, nay more the supreme truth of Holy Scripture, he extolled the dictates of the human reason in many things. Whence, like a second Lucifer estimating and elevating himself above others, he revived certain poisonous heresies already condemned and added new ones of a sufficiently dangerous kind.'[2] Of Pecock's attitude to the scriptures, Gascoigne says: 'he put forward the law of nature above the scriptures and above the sacraments', and he complains bitterly of Pecock's rejection of St Gregory's maxim, *Fides non habet meritum cui ratio humana praebet experimentum.* Even more distressing to Gascoigne was Pecock's apparent 'vilipending' of the Fathers: the second great complaint against the bishop, he said, was that he set little value upon or actually repudiated the works and writings of the holy doctors of the Church, St Jerome, St Augustine, and the blessed Ambrose, saying *Vath* about their writings, unless they proved their sayings by natural reason.[3]

Both in the *Repressor* and in the *Book of Faith* Pecock maintained that if the Church holds any article as faith, every member of the Church is bound under pain of damnation to accept it as such, and obey the Church, even though the Church is in error, unless he can surely prove the Church to be wrong—which Pecock thought the Lollards unable to do. If it so be that the Church is mistaken, in spite of all its efforts to discover the truth, it must be excused of God, and so must the laity who have been so guided by it. This admission, that the Church can err, is of a purely theoretical kind. It is a thinkable proposition, but it does not follow from one's statement of it that the Church actually *does* err. When Pecock, in the passage we quoted above, maintains that we ought to believe a syllogism even though the angels in heaven denied it, he is saying the same sort of thing: and in the latter

[1] *Reule*, pp. 421, 423.
[2] *Three Fifteenth-Century Chronicles*, p. 167.
[3] *Loci*, pp. 211, 214.

context he significantly adds: 'Nevertheless, sone, of this that y
now have grauntid to thee, folowith not that the chirche in erthe
errith, or may erre in mater of faith, no more than folowith of my
graunt that the chirche now in hevene errith or may erre in feith.'[1]

Pecock's views on the authority of the Fathers were strongly
influenced by the historical cast of his mind. It was, within the
limits of its age, a sceptical mind, as it reflected, for example, on
the difficulties of securing agreement among the eyewitnesses of
an historical event:

Verili, as y may trowe, thorouȝ al the tyme of werre during these xl
ȝeer bitwixe Ynglond and Fraunce, wist y not scant iii or iiii men,
whiche wolden accorde thorouȝ out, in telling how a toun or a castel
was wonne in Fraunce, or hou a batel was doon there, thouȝ thilk men
were holden riȝt feithful men and trewe, and thouȝ ech of hem wolde
have swore that it was trewe what he tolde, and that he was present and
sawe it.

A tale after it has run through three or four men's mouths 'takith
pacchis and cloutis, and is chaungid in dyvers parties, and turned
into lesingis, and al for defaute of therof the writing'.[2] Yet the
writing needs careful examination, particularly if it is of a con-
troversial nature like the Donation of Constantine which he feels
bound to reject, principally on the ground of the testimony of
Eusebius that Constantine was baptized in Nicomedia after Pope
Silvester was dead: if Constantine made any gift, it was 'oonli with
possessions competentli and mesurabli', for the great estates of the
Roman Church 'came by othere persoones long after Constantyn'.[3]
Again, in the *Book of Faith*, he argues that Moses and Esdras
wrote from existing written records and not from divine inspiration; and in the *Donet* he maintains that the Apostles' Creed was
not in fact composed by the Apostles, but by 'prelatis of the
Chirche after the tyme of the apostlis'. This led him, as we noted,
to reject the contention of Duns Scotus that it was a necessary
article of faith that Christ after death descended into Hell: 'in the
tyme of Austyn, and of othere holi clerkis about Austyn's tyme,
the comune crede hadde not withynne himself this seid article.
. . .'[4] Though his book on the *Just Apprising of Doctors* has perished, his views are clear enough: constantly he reverts to the

---

[1] *Book of Faith*, p. 176.
[2] Ibid., pp. 251–2.
[3] *Repressor*, ii. 351–3, 358–9.
[4] *Book of Faith*, p. 304.

c

theme that the writings of doctors, even of the Fathers, must be
judged according to the canons of reason:[1] they must not be
regarded as inspired or accorded any special authority, save only
that in matters of faith we should pay special heed to 'wise holi
lettred clerks whiche lyued in tyme of the apostlis as holy jerotheus,
holy dyonise, and suche othere if eny mo suche be founde'.[2]
When he came to discuss the earliest forms of monasticism, it is
interesting to find him citing, along with St Jerome's letter xxii
(ad Eustochium), as 'moost groundabli of alle other witnessing'
the statements of Philo of Alexandria preserved in Eusebius about
what he saw in Rome during the time of the Emperor Claudius.[3]
His patristic range, while eclectic, is considerable: he knew Chry-
sostom as well as any Lollard apologist.

As far as matters of faith are concerned the authority of the
Bible was for Pecock unquestionable. To ground truths of faith
is, he says, the primary function of scripture: 'it witnesseth al
the feith, or ellis at the lest, well nygh al the feith which Christ
seeketh of us'.[4] But he drew a distinction between the authority
of different parts of holy scripture. In the *Reule* he could segregate
three types of material to be found there. First, the truths of faith,
beyond the scope of reason, though not repugnant to it, such as
the Trinity of Persons in the Unity of substance. Here the text
should be taken, as far as possible, in the literal sense, and the
function of reason is merely to determine what that sense is, if
necessary reconciling the inconsistencies. Secondly, historical
statements of fact, e.g. that this or that king 'dide such a victorie'
or that 'such a persoon came of such a fadir and hadde such a
progenie'. In this, Pecock is referring to historical matter of a
non-supernatural kind (supernatural historical facts like the

[1] E.g. *Repressor*, ii. 320; *Folewer*, pp. 66–7; *Reule*, p. 464.

[2] Ibid., p. 462. Pecock's devotion to the Pseudo-Denys is marked: cf.
especially *Repressor*, i. 61, 170; ii. 418, 425, 446, 459, 460, 532; *Book of
Faith*, pp. 185, 188, 189, 193 ('holi and wys and passing clerk Denyse,
the disciple of Paul'), 257; *Reule*, pp. 313, 462. He refers to the *De Celesti
Hierarchia* ('Hevenly Ierarchie'), the *De Ecclesiastica Hierarchia* ('Chirchis
Ierarchie') and the *De Divinis Nominibus* ('Goddis Namyngis'), which he
may have known in the versions by Grosseteste (S. Harrison Thomson,
The Writings of Robert Grosseteste, p. 55); he may, like both Utred of
Boldon and Wyclif, have had access to Grosseteste's commentaries on
these works (described by Thomson, op. cit., pp. 78–9). Traditionally,
Pecock took the Pseudo-Denys for St Paul's disciple.

[3] *Reule*, p. 422.

[4] *Book of Faith*, p. 253.

Creation, the Incarnation, &c. he classified as truths of faith). To such matter we should give 'credence', if our reason assures us that the source of the statement is trustworthy. Thirdly, there are moral and spiritual imperatives which commend themselves to natural reason: e.g. that prayer and praise should be given to God, that we should be truthful, behave decently to other Christians, be temperate, and so forth. Their acceptance depends on their being shown to be 'ful accordaunt to the doom of natural resoun'.[1] A good example of his method, particularly as concerns the third category, is seen in the passage of the *Donet* where he examines the interpretation of the Third (our Fourth) Commandment, *Remember to keep holy the Sabbath day*. Certain doctors, he says, read into this commandment the implication that everyone should set aside a special time for the service of God, and that this special time should be Saturday. The first of these ideas, says Pecock, is 'moral in law of kynde': it applies to Jews, Christians, 'and all nations' because to devote certain times to prayer and thanksgiving to God is enjoined by natural reason, and the keeping of holidays and festivals 'lawfully ordeined by comune assent of the Chirche' is part of the duty of Christian people; but as regards the observance of the actual day, it cannot be proved that Christ substituted the Christian Sunday for the Jewish Saturday, nor indeed that the Apostles made any specific ordinance for the keeping of Sunday: the hallowing of Sunday, the day of Christ's resurrection, grew up in the course of time 'bi doom of good pollitik resoun and profitable governaunce and good reule' and people observed it 'withoute comaunding of þe prelatis in þo daies'.[2]

In the *Folewer to the Donet* Pecock lays down that reason is the final authority for all matters of divinity other than beliefs acceptable as truths of faith. All books have for their final authority the Bible or the doom of reason.[3] But the clearest statement of his attitude towards scripture comes in the *Repressor*. Here in the first part he is inveighing against three 'trowings' or opinions of the Lollards: (1) That no ordinance of governance of the Church is to be deemed a law of God unless it is grounded in the New Testament or the Old. (2) That every humbleminded Christian shall without fail arrive at the true sense of every passage of scripture. (3) That when the true sense of scripture has been

[1] *Reule*, pp. 461–2.
[2] *Donet*, pp. 128–32.
[3] *Folewer*, pp. 8–11.

discovered in the manner aforesaid, the discoverer should listen to
no argument of clerks to the contrary.[1] In refuting (1) he shows
that no truth of God's moral law is fully taught by scripture alone;
and consequently no truth of natural religion is grounded on
scripture. He argues that that only is the *ground* of anything upon
which it would rest if you took away all other alleged grounds;
but the truth of the moral law, God's law, does not in fact rest
upon scripture, but on the judgement of the reason. For on many
points of right conduct and behaviour scripture is silent:

I preie thee Sir, seie to me where in Holi Scripture is ʒoven the hundrid
parte of the teching upon Matrimonie which y teche in a book mad
upon *Matrimonie*, and the *firste* parte of *Christen religioun*; and ʒit rede
who so wole thilk book *Of matrimonie*, and he schal fynde al the hool
teching of thilk book litel ynouʒ or over litle forto teche al what is
necessarie to be leerned and kunnen upon matrimonie. . . . For thouʒ
Paul bidde ofte that a man schulde love his wif and that the wiyf
schulde obeie to hir husbande, ʒit what is this to kunnyng of matri-
monye in it silf, and into the propirtees of it, and into the circumstauncis
of it, withoute which matrimonie is not vertuose?

Seie to me al where in Holi Scripture is ʒoven the hundrid parti of the
teching which is ʒoven upon usure in the thridde parte of the book
yclepid *The filling of the iiij tablis*. . . . Is there eny more writen of vsure
in al the Newe Testament save this, Luke vjº c(apitulo) *ʒeue ʒe loone,
hoping no thing ther of?*[2]

Pecock argues that the moral law is not founded on the Old or
New Testament, but is written 'in the book of lawe of kinde
written in mennis soulis with finger of God as it was so grounded
and written before the daies of Abraham and of Jewis'.

Again, whatever provides incentives to men to keep certain
laws does not thereby become the *ground* of those laws: it is no use
mistaking an agency for a fundamental and originating cause; and
he takes an example:

If the King of Ynglond dwellid in Gascony, and wolde sende a noble
longe letter or epistle into Englond, both to iugis and to othere men that
each of them schulde kepe the pointis of the lawe of Englond, and thouʒ
he wolde reherce the pointis and governauncis, vertues and trouthis
of the lawe; . . . ʒit it ouʒte not to be seid that thilk epistle grounded
eny of the lawis or governauncis of Englond, for her ground is had to
hem before thilk epistle of the king, and that by acte and decre of the

---

[1] *Repressor*, i. 5–7.
[2] Ibid., pp. 15–16.

hool Parliament of Englond which is verry ground to alle the lawis of Englond, thouȝ thilk epistle of the king or of the Duke had not be writun. . . .[1]

Pecock's answer to the Lollard theology lies in a definition of faith which emphasizes the intellectual element. Faith is the species of knowledge that man acquires, not by his natural reason, but from another person who may not lie, or from God.[2] Reason comes in when, in order to believe, we are called upon to determine the probability of the evidence; and in that evidence there may be degrees of likelihood, ranging from strong probability to the certainty attaching to revelation. Faith, then, is a kind of knowing ('kunning') and involves a certain exercise of rationality. The definition is obviously influenced by the well-known assertion of St Thomas that faith is *cognitio quaedem*: but, St Thomas continues, *deficit a ratione cognitionis quae est in scientia*.[3] Pecock, however, impressed by the varying quality of the assurance of certainty, is led into an un-Thomist distinction between 'opinional' and 'sciential' faith, which his opponents were not slow to mark.[4] It is quite true, as St Thomas maintains, that faith must command the assent of the intellect; but the assent is given not because the thing believed is reasonably likely, but because it is a supernatural truth related to the ultimate end of man.[5] To put faith, as Pecock in the *Folewer* did, among the 'kunningall virtues' enhances neither faith nor the intellect.[6]

Just as it is the function of scripture to teach and reveal truths of faith, so commonly it is to be inferred that the scriptures must be reasonable if they are to be believed. Besides grounding truths of faith, the other function of scripture is to 'reherse and witnesse

---

[1] Ibid., pp. 21–2.

[2] *Book of Faith*, pp. 123–4. 'Feiþ takun propirli is a knowyng wherbi we assenten to enyþing as to trouþ, for as mych as we have sure euydencis, or ful notable likeli euydencis grettir þan to the contrari, þat it is toold and affermyd to us to be trewe bi him of whom we have sure euydencis, or notable likeli euydencis grettir þan to þe contrari, þat þerinne he not lyed', *Folewer*, p. 62.

[3] *Summa Theologica*, i. 12, art. 13, *ad* 3.

[4] *Book of Faith*, book i, ch. iii: *Folewer*, pp. 63–4.

[5] *Summa Theologica*, ii. 22, art. 3, *concl.*

[6] 'Nous ne saurions voir dans la croyance une violence quelconque imposée à notre raison. La foi à l'incompréhensible confère, au contraire, à la connaissance rationelle sa perfection et son achèvement', E. Gilson, *Le Thomisme* (1927), p. 47.

moral trouthis of law of kinde grounded in moral philosophie;
that is to say in doom of reason'. The reader of Pecock's works
will find it hard to give a single all-sufficing definition of this key
expression which constantly recurs. Sometimes doom of reason
seems to mean philosophy as such: sometimes it is made identical
with the law of God, constituting with the will a natural virtue;
in which case it is a sort of moral imperative, and to Pecock, as
Mr Green has aptly put it, the natural virtues, of which reason
is the chief, are 'the real potentials of human action, the com-
manders of the kunningall and moral virtues which in themselves
cover most aspects of thinking and acting'.[1] On other occasions
doom of reason seems to stand for the conclusions reached by the
dialectical process. In whatever sense he uses the term, it does,
however, seem that he had pondered with more care than most
the famous Quaestio II of Part I of the *Summa Theologica: utrum
Deum esse sit demonstrabile*, where St Thomas is arguing that the
facts about God which reason can discover are not articles of
faith, but preambles to those articles:[2] we may prove that God
exists and that he is one, but not that there are Three Persons; we
may find arguments for the immortality of the soul but not—he
might have added—for the resurrection of the body. Faith, as
St Thomas says, presupposes natural knowledge and perfects it.
The truth is that reason can establish conclusions preliminary to
the fuller understanding that comes only through faith.

Sic enim fides praesupponit cognitionem naturalem. If Pecock had
made *doom of reason* the intuition of a verity which is the natural
precursor to what we are asked, in scripture or revelation, to
believe about it, all would have been well. But he went beyond
this Thomist foundation, not only to expound his own version
of the Creed, but to offer a new list of moral virtues, which he
claimed to be better and more comprehensive than the ten commandments, in his *Four Tables* of the 'meenal' and 'eendal'
virtues: more comprehensive, since the Commandments did not
claim to be all-inclusive, and Our Lord clearly implied that they
were not.[3] It seems therefore that in condemning Pecock's *Four
Tables* and his Creed, the English Church authorities were on
firm ground. But the destruction of the carefully corrected philo-

[1] Green, pp. 133–4.
[2] i. 2, art. 2, *ad* 1. Cf. W. H. V. Reade, *The Christian Challenge to
Philosophy* (1951), p. 101.
[3] *Reule*, pp. 365–6, 378 f.

sophical works was, if inevitable, a more unfortunate thing, and it is here legitimate to see, in its united effect, the influence of two main parties: first the academic philosophers proper, the fifteenth-century followers of teachers like Wodham and Holcot, who had moved far in the direction of logical scepticism, even so far as to maintain, as Richard Billingham did, that all experience may be illusory, since the certainty contained in a cognition does not afford evidence of the existence of anything beyond the cognition, and does not even guarantee the existence of the self, as Augustine contended. The origin of much of this type of argument lay in Ockham's declaration that God could produce an intuition without producing its corresponding object. Along with this scepticism which represented reasoning as the logic of signs and seemed to deny the existence of metaphysics as the Thomist and Scotists had understood it, went a theology which denied the possibility of intuition and maintained that our concepts of the deity being nominal, we having no means of comparing them with the real; that all judgements proceed from faith, and the truths that we are incapable of knowing save by revelation cannot be known as we know other truths.[1] One can imagine with what impatience Ockhamists of this school would read Pecock's passages upon doom of reason. The great separation of philosophy and theology had taken place in the fourteenth century, and there was no resisting the current now. It is to be noted in passing that immediate steps were taken in Oxford to counteract Pecock's doctrines. Not only did the university write on 11 November 1457 to Bourgchier asking for copies of the works of a certain reverend father who had put before the people a new doctrine and discovered a new faith:[2] but the king in 1458 wrote to the university asking that the doctor's degree in theology should not be granted to Master John Harlow, a supporter of Pecock, who was about to incept. Henry directed that any supporter of Pecock should be prevented from taking 'any further degree there'. The king had heard that Harlow had various books compiled by Pecock in his possession for which he asked that search should be made; any discovered were to be sent either to himself or to Archbishop Bourgchier, and Harlow was to be put in custody until further directions as to his disposal were sent.[3]

[1] M. H. Carré, *Phases of Thought in England*, pp. 157 f.
[2] *Epistolae Academicae*, ed. Anstey, pp. 337-9.
[3] MS. Ashmole 789, fo. 324.

In the second place there were a great many sincere and reform-
ist churchmen, who did not deny the competence of reason, but
its utility. The Church, if we may take men like Gascoigne or
Archbishop Rotherham as representative, was not trying to defend
its own authority and conduct, but to preserve the ardour of
faith, from which alone, they thought, reform could come. Such
men could not be charged with blindness to philosophical argument; but they thought that the devotional life was all-important,
closely attuned as it was to the English genius, with its leaning
towards the poetic, the artistic and even the mysterious. The
fifteenth-century Englishman was compounded of opposites: he
was a hard-headed bargainer with a thick skin and an acquisitive
temper; but he had a streak of poetic imagination, and sometimes
a vivid sense of beauty, like sunlight on a stormy evening, lit for
a transient moment his religious life.

In this connexion it is important to note the character of much
contemporary English devotional writing.[1] Miss Phyllis Hodgson
in her edition of the Middle English treatises, the *Cloud of Unknowing* and the *Book of Privy Counselling*, discovered seventeen
different texts of the *Cloud* and ten of the *Book*: the majority of
these are in fifteenth-century hands. These treatises, written for
those who are seeking to know what the contemplative life means,
are both in the tradition of the negative philosophy which we
associate with the Pseudo-Denys.[2] They give instruction 'how to
be knit to God in spirit and in one head of love and accordance
of will'. The *Cloud* treats almost exclusively of an exercise of will
which will overcome the separation and lead to union. It is a difficult exercise 'hard and straight in the beginning'. God is infinite
and the finite mind can grasp only finite things; man's highest
knowledge falls short of God, and what he affirms of God falls
short of the truth. It is far safer to say what God is not than what
he is; for the discursive reason can never comprehend God, and
its activities are, after a certain stage, a hindrance to the work of
contemplation. The author of the *Cloud* finds it necessary to
silence reason by concentrating all his intellectual powers in a

[1] M. D. Knowles, *The English Mystical Tradition*, 1963, covers this
very significant movement, particularly strong in East Anglia.

[2] *The Cloud of Unknowing and the Book of Privy Counselling*, Introd.,
lviii (cf. p. 125): 'it is very unlikely that the author of the *Cloud* knew the
works of Dionysius in their original form. He was probably acquainted
with some of the many translations and commentaries.'

straining towards one single point, God as he knew him through a blind intuition of faith. And this at first reduces the mind to a state of darkness: 'the first time when þou doest it, þou fyndest bot a derknes, and as it were a cloude of unknowyng'.[1] But persevere in the darkness with faith, keeping the reason and the senses from their usual activities by placing a cloud of unknowing between self and the thoughts and images of all creation, and God 'wil sumtyme paraventure seend oute a beme of goostly liȝt, peersyng þis cloude of unknowing þat is betwix thee and hym, and shewe thee some of his privete'.[2] The deliberate concentration and rigorous focusing of the attention gives place to a spontaneous up-reaching of love.

The plunge into the darkness of unknowing is therefore only a vivid image of the decision of faith to love and to press towards a God whom the understanding cannot comprehend, and belief in the power of faith impelled such doctors as St Bernard, St Bonaventure, Hugh and Richard of St Victor to exalt affection above the reason in the act of contemplation. Love, as Aquinas said is *magis unitivus quam cognitio*. The contemplative must learn to discriminate between ideas and thoughts that come 'into the body by the windows of our wits'.

But þis I may sey þee of þoo sounes and of þoo swetnes that comen in by þe wyndowes of þi wittes, þe whiche mowe be boþe good and iuel. Use þee contynowly in þis blynde and deuoute and þis listy steryng of love that I tell þee: and þan I haue no doute þat he schal wel kun telle þe of hem.[3]

This, needless to say, is advice for the contemplative: what, then, of the ordinary, educated, receptive layman, whose life was not ruled by ascetic practice? The early printing press gives some indication. Of 74 works published or republished by Caxton between 1470 and 1490, 29 at least are works of piety and devotion. With Wynkyn de Worde the proportion is higher: between 1491 and 1500, 30 out of a total of 54. Much the same holds for printers like Julian Notary or Richard Pynson. For the whole picture, one turns to the British Museum *Catalogue of Early Printed Books* (between 1468 and 1530). There are 349 titles, of

[1] *Cloud*, pp. 16–17.
[2] Ibid., p. 62.
[3] Ibid., p. 92.

which 176 are religious: religious devotion and instruction claim
106; liturgical works number 58.[1]

It would not be fair on Pecock to say that he had no place for
such an approach to the deity. But mysticism and the mystic's
illumination was not part of his constitution, just as a nineteenth-
century liberal theologian could hardly be expected to understand
the system of Karl Barth. It was his purpose to show that scholas-
ticism could be adapted to the understanding of lay people, and
could provide the rational basis required for the moral liberty of
the individual. He contended that a respect for the reason-judge-
ment need not endanger an individual's faith. His aim was not
only by argument to convince the Lollards of the absurdity of
their revolt against the Church, and of their criticism of its practices, but also to correct that weakness in the Church which, to
him, was the real cause of lay unrest—its reliance upon mystic
formulae instead of plain, and, so far as possible, rational declaration of doctrine and morality. The failure of this earnest, humour-
less, pedantic, but strangely pathetic and engaging figure does not
point to the spiritual deadness of the age but to the preponderance
of the English devotional tradition.

[1] P. Janelle, *L'Angleterre catholique à la veille du Schisme* (1935), p. 14,
n. 6.

Chapter II
Archbishop John Stafford

The English bishops of the fifteenth century seldom arouse the historian's enthusiasm. They seem, like their registers, too concerned with ecclesiastical routine, too governmental and orthodox for any that might still expect to find elements of heroism in the later medieval Church. John Stafford is a fair example. He has suffered from the dislike of Thomas Gascoigne and in later times from the coolness of Bishop Stubbs. Gascoigne, who suspected his origins, charged him with begetting offspring by a nun;[1] Stubbs, more anxious to be fair, concluded that 'if he had done little good, he had done no harm'.[2] Sir James Ramsay, who admitted his administrative ability, wrote of him as 'a Beaufort partisan',[3] while Mr Kingsford was cautious and non-commital.[4] Now Stafford was one of Archbishop Chichele's best lawyers and a close associate: he was also the successor strongly recommended to the pope by the archbishop, and in 1443 the succession to Canterbury was no passing matter.

John Stafford was the natural son of Sir Humphrey Stafford of Southwick in Wiltshire and Hooke in Dorset. His illegitimacy a papal dispensation of 1408 puts beyond all doubt.[5] His mother was a local girl, Emma of North Bradley, in which the manor of Southwick lay.[6] On the father's side, his grandmother was a daughter of Ralph, first earl of Stafford, who fought in the king's division at Crécy, and took part in the negotiations leading to the treaty of Brétigny. He was therefore a kinsman of Humphrey, the sixth earl, first duke of Buckingham, the most resplendent of the Staffords, killed at Northampton in 1460. John Stafford's father, who died in 1413, was a shire knight of standing and influence, who

---

[1] *Loci libro veritatum*, ed. J. E. Thorold Rogers (Oxford, 1881), p. 231. His bastardy is also referred to on p. 40.

[2] *Constitutional History* (5th ed., Oxford, 1903), iii. 148.

[3] *Lancaster and York* (Oxford, 1892), ii. 55.

[4] *D.N.B.*, liii. 454–5.

[5] *C.P.L.*, vii. 252.

[6] Selwood Forest: *Victoria County History, Wiltshire*, iv. 414. J. Hutchins (*History of Dorset* (London, 1774), i. 292) thought Southwick to be the Hampshire place.

has been termed 'one of the wealthiest commoners in England', holding lands in Staffordshire and Cornwall besides his patrimony in Dorset and Wiltshire. These southern Staffords should be distinguished from the Grafton Staffords, the Worcestershire branch of the family, domiciled in Warwickshire, Staffordshire and Northamptonshire. Great confusion has been caused by the common family Christian name of Humphrey which both lines, as well as the earls, bore. They were not all Lancastrians. It was a Worcestershire Stafford, Sir Humphrey of Grafton, who helped to check the duke of Buckingham's rebellion and for his aid was given the doubtful honour of being sheriff of Worcestershire for life. It was a Stafford Humphrey, great grandson of John Stafford's father, whom Edward IV brought into his camp to be made lord Stafford of Southwick in 1461 and earl of Devon in 1469. John Stafford's half-brother was Sir Humphrey Stafford of Hooke in Dorset, nine times knight of the shire for Dorset, sheriff of Staffordshire in 1403–4 and of Dorset and Somerset in 1415–16, 1423–4, a big landowner who by his own marriage and the marriages of his sons and daughters made himself a territorial power both in the Midlands and western England. The relationship between this figure and his clerical half-brother was evidently close. In his will, made on 14 December 1442, Humphrey left to his brother 'by divine pity bishop of Bath and Wells' a pair of silver-gilt flagons and a silver-gilt figure of the beheading of St John the Baptist and a great Arras tapestry. He died on 27 May 1443 and was buried in the chapel of St Anne in the Benedictine abbey church of Abbotsbury, the chapel which he himself had built and to which in his will he left a number of precious ornaments and vestments (for he was evidently a connoisseur and collector). The bishop was his principal executor.[1]

Like another future archbishop, Laurence Booth of York, John Stafford had to be dispensed for promotion to holy orders in 1408.[2] He was ordained accolite and subdeacon on 6 April 1409 in the diocese of Bath and Wells. This suggests that the latest date for his birth may have been 1388; but well before 1409, while he was simply a tonsured clerk, he had been collecting benefices: he was rector of Hulcott, Buckinghamshire, to which he was presented on 14 December 1404; collated to the rectory of St Nicholas, Durham,

---

[1] *Reg. Chichele*, ii. 620–4.
[2] *C.P.L.*, vii. 252.

on 1 January 1407, by Thomas Langley, always a friend of the Staffords; instituted to the rectory of Farmborough, Somerset, on 25 September 1408; and collated as a portioner of St Teath, Cornwall, somewhere in 1409.[1] By that year he had a papal dispensation to hold any number of compatible benefices,[2] and he got one more at the University stage in his career, Bathampton in Somerset, which he had vacated by July 1410.[3]

Like Chichele, he took the doctorate in civil law before the end of 1413, but unlike Chichele he does not appear to have practised before he took it. We know little about his Oxford days. He was present in convocation on 4 March 1414 and was named as one of the doctors to appear before Bishop Repingdon visiting Oxford to inquire into the Lollard activities of 'certain sons who', in the bishop's words, 'are anxious to walk before they can crawl'.[4] Just over a month later Stafford was ordained priest by Bishop Nicholas Bubwith in the diocese that was to be his own. The young lawyer was by that time becoming known. Chichele, newly appointed to Canterbury, made him an advocate in the court of Arches on 5 December 1414[5] and by 1419 he was the archbishop's auditor, a colleague of Lyndwood and in the heart of the provincial system.[6] By this time also he was a member of the council of the prior of Christ Church, Canterbury, mentioned in Molasshe's register in 1416.[7] His first prebend was Barton, appropriately in Wells, to which he was instituted on 11 November 1413; others had followed, a canonry of Exeter in April 1414, the Salisbury archdeaconry already mentioned which he vacated for the chancellorship and the prebend of Brixworth on 2 December 1420. This he had vacated by March 1422 for a canonry and the prebend of Highworth in the same church and in the bishop's gift. As he rose, he secured the necessary dispensations: first, to hold two incom-

---

[1] Listed in A. B. Emden, *A Biographical Register of the University of Oxford to A.D. 1500* (Oxford, 1957-9), iii. 1751.

[2] *C.P.L.*, vii, loc. cit.

[3] Emden, op. cit., loc. cit.

[4] *Snappe's Formulary*, ed. H. E. Salter (Oxf. Hist. Soc., lxxx, 1924), p. 184. It may have been as a representative of Oxford that he was placed in 1417 on the committee of the Canterbury Convocation appointed to consider methods of securing more effective promotion for University graduates; *Reg. Chichele*, iii. 37.

[5] *Reg. Chichele*, iv. 110.

[6] Ibid., iv. 641.

[7] Bodl. Lib., Tanner MS. 165, fo. 124.

patibles and, between 1419 and 1422, to hold three incompatibles for five years together.[1]

Those three years were crucial for his career, for he was emerging into the royal view. In 1418, a year before he took the auditorship, a royal patent joined him with William Lyndwood and Dr Thomas Kington in hearing an appeal against a judgement of Bedford's lieutenant, Sir Robert Denny, in the military court (the court of the constable) awarding a ransom which one party claimed as inadequate:[2] and the same year he was appointed to a panel of judges, partly ecclesiastical, partly civic, to hear an appeal from a judgement in the admiralty court brought by two citizens of London.[3] Then there is a gap for two years, and on 25 February 1421 the young auditor passed to the royal service as keeper of the privy seal.

The seal carried with it regular working membership of the council, of which the chancellor, Thomas Langley, had become a leading figure. Bedford now presided, but the organization of the council was in the hands of Langley. A duplicate of the privy seal, under the keepership of Bishop John Kemp, had gone in 1417 to Normandy to be with the king. When Henry returned at the end of January 1421 Kemp was left behind as chancellor of Normandy, and the day after Queen Catherine's coronation, Stafford took his place. The growth of the privy seal office had been, perhaps, the most important administrative feature of Henry IV's reign, for Henry used it more abundantly than the signet and frequently directed it orally. His son continued and even augmented the practice. The department now held an essential position in the royal administration, its range was ubiquitous.

One of its more important functions was in diplomacy: in commissions to envoys, appointments of embassies as well as in correspondence with foreign powers. Stafford had had personal experience of diplomatic missions: on 23 February 1419 he had been commissioned to participate in the preliminary stages of the conference of Melun;[4] his conduct in these negotiations entitled him to be appointed next year (15 July 1420) as an envoy to Brittany about the observance of the treaty of Troyes,[5] and in

[1] Emden, op. cit., iii. 1751.
[2] *C.P.R., 1416–22*, p. 134.
[3] Ibid., p. 174.
[4] Rymer, *Fœdera* (The Hague edn.), iv. ii. 95.
[5] Ibid., iv. iii. 183.

May 1421 to be designated as a negotiator to confer with the Genoese envoys in England for an alliance.[1] Two years later Stafford was brought in to the bargaining over the release of James I, king of the Scots, which ended in the treaty of London of 4 December 1423, determining the payment James had to make and naming the twenty-one noble Scots acting as hostages.[2]

He was only keeper of the privy seal for the brief year and a fraction that remained to Henry V. When the blow fell and the mainspring of all English government died, the appointment of Stafford to the treasurer's office cannot have been a surprise. In that last year, with the preparation that had to be made for strengthening the English occupation of Normandy and France after the defeat of Baugé, with all the loans that had to be confirmed following upon the king's journey round the counties, the privy seal office had been working to capacity, with a clerk only barely mature directing the machine.

On the demise of the Crown all officers lost their commissions, but Gloucester and the *domini et proceres* tided over the interregnum by issuing writs for parliament to meet on 9 November 1422. In the assembly Langley, Stafford and Kinwolmarsh were re-appointed as chancellor, keeper of the privy seal and treasurer respectively. Within a week Kinwolmarsh was dead and Stafford was chosen to succeed him. Should we be right in seeing Beaufort's hand here? If at this early stage Stafford is to be grouped with anybody, it is likely to have been with his old patron the archbishop, who had to stand between the regality and the oligarchs, rather than with Beaufort himself. In 1426, when he resigned the treasury, he stood with the bishop of Winchester, but it will be noticed that he never left the council during that crucial year, much as he may have disliked the way in which the bishop was treated. He was essentially the civil servant.

As treasurer, Stafford had to implement the council's policy of retrenchment after the expansionist demands of Henry V. Kinwolmarsh had left some £6,000 cash in the treasury[3] and the casual revenue was augmented by the treasurer asking for the renewal, which meant repurchase, of all kinds of immunity and franchise. But the fall in cash receipts during the first exchequer year had to

[1] Ibid., IV. iv. 28–30.

[2] The diplomatic documents are in E. W. M. Balfour-Melville, *James I, King of Scots, 1406–1437* (London, 1936), pp. 96–8.

[3] A. B. Steel, *The Receipt of the Exchequer* (Cambridge, 1954), p. 166.

be seriously taken into account. Stafford asked for no subsidy from the Commons in 1422 or in November 1423; the only grant he secured, at the Westminster parliament of 1425, was the prolongation of existing customs dues for two years and the privilege of exacting tunnage and poundage from denizens for one year.[1] Until Michaelmas 1425 the buoyancy of the customs, which carried the assignments made so liberally upon them, was just enough to counteract the absence of parliamentary taxation, but, as Principal Steel has pointed out, in October 1424 the treasurer of the household, Sir John Hotoft, was unable to collect £1,300 in 21 tallies on the customs, while on 17 February 1425 the customs again defaulted to the tune of nearly £1,500 in 17 tallies belonging to the earl of Northumberland.[2] These facts pointed, on the assumption that expenditure could not be cut in sufficient quantity, to the need for fresh money in the form of loans, and £22,000 was the figure projected by Christmas 1425, though in fact less than £10,000 had been borrowed by March 1426, to which on 22 May another £6,566 13s. were added (Beaufort lent over £4,000). Stafford's period as treasurer saw the government forsaking the small lender for the large capitalist, relying chiefly on two or three bishops, certain London citizens and the magnates, particularly northern magnates.

Meanwhile in less than four years Stafford had greatly improved his position. Like the keeper of the privy seal, he drew 20s. a day for his salary and he had 200 marks annually as a member of the council. On 28 July 1423 the canons of Wells received licence from Bishop Bubwith to elect a dean in place of Walter Medford, and Stafford was chosen. In September 1424 he became canon of Lincoln and prebendary of Milton Manor which in December that year he exchanged for St Mary Stowe.[3] He had already entered the inevitable competition for bishoprics. The council was arranging a number of appointments and changes in the English dioceses, which had begun with the death of Henry Bowet, archbishop of York.

To illustrate these manœuvres there are two groups of his letters extant, preserved in the collection made by the English proctor at the Curia, William Swan.[4] The first were written in 1424–5,

---

[1] Rot[uli] Parl[iamentorum], iv. 275–6.
[2] Steel, op. cit., p. 168.
[3] Reg. Chichele, i. 326, 335.
[4] The subject of the next chapter.

the other in a group of 1428, when Martin had launched his
formidable attack on the Statute of Provisors and the bishops were
torn between loyalty to the Holy See and respect for the statutes
made in their own parliament. Let us take the first. On 21 February 1424 (this is before Bubwith died) Stafford wrote to Swan,
thanking him for letters dated at Rome on January 10, in which
Swan had related his efforts to persuade the pope and cardinals to
translate Morgan to York, and so leave Worcester vacant for
Stafford. This good work ought to be continued. Stafford is sending new royal letters both to the pope and to the college of cardinals, and in particular to Cardinal Orsini, who was, according to
Swan, favourable to him. Swan has assured him that the reason for
the delay in settling the matter is not Stafford's simplicity, but
another consideration, and that he has no doubt that, whatever
happens, Stafford will at least be provided to Hereford or Chichester. In this case, does Stafford wish him to sue for the bulls?
Stafford replied that he did not. It would not satisfy the lords of
the council. Swan is to apply only for Worcester or a second church
whose name is omitted, until he shall hear again 'in a few days of
yet another church'. His expenses will, of course, be paid.[1] The
other church may very well have been Norwich, for in a summary
list of provisions in Armaria XII of the Vatican archives[2] Stafford's
name occurs as provided to that see.

In point of fact, Stafford was provided to Bath and Wells. A
letter from Swan to Stafford shows that the disappointed Stafford
had accused Swan of sacrificing his interests to those of the bishop
of Chichester (Polton). The tone of Swan's letter is one of right-
eous indignation. It is usual, Swan points out, to consider the
character of a friend or a servant before trusting him with one's
affairs, and astonishing that having confided in him he should
listen to the whispers of scandal. *Sapiens enim non omni spiritui
credit.* Moreover, Stafford says that Swan had brought discredit on
him by publishing the statement that Stafford had given him only
twenty shillings when in fact he had paid him three nobles. None
of the charges is true. Swan can prove that the translation was
settled a month before he returned to the Curia and that he did all
he could, first to secure Stafford's provision to Worcester, and
then, when hope of that was lost, to one of the best churches in the
kingdom. He even exceeded the royal mandate in urging Stafford's

[1] B.M., Cotton. MS. Cleopatra C.iv, fos. 168v–169r.
[2] Fo. 121. Information kindly supplied by Dr Dorothy Sarmiento.

D

claim. Nor did he make any secret arrangement with the bishop of Chichester and discuss the matter of money.[1] It may be that Swan had nothing to do with Polton's translation to Worcester, but as John Kemp's letters show, Swan was encouraging Kemp to seek promotion in 1424 when this promotion was bound to upset Stafford's plans. It was clearly more to the interest of the proctor than the client that the negotiations with the Curia should be conducted in an atmosphere of secrecy and anxious anticipation, but there was no alternative in that period of divided authority within the council. The candidate who was uncertain of support might find himself at the mercy of the Statute of Provisors, as Richard Fleming did, if he intrigued too openly in the Roman Curia.

The Stafford letters of 1428 show him, when the council was effectively blocking Martin V's campaign for the revocation of Provisors, doing all that an English bishop, who was also a member of the council, could under these circumstances do: making loud professions of devotion to the liberty of the Church. On 16 January 1428 he wrote to Swan, thanking him for letters sent from Rome on 23 October and received here on 24 December. Swan has made him extremely nervous by telling him that the pope has remarked that *before Stafford's promotion* he had heard many things in his favour. Swan has not explained the meaning of these words and Stafford, although, as he says, not an imaginative man, is afraid that they are a sign of papal displeasure (*quod a tempore infancie ymaginativus non eram neque pronus praesertim de et super incertis aliqualiter iudicare*). He fears that the pope is offended because he has omitted to send anything since his promotion. He will make good this defect in a short time, and meanwhile assures Swan that he has paid his annual pension of 10 marks to Swan's brother, as arranged, and that he will do his best to secure the promotion of his nephew. The latest news, with which he concludes, is that both archbishops and other prelates are working most diligently in the present parliament for the abolition of the Statute of Provisors, of which he hopes to send good news presently.[2]

Stafford therefore had been obliged to make the best of Bath and Wells. He was consecrated at Blackfriars on Whitsunday 1425 by Henry Beaufort; the enthronement was at Wells on 16 September. Holding the office he did, the bishop was bound to be an

[1] Cotton. MS. Cleopatra C.iv, fos. 152r–153v.
[2] Ibid., fos. 173r–173v.

absentee from his diocese. When he had time for diocesan duties, he was seldom in the palace at Wells or in his house at Bath; his favourite residences were Wookey near Wells, and Dogmersfield in Hampshire, where he had Beaufort's licence to ordain, as the place was in the Winchester diocese. He did a good deal of diocesan business at his London house, in the parish of St Clement Danes outside Temple Bar (the Somerset House neighbourhood).

The register kept for him, a substantial volume of 252 leaves, appears not to have left the hands of his commissaries in the diocese. Neither the writing itself nor the method of entry or the arrangement of the gatherings suggests that any parts of it were written in London. Evidently copies of the bishop's London *acta* were brought down to Wells and written into the quires in his registrar's keeping. The registrar acted under the direction of the commissary-general, John Bernard, who was in fact vicar-general, but in the Wells diocese a good deal more: for there might be three or four vicars-general appointed, as happened when Stafford went to France with Henry VI.[1] Episcopal duties, ordinations, dedications, reconciliations, the making of chrism and so forth were mainly performed by an Irish bishop, Richard of Inniscattery. The commissary-general acted as judge in the consistory court and had Stafford's commission to inquire, correct and punish as well as to open, insinuate, prove and approve testaments.[2] His official was John Storthwayt, who presided in the absence of the commissary-general. In the later stage of his pontificate he had as commissary-general the accomplished and experienced west-country lawyer John Stevens, who had been in Archbishop Chichele's service (the owner of the formulary, All Souls College 182) before 1415 and became a canon of Exeter, a man whom Stafford was to bring with him to Canterbury as his examiner-general.

Stafford was continually aware of the conflict of spiritual and temporal duty, deploring his immersion in temporal business and even speaking of the 'sleep of negligence'. When he went to France with Henry VI it was *voluntate et mandato principis et domini et eciam de avisamento totius consilii sui*.[3] In 1426, when he resigned the treasurership, he could give himself, with a sigh

[1] [The] Reg[ister of John] Stafford, ed. T. S. Holmes, i (Somerset Record Soc., xxxi, 1915), p. 87.

[2] Ibid., p. 28.

[3] Reg. Stafford, p. 87.

of relief, 'now that secular business is removed, to the profit and salvation of the souls of our subjects',[1] and begin a visitation of his see. Bath and Wells was on the whole a peaceful diocese and not too poor. The list of *exilia beneficia*, those under 12 marks in annual value, was not as large as in the see of Canterbury. It was kept from being a dull diocese by the exploits of the Bristol Lollards which had greatly troubled Bishop Bubwith, and by the militant Nicholas Calton, archdeacon of Taunton,[2] whom no bishop seemed able to tame. He looked upon himself practically as a diocesan, insisted, to the surprise of the court of Canterbury, on proving wills which should have gone either to Ivy Lane or to the commissary-general's court, and got as far as exacting double procurations, both food and money, in the places he visited.[3] Stafford, when he could give the time, was a vigilant diocesan—not a John Kemp. The inquiry which he undertook into the income of the vicarage led him to insist on a *portio congrua* for the incumbents of the religious houses. Bruton, upon which he passed a severe verdict after his visitation, had allowed the portions of the vicars to decline, and in one case, that of Shepton Montis, left the living without any incumbent. They were admonished both to present a parson and to augment the stipend.[4] At the same time the bishop was watching the upkeep of prebendal houses. Nicholas Calton, the difficult archdeacon, had been allowing dilapidations to accumulate on his prebendal estates, and the president of the chapter was warned to be vigilant over this.[5] On the personal residence of incumbents Stafford laid much emphasis.[6] William Russell, parson of the united benefice of East Pennard and Bradley, was charged with not giving proper time and attention to Bradley and had to promise to 'say masses and offices there'.

Stafford, as the register shows him, was keenly alive to the curious magical practices found throughout his country diocese. He stigmatized them as the crime of perjury—a country professing Christianity, but practising paganism. Bogus medicals (*sapientes et aliter medicos*) caused him serious alarm. Through such magic, he wrote, the famous kingdom of England had twice lost the crown

[1] *Reg. Stafford*, pp. 48 f.

[2] On whom see *The Register of Nicholas Bubwith*, ed. T. S. Holmes, i (Somerset Record Soc., xxix, 1914), pp. lxxi–lxxiii.

[3] *Reg. Stafford*, p. 93.

[4] Ibid., p. 94.

[5] E.g. ibid., no. 379, p. 111.

[6] E.g. ibid., no. 676.

of glory, as the chroniclers say, by conquest.[1] One of these occasions must have been the Norman Conquest, for he had evidently been reading William of Malmesbury on the Anglo-Saxons. But the other? Stafford directed that proclamations should be made in the City of Wells and in all churches 'that magic arts, sorceries and incantations can bring no remedies to the illnesses of men nor cure sick animals, but are the snares and wiles of the ancient enemy'. The proclamation ended by prohibiting the translation of any part of scripture into English (as the Constitutions of Archbishop Arundel at St Paul's in 1409 had done) and by ordering that all such translations should be given up to the ordinary.[2]

This was in 1431, as soon as he had returned from France. Only a short while before a famous victory-working magician had been burned at Rouen. A people which believed in the magical powers of the Maid was not easily converted from credulity. Some years later (1438) Stafford had before him an interesting example of a woman healer and quack, Alice Hancock, who had previously appeared before John Stevens, the commissary-general.[3] She used to assert that by merely looking at the shirt, girdle or shoes of a sick person, or at some other article of clothing, she knew how to discern as truth when the illness made its first onset, even though she had never seen the person afflicted. Furthermore she said that by looking at it she could tell whether the sick person would die of the disease or get better. She used to send such persons a health remedy by blessing the girdle, shirt or garment of the diseased, though she never saw or touched the patient; and this art she publicly professed on Mondays, Wednesdays and Fridays, *spretis aliis diebus*.

Among other achievements, she professed to heal boys who were touched or damaged by spirits of the air 'which the people call "fairy"', and she asserted that she had communication with these unclean spirits and sought from them replies when she wished. When she appeared before Stafford, she told him that she supplied medicine to sick people who flocked to her, by virtue of certain prayers which she said she knew and repeated. Then Stafford ordered Alice to say the prayers aloud before him: as he listened, he heard *quaedam verba extranea et incognita* which

[1] 'Bina vice': *Reg. Stafford*, ed. T. S. Holmes (Somerset Record Soc.), i (1915), 105.
[2] Ibid., p. 107.
[3] Ibid., ii. 126–7.

Alice could not interpret or declare in common speech. The bishop
dealt gently with her, relaxed the penalty and made her abjure the
articles she professed and 'all acts of divination and heresy'. Other
soothsaying women were also made to abjure the *crimen sortilegii et
maleficii hujusmodi et omnem speciem heresis*. 1441 seems to have
been a peak year for Lollardy in the diocese. We hear of a man
lending out for hire books translated into the vulgar tongue.[1]
Evidently the bishop's prison at Wells, irreverently called 'the
cowhouse', must have been well tenanted.

But to return to public affairs. On 14 March 1426 Beaufort had
resigned the chancellorship. Stafford had been a member of the
commission of adjudicators which accepted Beaufort's defence
against the charges brought by Duke Humphrey of Gloucester.
Although in the parliament of Leicester, the bishop had been
declared a *trewe* subject, the Beaufort-Gloucester fracas had
strengthened the opponents of the bishop of Winchester. The
most likely explanation of Stafford's resignation also was suggested
by Mr McFarlane, who saw him involved in the odium which
Beaufort incurred when the treasury accepted much too low a
valuation for the jewels pledged to Beaufort as security for a loan
of £4,000, part of the loans which the council was empowered by
parliament to raise in 1424.[2] One can imagine that the valuation
must have been a highly contentious matter in the council, but
Stafford was too useful to that body to be forced out altogether,
and he can be seen subscribing a petition among the other lords
on 1 July 1426,[3] while on 11 July he was engaged in discussions
about recovering pledged jewels belonging to the king from persons holding them as security.[4] Stafford's name is in a list of
'lords of the king's council' when on 24 November 1426 the council
minuted the rules it had established for the handling of business,
especially the consideration of petitions. He attended assiduously,
like Chichele and Kemp: and he was also present, as a bishop, in

---

[1] *Reg. Stafford*, ii. 266-7.

[2] 'He (Beaufort) was driven from office on 14 March 1426, and with him
went his colleague, John Stafford, the treasurer, as part of the compromise negotiated by Bedford and the other lords in the Parliament of
Bats.' K. B. McFarlane, 'At the deathbed of Cardinal Beaufort', *Studies
in Medieval History presented to F. M. Powicke* (Oxford, 1948), p. 419.
On the council's order to the treasurer to agree with Beaufort on the value
of the jewels to be pledged, cf. ibid., pp. 416-18.

[3] *Proc. and Ord. Privy Council*, iii. 199.

[4] Ibid., p. 200.

convocation. Before 1426 and again when he had become chancellor, he acted as the *organum vocis* of the council putting the case to the clergy for a ruling. In 1432 he was present when convocation debated its attitude towards the papal bull dissolving the council of Basel,[1] an issue in which the council as well as the English Church was interested. In 1433, 1434 and 1437 he addressed convocation, standing among the secular lords of the council, to state his case—and probably not, like the secular lords, to withdraw; and on none of these occasions did the clergy fail to make their contribution.[2]

Stafford's appointment as chancellor, on 4 March 1432, need not be viewed as a victory for the supporters of the cardinal of Winchester. He was the most eligible successor to Kemp, if it was still the policy of the council to have a permanent official in that position. Now there are two aspects of the chancellor's work that need consideration. In the first place, his spokesmanship of the council in parliament. For eighteen years, whether as bishop or archbishop, Stafford was doing this. The *pronuntiatio* or chancellor's speech on the first day contained an announcement of important events or matters on which the council desired to have advice; if there were none, the chancellor passed to a theme prefacing a moralizing sermon, which led him to the causes of the summons; and the speech ended with directions to the Commons to choose their speaker, an assurance from the king that estates, the lords and commons, should enjoy their liberties and franchise, and with the appointment of receivers of petitions. On several occasions Stafford had to communicate news: in 1435 there was information about the duke of Burgundy, who *ipso Domino rege inconsulto* had summoned a congress to Arras. Although this was plainly against the treaty of Troyes, confirmed by the three estates of both kingdoms, and still more so the fact that, as the king has heard, the duke has entered into peace negotiations with France, the king must consult parliament as to whether he is to let this deceptive and derisive treatment stand or defend his title with armed force.[3] In 1444 he announced the journey of Suffolk overseas to arrange Henry's marriage, this on the text *justitia et pax*

---

[1] Present in convocation: *Reg. Chichele*, iii. 173, 175, 179, 183, 185, 189, 191, 196, 201, 210, 212, 226, 256; as royal envoy in convocation, ibid., iii. 91, 103, 110, 233, 247, 259, 282–3.

[2] See footnote 3 on previous page.

[3] *Rot. Parl.*, iv. 481.

osculate sunt;[1] and in 1447, under the text *Qui autem ineunt pacis consilia, sequitur illos gaudium*, he referred to the projected meeting of Henry VI *cum avunculo suo*, to be Charles VII.[2] Now, under the texts adopted as the theme, the indications of his political doctrine are sometimes worth scrutinizing, however near some of them verge to the platitudinous. Unity, such as inspired the people of Israel against Gibeah, and obedience unfeigned, are the subjects of his advocacy; under each heading, after the moralizing explanation of the actual words of the text, familiar in medieval sermons, he amplifies his point: *per nonulla auctoritates historias et exempla demonstravit*.[3]

In the second place the chancellor was the official by whom the royal prerogative in matters of law was mediated and communicated to his subjects. The chancellor kept and declared the conscience of the lord king. This duty increased very greatly under Henry V, when after 1417 the king was on active service and unable to consider the *clamores regni*, and petitions went to the chancellor, Thomas Langley. Stafford was chancellor for eighteen years, both as bishop of Bath and Wells and as archbishop, but that length of time alone would not account for the large number of petitions to him that have survived. Contained among the Early Chancery Proceedings (Public Record Office), it is probably the most copious collection for any late medieval chancellorship.

It should not, of course, be imagined that the chancellor saw all petitions on the English side of the chancery. The masters would distribute many among themselves; nor do we know whether the subpoena to the defendant normally asked for was automatically granted: a good many inquiries, purely departmental work, would have to be made first; but in all periods there are petitions from important personages which the chancellor would be obliged to see, particularly in the thirties and forties of the fifteenth century, when justice was being increasingly deflected in private and special interests. There is, for instance, a personal letter of Duke Humphrey to Stafford asking him not to remit to the admiralty court a plea in which Sir John Fastolf was suing certain men of the Cinque Ports for trespass on the high seas (the duke was warden at the time), 'in eschewing the hurt that

---

[1] *Rot. Parl.*, v. 66.
[2] Ibid., v. 128.
[3] Especially ibid., iv. 419; v. 3; v. 35 (on the throne).

peradventure might inconveniently befall to our said admiralty, if the said ports be that intent'. He would rather Stafford tried the case.[1] Another comes from Queen Margaret about a long-standing debt owed by a York tradesman to a merchant, Baldwin Sehenny (of Siena) of the firm of the Spinelli, under her protection. She approaches Stafford 'sith you have been at all times for our sake unto the said Baldwin good and special lord in his right'.[2] The big personages apart, certain types of case seem to be growing in frequency as the century advances: non-fulfilment of contract or agreement owing to disturbed or abnormal conditions;[3] refusal to produce documents in evidence essential to a case;[4] causing civil commotion in order to avoid arrest;[5] or intimidation preventing execution of judgement; cases connected with the ransom of prisoners: piracy of all sorts; and a group which would have been of special interest to a former member of the court of Canterbury, later to be its chief justice himself,—cases connected with the ecclesiastical jurisdiction: refusal to obey finding or awards of the court of Arches[6] or of the archbishop's prerogative jurisdiction,[7] non-performance of clauses in wills by executors[8] or by feoffees to use appointed by the deceased; generally the executor sued, sometimes the beneficiary of the will. The chancellor seems in principle to have stood behind the testator, and supervisors of wills did not hesitate to resort to his jurisdiction where the dead man's intentions were frustrated.

On 10 April 1442 Henry Chichele wrote a letter to the pope asking to be allowed to resign the archbishopric, *multis quidem oneribus et curis, . . . fractus atque fatigatus.* The letter, *Dimittite me, beatissime pater,* recommended 'confidently and securely' the chancellor of England, *ut patrem maxime meritum*; and the archbishop went on to develop his qualities, his intellectual gifts

[1] P.R.O., SC.1/44/8.

[2] S.C.1/44/13.

[3] C.1/15/1.

[4] C.1/16/317.

[5] C.1/15/4.

[6] C.1/15/30. In this case the chancellor is asked to implement the findings of the court of Arches which excommunicated the defendant 'with book, belle and candille'. Lord Grey of Ruthin took no notice, hence the action. The plaintiff 'is not of poure ne dare sue for common lawe against the said Sir Henry because of his grete supportacion'.

[7] C.1/16/287.

[8] C.1/16/298a.

(*scientia*), in which he easily surpassed others, his nobility of birth, the power of his friends and those intimately connected with him (*necessariorum suorum*) and the grace of his hospitality: then his Christian virtues, his faith, loyalty, zeal, and the services which he had done to the Roman see and continually did.[1] Henry VI wrote also, supporting the archbishop's request, and testifying to his services in the Church.[2] The pope, who believed in the counsel of old men, would not comply. But when next year (12 April) Chichele died, Henry wrote again, recommending the translation of Bath to Canterbury

both on grounds of his wisdom, his piety and his humanity (*mansuetudinem*): as well as because now for many years he has borne himself with great industry and prudence in the office of chancellor, having always been engaged in the highest affairs; and, what is difficult enough among mortals, in administering justice to our subjects he has emerged greatly loved of all (*plurimum dilectus evaserit*).[3]

The pope assented. The bull of provision was dated 3 Ides May 13 Eugenius IV, 13 May 1443[4] (about an average interval, for Chichele had died on 12 April), and was presented to him as elect and confirmed in a room of his inn in the parish of St Clement (St Clement Danes, not St Clement Eastcheap) 'outside the Bar of the New Temple'.[5] On 6 August he took the oath of fealty and did homage to Henry VI at Eltham, with Huntingdon, his cousin Humphrey Stafford, Suffolk, Lord Sudeley and Adam Moleyns, dean of Salisbury, present. The pallium was brought over by the Dominican professor Thomas Bird and conferred by William Wells, bishop of Rochester, the *juramentum* to the pope following the usual form till the last clause:

regulas sanctorum patrum, decreta, ordinaciones, sentencias, desposiciones, reservaciones, provisiones et mandata apostolica totis viribus observabo et faciam ab aliis observari.[6]

This is not the *juramentum* taken by Henry Chichele: it follows Martin V's oath of canonical obedience for the suffragans of Canterbury. To have made any such promises in Henry V's time

[1] [*Official*] *Corresp[ondence of T.] Bekynton*, ed. G. Williams (Rolls Series, 1872), i. 147.
[2] Ibid., p. 149.
[3] *Corresp. Bekynton*, ii. 75–6.
[4] Lambeth Palace Lib., Reg. Stafford, fo. 1r.
[5] Reg. Stafford, fo. 1v.
[6] Ibid., fo. 4v.

might have involved the bishop or archbishop in the penalties of *Praemunire*.

To a reader accustomed to the order and neatness of Chichele's register, as well as to the comparative fullness of the registration, the record of John Stafford in 210 folios may appear a little disappointing. Of course, only nine years are in question: yet it begins correctly enough with the bulls of provision and the various documents of appointment,[1] followed by commissions (fos. 59v–74) to his legal, pastoral and temporal officers. The institutions to the Canterbury livings (fos. 74 f.) and to vacant sees are reasonably full, and the ordinations are complete. There is an excellent register of testaments: incidentally in the commission to Alexander Bowet, as commissary of the prerogative, the archbishop reserves to himself the proof of wills of bishops, dukes, earls, knights and other nobles as well as of the seals and signets of the defunct[2]—a definition of those testaments which the archbishop proved personally, though not quite complete, since *dominus* did in fact prove wills of important London citizens. But there is no register of royal writs included, no significations of excommunication, no section of miscellaneous letters, only a handful of commissions to his law officers to show what was going on in the Audience or the Arches, and no minutes of convocation. There are only two incompletely recorded visitations, Canterbury and Rochester.[3] It looks as if Audience as well as Arches had its own register and indeed Mr John Gerebert's commission (15 August 1443) as principal registrar, *Registrarium Curie nostre principalem*, with oversight of the registers and 'of all muniments and all other documents of the kind'[4] suggests that there was some devolution of duties in the archbishop's chancery. Presently we shall find a scribal registrar, Master Robert Growte, appearing, and in quite important company, but he must have been working under John Gerebert. He had—if indeed it was Robert who made the entries —a distinctive hand, appearing only in certain contexts.

[1] An interesting one is that of James Fiennes (treasurer 1449, 1st lord Say and Sele) as steward, drawing £20 annually from the manor of Otford, and £20 from Aldington. This was a royal job: *Considerantes quam valde et sinceriter prefatus Jacobus per literas regias et viva sue celsitudinis voce ad dictum officim extitit nobis recommissus.* Reg. Stafford (Canterbury), fo. 7.

[2] *Signis tamen et signetis quibuscumque dictorum defunctorum nobis et cancellario nostro specialiter reservatis,* ibid., fo. 5v.

[3] Fos. 42r–42v.

[4] Fo. 5v (25 August 1443).

Fortunately, two matters out of the run of ordinary administration and of importance to the archbishop are preserved. One may be briefly touched upon: the other we must deal with at length. In the convocation record of Chichele in 1439 stands a petition of the Canterbury convocation made to Henry VI, written in French, that the writ *præmuniri facias* should apply only to suits carried to the court of Rome or outside England, as was its original intention and should not be used to limit the scope of ecclesiastical jurisdiction within the country.[1] Evidently the convocations had had no satisfactory reply. The first time the request was made, the convocation of York presenting a similar petition, the answer was given (11 December 1439) that the king had not discussed the matter with the council, but was willing to give all his officers instructions that no writ of *præmuniri facias* was to be issued until the next parliament unless the king and council had discussed the matter and had decided whether the writ should issue. The petition suggests that the writ was being used like an ordinary writ of prohibition to stop a case in the church courts. The 'next parliament' had come and gone, but the council had not given its verdict. Now early in 1446 the two archbishops decided that a further approach must be made about a restriction which the clergy in 1439 had, in petitioning parliament for redress, grouped with the complaint against the fraudulent indictment of clerks. Their petition to the king in parliament is in English.[2] There is no surviving minute of the council on this topic and we do not know the result of these overtures.

The care which Stafford exercised in his relations with the Holy See is best exemplified in the record of the proceedings between 1444 and 1446 when Eugenius was pressing for a crusading tenth for defence against the Turks.[3] Throughout, Stafford had what his predecessor never possessed—the friendly help of a papal domestic prelate, no less than the Castilian doctor Vincent Clement,[4] acting as an unofficial liaison with Rome: for after the events of Chichele's pontificate and the drastic way in which the

---

[1] *Reg. Chichele*, iii. 283–4.

[2] Reg. Stafford (Canterbury), fo. 24.

[3] Fos. 45–7.

[4] On this important man, who became collector in 1450 and was, to Gascoigne's disquiet, made S.T.P. at Oxford, cf. Johannes Haller, *Piero da Monte* (1941), pp. 83*, 91*, and letters 98, 102, 119, 121, 131, 133; *Corresp. Bekynton*, i. 160, 174, 178, 185. Wylie refers to his 'naturalization' in 1437: *The Reign of Henry V* (Cambridge, 1914), i. 193 n. 8.

papacy had treated the archbishop in 1425–7, the greatest caution
was necessary to prevent Rome regarding any delay or refusal to
carry out papal mandates on the part of England as an occasion
for censure or even for the suspension of the archbishop—Canterbury was not a *dilectus filius* from the papal point of view.

It was important therefore that the acts of the archbishop, in
any set of dealings with Rome, should be meticulously registered,
so that the English case should go on record fully and accurately.
Unfortunately it is characteristic of David Wilkins that, when he
came to print the main letters and documents in these years, he
omitted the registrar's connecting and chronologically exact narrative. The registrar himself he fails to recognize: he renders him
as *magistri Roberti Registri*. In the register the abbreviation is
plain: it is *registrarii*, and at a moment so rare in registers, Master
Robert Growte[1] speaks in the first person. The occasion for it was
the visit of Giovanni Battista Legname, bishop elect of Concordia, to England, to ask for the subsidy in aid of the proposed
crusade. The matter had been discussed in a convocation no record
of which has survived, save the message which had to be conveyed
to the bishop of Concordia by a group of three—the bishop of
Bath and Wells (Thomas Bekynton, Stafford's successor to the
see), the abbot of Gloucester and Master Vincent Clement,
ex parte prelatorum Anglie. These were to welcome the pope's
intention of liberating the Holy Land: to report that the king had
'asked the prelates here in parliament' to bear in mind the cause
of God and try to do something; to promise a gift to the bishop,
notwithstanding the claims upon them, of 6,000 ducats of the
Curia, and to proclaim and carry out the indulgences for the crusade; and finally to state, on behalf of Henry VI, that 'the king's
highness has decreed that letters are to be sent to our holy lord the
pope with effect that, if the highest grant it, peace is to be concluded between the kings of England and France, and that his
highness the king will so act, that his holiness, the Roman Church
and the whole of Christendom may be contented thereat'. The
bishop of Concordia was asked by the prelates 'in all things to
remember the fervour and diligence of the very reverent father in
God the lord archbishop which he had in the execution of such

---

[1] The surname identified on the strength of later testimony (Reg.
Morton, fo. 237v) by I. J. Churchill, *Canterbury Administration* (London,
1933) i. 24. Growte had been Stafford's 'scribe and registrar' at Bath and
Wells in 1440: *Reg. Stafford* (B. and W.), ii. 251.

matters'. Concordia's reply was exemplary: he was deeply grateful to the king and the prelates for the present: he said that he
understood the delicacy of his task and protested that it was not
the intention of the pope to extract anything against English
wishes. Accordingly the collection for the crusade was put, unen-
forced by canonical penalties, to the English dioceses by Stafford,
and the register of Thomas Brouns of Norwich records both the
archbishop's letter and the local instructions to the clergy.[1] Concordia had been too true to his name. Evidently he was too
pleasant and compliant, so that, in view of what was coming, the
registrar Master Robert now begins:

About to register the things said and done in the business of the
said tithe imposed throughout all Christendom as well as in this kingdom of England, I will begin a little farther back (*altius*), from the
deeds and sayings of the elect of Concordia the previous year, 1445;
although the registers[2] record his deeds and words very plentifully, I
thought it would be necessary to add certain particulars, to make the
evidence clearer. The said bishop of Concordia, in all his dealings with
the said lord of Canterbury in the matter of the subsidy, never showed
him any bull requiring the said subsidy nor entered upon (*ingressus est*)
the matter of the tenth itself, nor was willing to enter upon it, as master
Lewis Cardona, now the orator of the said lord pope, then his clerk, did
of late on the last day of October 1446 before the king's highness and
all the lords of the council, the said most reverent father the archbishop
requiring him to do so, and publicly giving witness to having done so.
There are other venerable persons, the abbot of Gloucester and Master
Vincent Clement, who said that they had heard this as the truth, and
this came out most clearly in the replies which the bishop of Concordia
gave on 12 March 1446 to the reverend father the bishop of Bath, the
abbot of Gloucester and lord Vincent Clement, who were sent to
answer the said bishop of Concordia on the matter of the subsidy.'

The register refers in some detail to the order of the conversations
on this topic.

Concordia therefore never presented the bull as an executive
order to Stafford and never tried to enforce it: all he did was to
talk about a contribution from the English dioceses and to ask
for it as nicely as possible; and Stafford took it up. But on 25
September 1446 a different sort of person arrived from Eugenius,
ab insperato in Angliam, 'a certain Lewis Cardona, professor of

[1] Wilkins, *Concilia*, iii. 541–4.

[2] What are the 'registers'? Separate registers of the provincial assemblies? Nothing survives in the register of Stafford itself.

Sacred Theology, a man of Toulouse, who presented two letters, one open, the other close'. By the first, the one which referred to the bull Concordia never presented, the pope announced the collection, throughout Christendom, of the tenth imposed on all benefices by the council of Basel and confirmed by the pope, and commanded the elect of Concordia and John bishop of Coutances, then apostolic notary, to convey his instructions to Archbishop Stafford along these lines:

although King Henry was willing that the said tenth should be collected by the bishop of Concordia and paid as his share 6000 florins of gold, yet the bishops, considering that the parsons of England were heavily burdened, did not execute the papal mandate. The pope therefore orders the said archbishop to exact and collect, within 6 months from the presentation of these letters, the said tenth.

The second letter was a strong exhortation to Stafford (after mentioning Henry VI's ardent wish for the crusade),

not only to consent to the tax, but to use your authority with the prelates and clergy of the kingdom and so work and do that all the prelates and the whole clergy will consent and pay: not only will the business appear commendable to them if they see you well disposed to pay, and eager to exhort them, but you will gain great recompense from God and much gratitude from ourselves.

By the end of September the council had heard of Cardona's visit and a royal letter under the signet dated 1 October reached the archbishop telling him to keep the legate engaged 'to tary hym and make hym to abide unto tyme we come to our cite of London which by God's mercy shal not be long'. Cardona found it much too long, he wondered greatly, says the account, at having to wait such a long time, which did not fit with the honour of his lord the pope, that the command of the pope should appear neglected. He was bitterly disappointed that at a preliminary meeting of convocation at the archbishop's house in St Clement's to discuss certain points about the bull which needed clarifying, no decision was taken. The registrar carefully reported his words. A long narrative of these discourses with Cardona is given. Anyhow Cardona did not see the king till 11 November in the second parliament chamber (*in secunda camera par[l]amenti*) of the palace of Westminster and at this meeting Cardona presented the king not only with an ornate address on the subject, but with a symbolical or mystic rose which the pope had sent him, and Stafford gave an address, *ex parte regie celsitudinis habens aliqua de misterio et significacione rose.*[1] The rose was sent as a gesture to the sovereigns whom Eugenius was approaching for the crusading tenth: but the mystic rose did not evoke the royal licence to gather the tenth, despite Henry VI's own anxiety to contribute; and the registrar notes with care and subtlety the way in which Stafford divested himself of the responsibility for the decision, which was to be conveyed to the pope by the royal messengers. Stafford immediately sent Eugenius his own messenger, Thomas Hope, and the register gives the instructions he received:

The said Hope two or three days after the king's proctor has presented the king's letters will come to the presence of our holy lord along with the proctor and all other venerable English in the Curia, and will have in his hands the letter of the archbishop, and will say as follows:

'Most holy lord, the humble creature of your holiness, the lord of Canterbury, commends himself with devotion and reverence, desiring always to hear of the safeness and prosperity of the person and estate of your holiness, and sends to your same beatitude his letter.' And he (Thomas Hope) will kiss that letter and give it into the hands of our lord and will add: 'the rest the proctor has at the command of the king's highness to your holiness'.

After Master Thomas Hope, the bearer of the letters, has presented them to the most reverent father and has read them, the king's proctor will say the following words:

'Most holy father at the command of the lord king I have to say to your holiness how on the matter of the tenth your humble creature of your holiness, the lord of Canterbury, has signified by his letter that action has been taken. But the orators of the lord king that are shortly to come will explain the whole matter from the beginning and the proposal of the lord king, the princes and lords of the noble kingdom of England clearly and in order.'

In the meantime before the arrival of the orators if he (the proctor) thinks that our holy lord has been adversely informed about the lord of Canterbury, he will come into the presence of the pope and say: 'Holy and truly blessed father, we have gathered that your holiness has received sinister information about the lord archbishop of Canterbury on the matter of the tenth; wherefore we wonder greatly that any one would be so perverse to suggest anything about the archbishop save that he is the most faithful and obedient servant of your holiness: those who

---

[1] One of the passages from the register printed by Wilkins, *Concilia*, iii. 557.

differ from this view are intending to make a great scandal between your holiness and the famous kingdom of England to gratify their own passions and frivolous desires.'

He is to inform the archbishop of anything which he hears and senses (*senciat*) in the matter of the tithe. The register continues:

The said most reverent father of Canterbury considering that the malice of certain persons both in this kingdom as well as in the Curia who try to bring this calamity upon the wretched clergy of England never ceases; like a good and dutiful (*pius*) father, altogether solicitous for the flock committed to him, in that he might the more powerfully resist their wickedness, sent certain remunerations to those working in the Curia in this most merciful cause for the defence of the hapless English Church: the more truly also to conserve obedience and faith to our holy lord pope, hitherto augmented in this kingdom, and by their wretched conduct now much diminished.

This may sound subservient, but what was an archbishop to do against the background of mistrust at Rome? It was not long since Martin had rated Chichele for sanctioning the Jubilee indulgence for St Thomas issued at Canterbury, and still less time since the archbishop himself had been suspended for his suspected support of the Statute of Provisors. The brave (but unconvincing) course was to make it clear to Eugenius that the termination of the French war had for England priority over the defence of Constantinople and the security of the Mediterranean. Henry VI got as far as the intimation that peace with France was round the corner, but it was impossible to extricate the English garrisons quickly enough, and Charles VII, on the up-grade, was not going to let them go so lightly.

Stafford was not a hero, but a diplomat seeking relief for his clergy heavily burdened by taxation for secular ends. That people had confidence in him can be seen at the crucial hour of Cade's rebellion, when he did not share the fate of Moleyns and Ayscough, but was appointed as one of the justices to hear the rebellion indictments in Kent.[1] His conduct here was likely, if the copious pardons on the Patent Roll give any guidance to the government's policy,[2] to have indicated mercy rather than vindictiveness. He was regarded as an able, just and merciful judge, human, patient and as open-handed in his hospitality: and that is not a bad reputation.

[1] *C.P.R., 1446–1452*, p. 388.
[2] Ibid., pp. 338–74.

E

Chapter III
To and From the Court of Rome in the Early Fifteenth Century

The history of the English Colony in Rome during the later Middle Ages has yet to be written. A great deal could be learned from it about the leading English personalities at the Papal Curia, and more still about their occupations; for English men and women did not live in Rome for culture or amusement. Some were connected with the two hospices, the Holy Trinity and St Thomas of Canterbury in the Via Monserrato, and St Chrysogonus and St Edmund in Trastevere; some were members of the Papal Court, living in houses which they leased from one or the other hospice, and some may have been there as commercial or banking agents. The archives of the English College,[1] built on the site of the hospital of St Thomas,[2] reveal the early activities of the English residents at Rome, as they acquired lands and houses for the foundation and support of the hospital and formed a fraternity in the place so founded.[3] The popular account is that so much inconvenience was experienced by the English visitors to the Jubilee of 1350 that the residents decided in 1361 to found a house for the reception of their fellow-countrymen. In actual fact there was always a demand for accommodation, for, besides the resident members of the Court of Rome, there was generally a stream of litigants and suitors from England, as contemporary correspondence makes clear.

During the fourteenth and fifteenth centuries there were generally three or four prominent English clerks at any one time in the Curia. Not all were of senior standing, for the way up was *via* the notariate and the writerships of the Chancery to the post of abbreviator, first of the 'lesser', then of the 'greater park'. The senior or 'major' abbreviators were men of great importance, for they were the guardians of Chancery traditions and could determine

---

[1] I was much indebted to the late Rt Rev. Mgr Godfrey, formerly Rector of the English College, for permission to study them in 1934.

[2] For an account, cf. (Cardinal) F. A. Gasquet, *A History of the Venerable English College*, Rome, pp. 27 ff.

[3] The deeds of 1361–2 are printed by W. J. D. Croke, *Atti del Congresso Internazionale di Scienze Storiche* (1903), iii. 568 ff.

the form in which Papal bulls, after the petitions evoking them had received the signature, were drafted. They could tell the Holy Father that such and such a kind of signature ought not to be given, because it was against Chancery practice, or that his bull could not be issued without the insertion of certain clauses. Such a person was Thomas Polton, Dean of York, who, after many years of experience of the Curia, where he was a senior abbreviator as well as proctor for Henry V, was appointed first to the see of Hereford, thence to Chichester, and finally to Worcester. The more one penetrates into the intricacies of Chancery procedure, the more one is forced to the conclusion that the Pope had to be a very constitutional monarch indeed with the heads of such a civil service watching him.

English nationals in the Papal service come before us mainly in the guise of proctors, whether commissioned permanently to represent a chapter, a convent or a bishop, or employed upon special cases in the Court of Rome. The business of a proctor was manifold.[1] In its most usual aspect it consisted in securing for a client or clients the bull he or they desired in the form that would give what was wanted; in paying, or in settling the payment of all incidental fees and expenses; and in advising or warning his client of any difficulties or problems that arose throughout the case. He was a mixture of solicitor and advocate. When there was litigation, he had to represent his client in any judicial proceedings, and if necessary he might retain counsel for a special opinion; he had to supply *informationes* or statements approved by his client which were lodged with the court for the elucidation of difficult points; and, as the party he represented was not always present, he had to use his initiative and his legal knowledge to the best of his ability and be prepared to be hauled over the coals if matters went wrong. It was difficult and responsible work, and nobody without special qualifications in canon law or 'both laws' could take it on.

At the beginning of the fifteenth century there were two English proctors of special importance resident at the Curia, Mr John Fraunceys and Mr John Ixworth: Fraunceys, a member of the Papal household, canon of Southwell and York and rector of Saltwood, had been William of Wykenham's representative and

---

[1] The best account of the rise of the proctor is given by R. von Heckel, 'Das Aufkommen der ständigen Prokuratoren an der päpstlichen Kurie', *Miscellanea Francesco Ehrle*, ii (Rome, 1924), 296 f.

had carried through all the difficult negotiations in connexion
with the foundation of the two St Mary Winton Colleges.[1]
Ixworth was canon of Chichester, Exeter, Salisbury, Southwell
and York, and had been at the Curia for some fifteen years.[2]
Along with these two senior people there were Mr Henry Har-
burgh, canon and later treasurer of Salisbury Cathedral,[3] and Mr
Robert Appleton, later canon of York and a representative of this
country at the Council of Constance.[4] In 1404 or 1405 (probably
the former) they were joined by a young Rochester clerk, from
Southfleet, whose letters are the subject of this little study: Mr
William Swan. He was an Oxford bachelor of decrees and a
clericus conjugatus—he was married and had two daughters. Lest
this should horrify the stricter reader, let it be said that it was
quite possible for a married clerk to hold a registrar's post, if he
was dispensed from the provincial constitution *cum ex eo quod
clerici conjugati*.[5]

Unlike his colleagues and less distinguished contemporaries
at the Curia, John Urry, John Blodewell, William Lovel or John
Forster (later canon of Lincoln), ecclesiastical lawyers of the
younger generation, Swan preserved his letters, and two collections have survived: his autograph book, now MS. Arch. Selden
B.23 in the Bodleian Library, and the almost contemporary copies
of a different series in Cotton, Cleopatra C. IV. The latter collection, which I shall not discuss here, is to be the subject of special
treatment by Mrs Sarmiento; it contains some of the more
celebrated suits that verge upon ecclesiastical politics. The
Bodleian manuscript, of which Mrs Sarmiento has made a valuable
MS. calendar,[6] is a letter-book pure and simple, not a formulary.

[1] H. Chitty and E. F. Jacob, 'Some Winchester College Muniments',
English Historical Review, XLIX (July, 1934), which gives a number of
bibliographical references to Chancery procedure.

[2] *C.P.L., 1362–1404*, p. 500; *1404–15*, pp. 66, 84.

[3] For his will, cf. *Reg. Chichele*, ii. 465–9 and p. 657 for biographical
note.

[4] Finke, *Acta Concilii Constanciensis*, ii. 898; von der Hardt, *Magnum
Œcumenicum Constantiense Concilium*, iv. 493, 592, 1100.

[5] A good instance is in *Reg. Chichele*, ii. 341: dispensation to Thomas
Colston, clerk of the diocese of Lincoln that, notwithstanding his mar-
riage, he may hold the office of scribe and registrar in any spiritual court.
The constitution is in Lyndwood, *Provinciale* (1679), p. 129.

[6] I should like to express my obligation to this work as well as to her
(as yet) unprinted thesis on William Swan, in the library of Manchester
University.

The names of addressor, addressee and the dates are frequently given; and though only certain sections of it are in Swan's own hand,[1] he has added headings to the majority of the contents. At the end (fo. 153v.) are the words: *Magister Willelmus Swan Anglicus*[2] *Roffensis diocesis clericus est huius libri dominus verus et patronus.* It is a large paper volume; and it is to this, I venture to think, that Swan makes allusion in one of the letters printed below —a book which he found 'very necessary' to him. It was necessary because it contained copies of the correspondence that passed in a number of long and intricate suits, e.g. the Fountains case (Frank *v.* Rypon), the suit concerning John Macclesfield and the Hospital of St Anthony in Threadneedle Street, the Stillington process and others.

Swan, who after the Council of Constance lived 'near the English Hospital', came to the Curia during the pontificate of Innocent VII, and was to prove a faithful follower of Gregory XII. From his letters in the Bodleian Manuscript we get a vivid picture of the hesitancies and fears of 'the son of the Venetian fisherman' (as Dietrich of Niem called Gregory) during 1407 and 1408, the later years of the Great Schism, when negotiations for union were in train with the more obdurate Benedict XIII.[3] Swan followed Gregory as the Papal court moved from one Italian town to another, gradually nearing the Gulf of Spezia, and Savona, the proposed meeting-place of the two *contendentes de papatu.* In his own hand he copied into his letter-book the story of Gregory's attempts to get legal sanctions for his refusal to meet Benedict XIII.[4] At one period the Pope was becoming so difficult and business so hard to transact that Swan contemplated leaving the Curia, but the *camerarius,* the Bishop of Bologna (Angelo Correr, who stiffened Gregory's resistance to abdication) persuaded him to stay.[5] Although Swan was fully alive to the fact that Gregory was under

[1] Correctly identified in *Summary Catalogue of Western Manuscripts,* i, no. 3351. Letters in Swan's own handwriting are on fos. 32v, 33, 41v, 42, 42v, 48–51, 124, 137v. Chapter IV deals with one of his outstanding cases.

[2] Needless to say, the word *Anglicus* shows that he had the book with him abroad.

[3] Fos. 18, 18v, 33, 48, 48v.

[4] Fo. 33. Cf. Noel Valois, *La France et le Grand Schisme d'Occident,* iii. 530–43; J. H. Wylie, *Henry IV,* iii. 29–31; M. Creighton, *History of the Papacy during the Reformation,* i. 209–11.

[5] Fo. 42v.

the thumb of his relatives, he held firm to his Papal master, even
during the Council of Pisa, and actually got into trouble in England
for procuring for a client bulls uttered by Gregory XII, when he
should have got them from Alexander V. While the Council of
Pisa was in session he followed Gregory to Rimini,[1] though one
correspondent at least (Thomas Polton) thought that he would
surely be going to the Council and asked Swan to find lodgings for
him at Pisa.[2] After Alexander V's election (1409) he wrote in a
very disillusioned way, as if he had no intention of returning to
his work at the Curia; evidently the decision of the Council of
Pisa and his master's discomfiture (as well as the uncomfortable
proximity of Ladislas of Naples) had seriously affected him, and
he proposed to sell out and go home. To Robert Ely, his proctor
in the Curia, he wrote (16 January, ?1410):

> Moreover, reverend sir, I would ask you to sell my goods there, (at
> Rome) as best you can, just as I wrote to you before; reserving only
> those things which I want you to have despatched to me by the firm of
> Albertini to Florence, according to my earlier list: I asked you to keep
> for me the Decisions of the Rota along with the Belial process[3] and
> other treatises bound in one book; the Formulary of the *Audiencia Con-
> tradictarum*[4] with the other contents in the same book; the Rules of the
> Chancery in one quire; various other papers and muniments and letters
> which are stored away in a sack; the quire with petitions, and the quire
> of medical matters. Please do not sell these, but get the Albertini to
> send them to Florence. And in case those three painted cloths, the bed-
> coverlet, the head-cloth and another of the same design and a fourth,
> a banker cunningly worked, cannot be sold profitably. Kindly send them
> to Florence too. All this should be done with the consent of Master
> John Bremour, who is to be given the proceeds of the sale of those
> goods, and the balance of the sum of 40 ducats still owing I shall pay
> from those proceeds and make over in cash to the Albertini firm before
> I decide what is to be sent to Florence. Your business and that of our
> friend Master Simon I have not dealt with yet, and the reason is that
> the ship in which are the registers has only come within the last three

---

[1] Fo. 54.

[2] Ibid.

[3] 'The subject of the book is a suit brought by canonical process by the
infernal powers against Christ for the spoliation of Hell', F. M. Powicke,
The Medieval Books of Merton College, p. 207. The work was by Giacomo
Pallordini, canon of Teramo.

[4] The official formulary: M. Tangl, 'Neue Forschungen über den
Liber Cancellariae Apostolicae', *Neues Archiv* 43 (1922), 565 n. 1.

days, and the *Camera* has not yet decided when it is to be definitely settled. Moreover, my dear friend, after I came to this place where I now am once again I felt ill unto death, wherefore I have decided to give up and return to England and there continue my study in the University of Oxford, until by God's grace better times return; and even if I were to remain in Italy, the goods I have there, with the exceptions I have made for preservation, would not be really necessary for me. So do not postpone their sale, and perhaps the Jews will give most for them. I beg and implore you to keep me informed about these and other matters, and please forward on to me, by the bearer of these presents, the letters sent to me from England. . . . I find contained in the indenture you sent me, the other part of which brother Walter has in his keeping, that the large paper-leaved book, in which letters etc. are written, has remained with William Godefader. He ought to have sent it to Rome, or it should be in your possession or among the other goods which he deposited there. The book is of great use and very necessary to me, wherefore please contrive to secure it and let it be sent to me.[1]

The 'large paper book' was duly secured by an agent at Bologna (1410).[2] If, as is suggested, the Bodleian manuscript is indeed the *liber magnus de papiro*, one can easily appreciate that it was worth recovering.

But Swan was to make many more insertions in his letter-book. In 1411–12 he was back again in England, and he has entered there letters he received asking him to do propaganda on behalf of Gregory XII.[3] As late as 25 August 1412, Gregory, who addressed him as 'Papal Secretary', was condoling with him on account of his 'adversity', and reminding him that his misfortunes were only making him the more worthy and amiable.[4] The adversity alluded to (if it was not illness) may have been some form of punishment for his continued devotion to Gregory. He does not seem to have continued his legal studies at Oxford; instead he returned to the Curia during the Council of Constance, for in January 1416 he

[1] *Infra*, Appendix A.

[2] Fo. 124.

[3] Fos. 58, 58v. The letter of 6 March 1412, from Cardinal Jacobinus de Torso, is very interesting. The Cardinal encourages Swan to use his influence in England to procure the restitution of obedience to Gregory XII, and tells him that the Bishop of Winchester (Henry Beaufort) is understood to be well disposed. Swan is to prevent the King of England falling into the net of Baldassare Cossa, who is pretending to hold a general council (Council of Rome).

[4] Fo. 59v.

was dealing with the very important Fountains case there.[1] It seems likely that he returned after the resignation of Gregory XII was generally admitted to be inevitable. He was in England at the end of 1418, but rejoined the Curia at Florence in 1419,[2] and thenceforth his position at the Curia seems to have been secure, and he appears to have resided there till 1429 or 1430. He never got possession of the canonries in Chichester and St Paul's which had been his earnest quest for a number of years: his pursuit of these dignities shows how strongly local competitive interests stood in the way;[3] on 20 November 1408, the Archbishop of York (Henry Bowet) made him registrar of his court of Audience[4] and the Archbishop addresses him both as that and as a member of his household.[5] After the Council of Constance his service as proctor to the Archbishop of Canterbury and the confidence which Chichele reposed in him brought the reward (1421) of the living of Newington (Surrey) in the Archbishop's peculiar juris-diction,[6] a benefice which in 1424 he exchanged for East Green-wich in Rochester.[7]

It was after 1419 that Swan was entrusted with his more im-portant private or official missions, like Kemp's promotion to York, where political consequences were involved: here is the Archbishop of Canterbury in communication with him after the conquest of Normandy, and urging him to secure the pro-motion of a monk of Christ Church, Canterbury:

Dear brother in Christ: We thank you warmly for the letter you sent from the Curia that gave us no small matter for rejoicing, in which we learned that yourself and our other friends were in your old health;

---

[1] Fo. 64v.

[2] For a narrative of his journey out, *via* Constance, see Appendix B, *infra*, pp. 74–77.

[3] The mandate to the *executores* to execute the provision to Swan of 'a canonry in either London or Chichester, with expectation of prebends in both Churches', was dated 17 Kal. Dec. 1404; fos. 2–3v.; but in September 1406 Swan was still seeking execution of the provision, fos. 29–30; his proctor took possession of the prebend of Fittleworth (Chichester) in May 1407 (fo. 35), but, though he got the royal ratification (*C.P.R. 1405–8*, p. 244), his representative was ejected by William Rede, brother of the bishop; fos. 35v–36v.

[4] Reg. Bowet, ii, fos. 16v–17.

[5] MS. Arch. Seld. B.23, fo. 52.

[6] *Reg. Chichele*, i. 196.

[7] Ibid., i. 218.

and we ask you to keep us informed of what goes on, and to write to us boldly about anything we can do for your aid and gratification, in the firm hope of obtaining what is reasonably within our power to bestow and accords with your desires. My friend, our dread lord the king sent the most holy lord Pope his letters of recommendation for the promotion of Master John Langdon, doctor in theology, our colleague and monk of Canterbury, to the Church of Lisieux in Normandy, and to procure this he also charged his ambassadors our brother of Lichfield and Master Thomas Polton; which promotion has not yet been made, wherefore his royal majesty is astonished, since in truth he will suffer no Frenchman in the Gallican Church, until the land is more quiet and peaceful. On this matter too Master John Forster had special instructions from the king by word of mouth, but, we are sorry to say, the said Master John in coming to the Curia from Normandy was captured and detained in France, notwithstanding the safe-conduct he had of our adversary of France and of the Duke of Burgundy as well. Whence, dear friend, we ask you, since at our advice Master John Langdon has appointed you and Master John Blodewell his proctors in the room of Mr. John Forster, and has transferred to you the money along with the documents in the case (*informaciones*), to do all you can with my brother of Lichfield, Master Thomas, and, if it behoves you to do so with our holy lord Pope himself, that the said promotion may take effect.[1] We shall solicit your friendly counsel and aid in promoting other matters, about which we intend to write more particularly, matters that affect us and our Church of Canterbury, of which you are an *alumnus*; for which you may be sure that we shall compensate your assistance as time and place permit. Farewell, and with increase of honour in all prosperity, as we desire. Written with our own hand[2] in our manor of Otford on 6 September (1419).[3]

The Archbishop's allusion to the capture of the royal messenger on his way through France to the Curia need cause no surprise. Going to the Curia was always a risky business, and Swan in his letter-book has recorded the experiences of a correspondent who may possibly be none other than Walter Medford, Dean of Wells, collector-general for the Papacy in England. The collector, who had in his valise the moneys gathered by him in England (40l. in English money) and all his notes on the suits and the *litterae de gratia* which he had promised to expedite, was

---

[1] This never took place. The see was granted to Cardinal Branda da Castiglione: Eubel, i. 304. In 1422 Langdon was made bishop of Rochester. The bull of provision is in *Reg. Chichele*, i. 79.

[2] *Propria manu* is most rare in Chichele's correspondence.

[3] M.S. Arch. Seld. B.23, fo. 68v.

relieved of his property by a rascally servant just when he was approaching Constance. It was the loss of these important memoranda, he bitterly complains, that was found to destroy all his credit in England, for without them he could not fulfil what he had promised to his clients. It was in vain that he laid his plight before the mayor of Constance and got the facts of the case attended to by a notary while the local authorities had a search made in the neighbourhood for the elusive villain. *Non est inventus locus eius.* 'I thought', writes the collector, 'that he was a simple man, nay a simpleton.' But the man was clever enough to get permission, when the party was nearing Constance (which was his home), to go on ahead in order to inquire about his mother and sister, and to slip off with the collector's luggage.[1] Swan has inserted the whole letter which the wretched official wrote to the presidents of the Camera, excusing himself for the loss of such valuable documents, and he himself may have been the notary who took down the account of the incident; for, writes the collector, Swan, who was riding with three horses, joined him at Canterbury on his way out from England 'and always stood by and gave no small consolation in the dangerous obstacles and fearful perils of so long and precarious a way'. It is relevant to note that a letter to or from Rome took from seven to eight weeks to reach its destination,[2] and individuals going to the Curia might well take longer.

During his early days in the Curia, Swan had had some difficult business to transact. The case which, as he complained, consumed most of his time was the Arundel-Talbot marriage. John de Arundel and Elizabeth Talbot, who after matrimony had discovered that they were related in the third and fourth degrees, wanted to get a dispensation to continue in the married state, and their case was promoted by Elizabeth's relative and guardian, Lord Furnival, Treasurer of England.[3] The Pope signed the supplication (1405), but it was held up in the Chancery and the Camera, and Swan, acting for Lord Furnival, was asked to pay 1,000 ducats, which he could not immediately do. After a month's delay the matter was settled in the Camera, and the bull of dispensation despatched from the Chancery. But the presidents of the Chancery inserted two clauses at their own discretion, one of which was to the effect

[1] Appendix B, *infra*, p. 76.
[2] Cf. fo. 29: Swan thanks his English correspondents for letters written in London on 8 July and received in Rome on 30 August.
[3] Fo. 26.

that John and Elizabeth must separate until a fresh dispensation had been made out, and could then marry again. This was to safeguard the right of their children. Swan, along with the merchant Simon de Albertini (who had the bull and did not want further delay in receiving payment for it) appealed to Innocent VII, who inquired how much it was agreed that John and Elizabeth should pay for the bull. In Swan's words:

> Our lord Pope wished to hear the final conclusion on this matter; and when the sum paid came to his ears, he blamed and reprehended the chamberlain and the clerks of the Camera who knew, and were responsible for, the agreement reached over the dispensation—for he said that John and Elizabeth would be persons born of royal birth and of noble stock, and had more than 100,000 marks worth of property; of which goods, he asserted, the third at their disposal of should have belonged to the apostolic Camera.[1]

Swan explained, he tells us, that they were young, and under the control of their parents, and had practically no money of their own, but the Pope insisted that a large sum must be paid. This caused further delays, and the matter would not have been settled if the merchants had not intervened and helped Swan to persuade the Pope to sign the dispensation and to take out the extra clauses. At this point the Chancery doubted the validity of the document, unless the two clauses were left in or at least the one about separation. Swan had then to employ two advocates to write opinions on the point for the seniors in the Chancery.

> The senior lords of the Chancery maintained categorically that never, all the days of their life, had any bull gone out in the form aforesaid, even if it was for a king, without the above-written clauses being added, unless this was done by an act of supreme favour.

The actual bull[2] bears no traces of these clauses, so the *maxima gratia* must have come into play, and Swan have been successful in spite of Chancery and cameral obstacles. But it was a laborious and intricate case. 'In truth', he writes, 'never in my life in any business did I suffer such worry and trouble, as in the said affair.'[3] He carried it through, hoping that the promoters of the suit would assist him in gaining from the king a licence to accept his Chiches-

---

[1] Fo. 26v.
[2] *C.P.L.*, vi. 71, 10 October 1405.
[3] Fo. 29.

ter or his London prebend[1] (*licenciam . . . regiam de libere exequendo gratiam meam*). 420 ducats was what he paid for the bull, so that he was successful in beating down the demands of the Camera.

This case makes it clear how important a factor in any suit at Rome was the standing of the legal representative and his knowledge of the persons as well as of the procedure of the Curia. Perhaps that is the point of the little testimonial conveyed in one of the letters in Swan's collection written to an anonymous abbot, where Swan is described as

Mr William Swan, bachelor in laws, proctor-general in the Roman Curia, who though young, is yet very wise and circumspect, faithful and diligent, and conducts himself with ability (*virtuose*) in all his doings. Wherefore, reverent father [continues the writer], I am sending him to your paternity to expedite the business which you are to prosecute in the Court of Rome, for I know that he will expedite your business faithfully and without delay, if it is in any way possible to expedite it and he is shortly to cross over to the Curia, as I told you verbally on a previous occasion.[2]

The letter may have been written in 1410 or 1411: it is certainly not the work of the Swan of 1419, and I suspect that it is the composition of a man trying to build up his practice after the Council of Pisa and an unlucky adherence to Gregory XII.

But, throughout, Swan was never one to underrate the value of his own services. If a bull has been difficult to secure, the fact is duly noted;[3] if the Pope is unusually sticky, Swan will certainly say so.[4] Only at one juncture does he show himself

[1] In another letter (4 September, 1406) Swan said that he was hoping for the aid of Lord Furnival and of John Macclesfield in getting a royal licence to accept his London prebend: fo. 28; he made similar overtures to Robert Mascall, bishop of Hereford, fo. 28v.

[2] Fos. 25v, 26.

[3] Fo. 29. 23 June 1406: a change in a petition has involved a corresponding change in the Papal signature, which has only been obtained with the greatest difficulty, and Swan hopes that his client will consider the trouble that he has taken. 4 September 1406: to the prior of Rochester, telling him that he (Swan) has obtained a bull for the appropriation of the Church of Boxley. This has been difficult to secure, as the Pope rarely grants appropriations nowadays.

[4] Fo. 29, 1406. The Pope has ordered that no one, least of all an Englishman, shall have more than one expectative grace and one collation, which rule is kept in the Chancery; cf. also fo. 42v, when Swan excuses himself for lack of success, 'because the pope is more difficult to deal with than usual'.

reluctant to get a bull for his client, and that is just before the Council of Pisa when union was in the air. In the letters for 1408, letters that are particularly interesting to historians of the Schism, there is one to a Mr John Bayley warning him not to apply for a provision, although he has the royal licence to do so, because, in the event of the hoped-for union of the Church, graces will be revoked;[1] and another to Mr William Dogge, in reply to his request for a new grace of provision, assuring him that he (Swan) would be ready to obtain this for him as he has obtained other graces, for the sake of the time when they were at Oxford together in the same dining-hall (sala), but that it would not be advisable for the moment on account of the union of the Church, which would mean the revocation of graces (as above).[2] He was of course prepared to advise in a case when he considered that a process should not have been brought in the Court of Rome at all. He knew enough of the English legislation about the acceptance of benefices from, and the bringing of suits in, the Curia, to discourage people litigating there instead of in the King's Bench at home: the king had the whip hand on such occasions when his court and the court of Rome were brought into comparison.[3]

For Swan the years 1406–8 were the most difficult financially. To his English clients like John Macclesfield, Robert Newton and his chief friend John Launce, rector of Southfleet and prebendary of Chichester, he makes frequent representations about the money that he has disbursed on their account.[4] His more important patrons have to be reminded that they have promised to reward him for his services;[5] and those for whom he has succeeded in getting bulls are given a broad hint that they should send him more than the price of the bull. One client, who is to pay £20, is told that he should be eternally grateful to Swan, for it was almost impossible to· obtain the two bulls which Swan succeeded in extracting, because of a Chancery rule against plurality.[6] In one letter he sends a list of the sums of money due for bulls and a list of debtors is given. Swan asserts that scarcely

[1] Fo. 50.

[2] Ibid.

[3] Fo. 51v. On fo. 45 there is a striking letter in which Swan warns a papal provisor to give up his claim to the prebend of Erpingham (Rutland) in the diocese of Lincoln because the King had already granted it away.

[4] Especially fos. 25–6, 27–8.

[5] E.g. fo. 28v to the bishop of Chichester (undated); fo. 30.

[6] Fo. 29.

any matter has been entrusted to him for which he has not been
able to obtain the Papal signature, and therefore asks for £20 to be
sent him without delay, so that he can transact more business and
can say to them: *Lord, the talent thou gavest me has gained ten
talents* (a conflation of St Matthew xxv. 20, and St Luke xix. 16).[1]

The financial stringency was increased by illness. In September
1407, Swan succumbed to dysentery at Viterbo and was removed
to the hospital of the Holy Ghost. He had a high temperature and

various illnesses different from one another, so that it was extremely
difficult, so the doctors said, to give me any medicine, for the medicine
that was good for one illness was very bad for another. The dysentery
continued for a month and more during which time I never rose from
my bed.

He was at Viterbo a little more than six weeks and prevented from
following the Curia, but the illness cost him 'a heavy, nay an
impossible pile of expenses'. 'I spent in doctors and medicines
and other expenses 41 ducats and 30 boloners': but there was an
Englishwoman to nurse him:

and undoubtedly if it had not been for Alice Tudor who came to me
two days after I had fallen ill, on account of your kind letter which she
bore with her, I should have died. But she was with me in all my
troubles and tribulations and never left me until I was well. She spent
many sleepless nights on my account. She could not have looked after
me better if she had been my mother, and in consequence I ought to
regard her as my mother, and all my friends are equally in her debt.
But women always treat me kindly (*sed vita mea valet inter omnes
feminas*). Blessings on her![2]

It is natural that Swan's wife, Joan, and Richard, his brother,
who was a London skinner, should have been anxious. On another
occasion, probably early in 1416, we are given a picture of the
Swan family waiting for news. John Launce, rector of Southfleet, the family home, thanks Swan for letters written from
Constance on 26 December, and received by him while he was
celebrating mass on the day of the Purification (2 February).
When mass was finished he went home to his rectory in the severe
cold, and there read the letter to Swan's wife and mother, who
sighed and thirsted for news. (They had probably been at mass,

[1] Fo. 29.

[2] Fo. 33v. Alice Tudor had a suit at the Curia and was evidently going
to interview her proctor; fos. 34v, 39. She was also called Alice Proude.

and Launce may have told them about the letter he had received and invited them in.) But because in one passage telling Launce that all was well there was no mention of Thomas, Swan's nephew, Swan's mother wrung her hands and groaned that Thomas was dead. She had jumped to the conclusion, a thing which no good lawyer does, Launce sententiously remarks. They were greatly consoled before the end of the letter to hear that Thomas, who had been ill, was getting better. Launce tells Swan that his wife and children, his mother, brother and sister are living together in amity, peace and charity; but that Richard and Agnes, Swan's sister, have been ill from time to time with fever. The rector of Gravesend and other people who are coming to the Curia will give Swan the news, and so Launce will not write more. Now that he is growing old and weak in the head he dislikes the fatigue of writing and asks to be excused.[1] The letter is signed *Totus vester Johannes R(ector) de Suthflete utinam vobis utilis.* We have another reference to Thomas in 1420 from John Seward, schoolmaster (*scholemaister*), who writes to tell Swan that his mother, wife, children and brothers (evidently including John the Pewterer[2]) are well, so too his kinsman Thomas, whom Seward was teaching.[3]

How Swan and his wife supported each other's absence there is only one letter to indicate. It is written—or rather the substance was written—by Joan, who, as she tells her husband, had difficulty in finding a scribe 'and if there are any unbecoming passages, greater or less, in this letter, they are to be imputed to the scribe, not to the sender'. The tone of the letter is apologetic and extremely deferential: the scribe had a very flowery style, which cannot have been Joan's.

Quanquam ex debito sacramenti et vinculi conjugalis fateor me, ut teneor et debeo, ad que(cun)que subjectionis et complacencie obsequia et servicia[4] vestre reverencie grata, statusque, honoris, utilisque vite incrementa obnixam et allegatam, forcius tamen et animosius incitant et provocant me merita innate probitatis et gratitudini(s) magnifica laude digna in absentia vestra mihi ostensa ut per gratas literas vestras mihi in egritudine[5] medicinales et consolatrices[6] sum experta vicibus iteratis.

---

[1] Fo. 124.
[2] *Cal. Close Rolls, 1422-9*, p. 388.
[3] Fos. 137v-138. Thomas may have been Richard's son.
[4] MS. *servicie.*
[5] MS. *egritudini.*
[6] MS. *consolatiores.*

A mouthful even for a dutiful wife in the fifteenth century.
Joan goes on to say that she is very sorry indeed that she has
appeared negligent and remiss in writing, but she has a valid
excuse because she has had a series of fevers and illnesses, which
have also assailed Swan's younger daughter and his brother
Richard as well. Then, after a number of family and business
details:

> My master and beloved lord, I have been troubled in the past and
> still am sad to know through your letters that you are annoyed (*quod
> absit*) with the reply which you thought I made in the missive I sent to
> your reverence concerning my coming to you and staying with you and
> learning the German language or what is in other words termed *gram-
> matica*. Reverend master, my lord husband, let not your accustomed
> kindness hold me to blame by construing my words in any sinister
> fashion. I understood your reverence to ask two things; to wit, that I
> should reside in Rome and learn the language. One part of this request
> I must admit to having refused, to wit, learning the vulgar tongue: but
> I never refused to come and stay with you there, if your reverence had
> decided that I should do so; for I would wish to be pleasing to you in
> my actions; nay I would rather be with you and eat mouldy and insipid
> rye bread than sustain your absence, as previously, with the unleavened
> bread of sugary sweetness.[1]

It is interesting to find that Joan Swan was told to learn German
as the *lingua vulgaris* at the Roman Curia. Was this when and
because the Curia was at Constance (1414–18)? The fact certainly
points to the nationality of a considerable part of the curial
personnel. Dietrich of Niem was clearly one of many Germans
in the curial service. But Joan's reply seems none the less intelligible
and humane. Her departure to Rome would have involved the
break-up of the home at Southfleet, and have left Swan's mother
stranded.

Swan's letters are scarcely distinguished for their literary
merit. That was not their purpose; but their significance as
documents of ecclesiastical administration is high; and their
often naïve humanity may perhaps justify a brief account of them
in a book dedicated to a scholar-friend and fellow-medievalist
who never thought anything human to be foreign to her interests.

[1] Fo. 137v, Appendix C: 'cum pane (v)iridi et tristi siliginoso quam
sustinere absenciam vestram ut prius asimo sucoro dulcorato.'

Letters

16 Jan. 1410.[1]

To Robert Ely, his proctor at the Curia

Vir venerabilis, amice confidentissime, praemissa recommendacione. Noveritis quod alias scripsi vobis pro illis instrumentis appellacionis et notificacionis concernentibus Ricardum fratrem meum quatenus ea instrumenta eidem fratri meo ad Angliam mitteretis una cum illo rescripto obtento pro eodem et directo, ut optabam, domino meo episcopo Roffensi, unde supplico ut alias quatenus cum omni festinacione ea transmittere curetis, si nondum transmissa fuerint, quia dicta instrumenta erunt sibi plurimum oportuna. Preterea, domine reverende, queso quatenus res meas ibidem existentes vendicioni exponere velitis modo meliori quo potestis, velut alias vobis scripsi, reservatis illis quas vellem mihi transmitti ad Florenciam per illos mercatores de Albertis, de quibus dudum misi informacionem, videlicet quod conservaretis mihi Decisiones Rote cum processu belial et aliis tractatibus simul legatis in uno libro, item Formularium Audiencie Contradictarum cum aliis contentis in eodem libro, item Regulas Cancellarie in uno quaterno, item diversas alias scripturas ac munimenta et literas in uno sacco reconditas, item quaternum cum supplicacionibus, item quaternum de medicinis. Ista non habetis vendere sed placeat ea michi mittere ad Florenciam per mercatores de Albertis supradictis. Et in casu quo non valeant bene vendi illi tres panni depicte, scilicet coopertorium ad lectum et capitale et alius pannus eiusdem picture necnon quartus pannus[2] scilicet unum bancale bene laboratum, michi eciam ad dictum locum Florencie destinare dignemini. Et michi placet quod ista fierent de consensu magistri Johannis Bremour cui detur quicquid ex vendicione predictarum rerum poterit acquiri, et residuum summe XL ducatorum non solute ex vendicione huiusmodi rerum solvam et[3] realiter tradam mercatoribus dictis de Albertis Florencie, antequam michi fiat deliberacio illarum rerum illuc destinandarum. Facta vestra et amici nostri magistri Simonis nondum expedivi, et racio quia navis in qua fuerunt registra infra triduum primo venit et nondum est ordinatum per Cameram quamprimo erit expedienda sine fallo. Insuper, singularissime amice, a tempore quo veni ad locum ubi nunc sum[4] iterato infirmabar ad mortem, quare deliberavi omnino ad Angliam redire et ibi continuare studium in Universitate Oxoniensi, donec tempora per dei graciam magis reddantur accomoda, et quamvis adhuc remanerem in Italia res ibidem existentes non essent plurimum michi necessarie, exceptis illis quas cupio conservare, quare ipsas res alias

---

[1] MS. Arch. Seld. B.23, fos. 60, 60v.
[2] MS. quartum pannum.
[3] MS. ut.
[4] Probably Rimini.

F

vendere non postponatis, et forsan Iudei melius ement. Supplico ex corde quatenus de premissis et singulis aliis ac novis occurrentibus, si que penes vos sint, me reddatis cerciorem, et literas si quas de Anglia transmissas (noveritis eas per latorem presencium) cupio michi destinare. Scripsi fratri meo de rescripto per vos in ipsa camera impetrato et misi informacionem etc., quare queso quatenus michi de tempore impetrati rescripti et quando illud misistis volueritis scribere et significare. Res mee Bononie dimisse salve sunt, ut intellexi. Reperio contentum in indentura penes fratrem Walterum dimissa primo quam[1] michi misistis quod ille liber magnus de papiro in quo scripte sunt litere etc., remansit apud dominum Willelmum Godefader, quem forsan tunc Rome debuit dimittere aut penes vos vel cum aliis rebus suis ibidem dimissis. Iste liber est michi multum utilis et valde necessarius, quare placeat laborare pro ipso habendo, et michi destinetur, etc. Non plura etc., sed vos conservet Altissimus. Scriptum xvj die Januarii [1410].

Per vestrum quem scitis.

22 Feb. 1419[2]
A Collector writes from Florence to the Staff of the Apostolic Camera

Reverendi in Christo patres, eximie et venerande gardiane post salutem in domino et post graciarum etsi non ad plenas, aliquales tamen impensas acciones. Potissime de expensis tam largifluis nuper iam in Anglia circa me caritative factis, ut vobis clare constare poterit ceterisque singulis quale fuerit infelicitatis mee dolorosum elogium, ut sic a casu simili quis cavere valeat, nosce[3] dignemini quod equitando de Anglia versus Romanam curiam cum itinere duorum dierum distarem a Constanciensi civitate ubi nuper fuerat sacrum generale concilium sanctissime celebratum familiaris quidam meus Constanciensis nacione Johannes autem nomine, quem mecum in Angliam duxeram et in Anglia continue in meis serviciis fuerat occupatus et quem iterum ex toto simplicem ymmo simplicissimum reputavi, maliciam finaliter subtilissimam et decepcionem cunctis admirabilem suadente diabolo penes seipsum nequiter ac dolose prochdolor adinvenit que mee iacture dampnosissime ymmo destruccionis omnimode, ni forsan dominus deus per aliquem inspiratum michi modum celerius provideat, infallanter est occasio. Nam quadam sacra die dominica hora prandii superveniente ad quoddam muratum[4] oppidum causa prandendi declinavi associante me quodam nobili venerandoque viro magistro Willelmo Swan Roffensis diocesis de villa que Suthflete nuncupatur in comitatu Cancie et

---

[1] MS. que.
[2] MS. Arch. Seld. B.23, fos. 46v, 47, 47v.
[3] I.e. nosse.
[4] MS. murratum.

prope Gravesende, qui quidem in Romana Curia non mediocrem tenet statum, est enim literarum apostoliarum scriptor et abbreviator, est insuper ubiquam tam auctoritate papali quam imperiali notarius ac tabellio publicus, qui licet cum tribus incederet equis me tamen sui gracia de Cantuaria ad antedictam curiam nusquam deseruit neque dereliquit, quinymmo michi cum equis eciam tribus equitanti semper astitit consolacionesque non paucas prebuit in tam prolixe periculoseque vie dispendiosis amfractibus et discriminibus timorosis. Cumque in hospicio per nos recepto in mensa collocati appositis vesceremur et traditor iste omni fallacia atque dolo plenus una cum aliis nostris familiaribus ipsum adiuvantibus nobis prout decuit personaliter ministraverit, de beneplacito mei antedicti socii venerandi omnibus familiaribus licenciando mandavi ut in mensa discumbendo celerius se reficerent et consequenter ad alterius iter nos quantocius expedirent. Cui ille, 'sedeant', inquit, 'alii quia ego non prandebo neque possum neque volo'. Confestim autem intencionem sue mentis et quid per hec verba dicere michi voluit diligencius inquisivi, sed ipse fraudem volens operire aliquantulum se difficilem reddere simulavit, finaliter tamen dolosissime fingendo dixit quod firmo se voto domino deo arcius se obligaverat quod nullo casu cibum sumeret nullumque potum degustaret sed nec in loco quovismodo sopiret quousque Constanciam [pervenisset] de matris sue statu atque predicte sororis, de quarum vita solicitus valde fuerat, ut asseruit, notitiam habiturus eoque [quod] pestis valida Constancienses post eius recessum virulenter invaserat. Cumque dictum votum velud stultum atque fatuum cunctis audientibus raciones assignando dare reprobarem, ipse tamen nullatenus acquievit dictum suum votum ficticium infringere, nec eciam, si ipsius mors ex ipsius observacione sequeretur, quovismodo violare, nos igitur sumpto cibo una cum isto fatuo sic recessimus quousque tetra noctis hora ab ulteriori itinere pausare nos coegit. Illo vero sero eundem iterum quem de mane simultatum modum penitus observavit, nostra iocose dicente hospita dictum familiarem in hoc Iudaizare, eo videlicet quod sacro die dominico se tali ieiunio maceravit. Eadem quoque nocte omnem lectum sprevit, in banco dumtaxat duro reficiens eius artus. Cui ego tunc mirum in modum compaciens et timens ne forte acceleracionis eius mortis fieri possem occasio, estimans eundem non fraudulenter quinpocius simpliciter incedere, summo mane diei lune sequentis ipsum congeriando usque Constanciam preire licenciavi, parentes ut esset revisurus et cibum aliquem gustaturus, ac ut demum circa sero michi venienti deberet obviam occurrere ut ad domum sue gentis quam non paucis laudibus perante sepius extulerat recta via duceret stricte precipiendo mandavi, pecuniam insuper in eius peram contuli quam daret pro navigio tam pro se quam pro equo quem insidebat pro vectura ultra quoddam flumen per quod ipsum pertransire necesse fuit. Iste vero furcorum filius quem tam tenere nutrieram, quem a carne

nuda usque ad superficiem, a vertice ad pedum plantas tam delicate
vestieram et quem a scoria deformi purgando ultra condignum in
tantum ornaveram, per viam aliam obliquam fugiens cum illo equo meo
forti et notabiliter quem equitare consueverat una cum valisia super-
posita in qua proculdubio omnia mea bona ac universa munera in
Anglia michi collata ad valorem quadraginta librarum aut circa in
pecunia Anglicana omnibus computis inclusa fuerant me sic subtiliter
spoliando depauperatum reliquit. Et quod deterius est omnia memor-
alia que in cartis scripseram causarum et graciarum quas expedire
debueram ad mentem michi reductiva una cum aliis abstulit de quibus
plus incomparabiliter quam de omnibus aliis meis bonis lugeo deo
teste, quia per hoc honorem in Anglia sine meis demeritis me pro
perpetuo ut vereor perdere fecit, eo quod expedire nequeo neque scio
illa que certitudinaliter expedire deo dante repromiseram et sine fallo.
Verumptamen per totum diem illum hec mea destruccio me vere latuit
quia infallanter estimavi ipsum in Constancia iuxta promissa reperisse.
Sed cum illuc hora serotina nil mali adhuc ymaginans eiusdem diei per-
venissem ipsumque in prompto non reperiens in loco per nos statuto
et illucente die martis tam ab eius matre quam ab aliis quorum interfuit
plenius fueram informatus quod ribaldellus ille nullatenus in Constancia advenisset, tunc ego licet totus alteratus et attonitus ad maiorem
civitatis quantocius accessi casum intimans consiliumque petens pariter
et favorem. Qui confestim meis expensis literas sui parte et Constanciensis civitatis ad loca circumiacencia que insignia sunt et ad que seu
ad eorum aliquod verisimile estimare potuit hunc proditorem declinare
vivaciter mitti fecit. Equites vero atque pedites Constanciam exierunt
ad istum sceleratum ubilibet capiendum, et ad eiusdem finem ibidem
longo mansi tempore, premissa tamen per me coram publico notario
canonica protestacione et coram testibus idoneis ad hoc specialiter
convocatis. Verumtamen totaliter incassum laboravi quia non est
inventus locus eius nec ipsius vestigia insequi quisquam novit, quare
et gravius dampnum notabiliter incurri dum post primam spoliacionem
per eundem factum plures pecunias pro eius inquisicione consumpsi
et pro mea interim mora et inibi longa mansione. Totus igitur anxiatus
iterum ad civitatis maiorem personaliter accessi humiliter supplicando
quatenus michi literam testimonialem de et super premissis ad meam
innocenciam potencius servandam concedere dignaretur. Ipse vero
concilio civitatis ad hoc maturius convocato literas eiusdem civitatis
sigillo roboratas saltem in quantum eis de veritate facti constare poterat
in eorum ydoneitate meis expensis de consiliariorum assensu benigne
prebuit, quas certe postea per notarium in Romana Curia in latinum
transferri feci et illum venerabilem virum itineris mei comitem supra-
dictum sub salario competenti iuridice requisivi eo quod notarius est
prout superius est expressum quatenus de omnibus et singulis que
premissa sunt utputa qui in omnibus presens extitit et de visu et de

certa sciencia super premissis deponere [et] testificare posset, quatinus unum aut plura instrumenta super hiis conficeret, quod et fideliter annuit et efficaciter adimplevit. . . . [7 *more lines.*]

Script' Florencie ubi est de presenti locus Romane Curie VIII. Kal. Marcii.

c. 1420[1]

To William Swan at the Curia.

Honorabili et amantissimo magistro et marito suo magistro Willelmo Swan in Romana Curia commoranti detur, etc.

In Christo coniuncte magister et amantissime marite: quanquam ex debito sacramenti et vinculi coniugalis fateor me, ut teneor et debeo, ad que[cun]que subiectionis et complacencie obsequia et servicia[2] vestre reverencie grata statusque et honoris utriusque vite incrementa obnixam et alligatam, forcius tamen et animosius invitant et provocant me merita innate probitatis et gratitudini[s] magnifica laude digna in absencia vestra mihi ostensarum ut per gratas literas vestras mihi in egritudine medicinales et consolatores sum experta vicibus iteratis. Scituri dilectissime magister et marite quod de negligenciis et obmissionibus scripture ex parte mea in literis vestris graciosis pretensis[3] et mihi impositis fides oculata usque in diem presentis scripture et notorietas in partibus, cum presencia vestra corporale[4] aderit, quam deus acceleret, vestris statu et honore semper saluis me reddent excusabilem, ymmo penes reverenciam vestram penitus excusatam. Precarissime marite, a festo Pasche citra insecute sunt me infirmitates diverse presertim febriles et fluxus continui, eciam et filiam vestram iuniorem et fratrem vestrum Ricardum. Die quarto etc., Altissimo laudes, iam incipimus reconvalescere ut speramus. Mater vestra eciam bina vice passa est et reconvaluit. Insuper magister et domine mi, frater vester Johannes premunivit me quod terram quam colui presenti anno ipse recepit[5] ad propriam suam sulcuram et usum. Item noveritis quod Iacobus Bere non solvit mihi nisi quatuor solidos pro litera quam sibi misistis et dicit se nolle plus solvere usque ad personalem adventum vestrum etc. Ad Gravesende non possum habere ultra duos solidos. De Ricardo Gense et Rogero Harwel nichil recipere possum. De istis alta discrecio vestra habet providere ut bene novit pro disposicione persone mee servule vestre et liberorum. Magister et domine mi amantissime, alias dolui et adhuc contristor intelligens per literas vestras vos indignari quod absit de responsione quam [per]penditis me fecisse in scriptis

---

[1] MS. Arch. Seld. B 23, fo. 137v.
[2] MS. servicie.
[3] MS. presensis.
[4] MS. corporali.
[5] MS. recipiit.

reverencie vestre per me missis quoad adventum meam et moram et addiscendum linguam Teutonicam seu aliis dictis grammaticam. Reverende magister et domine mi marite, non capiat me queso grata benignitas vestra consueta in verbis sinistro modo, duo enim intellexi reverenciam vestram demandasse, videlicit moram meam ibidem et erudicionem lingue. Unam partem confessa sum me recusare, videlicet erudicionem vulgaris lingue, set non negavi venire et ibi vobiscum morari, si et illud fieri decrevisset vestra reverencia graciosa, operis per effectum, ymmo ocius vellem vobiscum esse cum pane [v]iridi et tristi siliginoso quam sustinere absenciam vestram ut prius asimo sucoro dulcorato. Verumptamen prout decreverit providencia vestra in premissis cum humili spiritu vestris ut decet parebo mandatis. Alia non restant pro presenti vestre reverencie scribi condigna. Personam vestram illuc illac et alias ubicunque conservet, regat et dirigat per tempora feliciter longeva dextera dulcis dei. Scriptum apud Suthflete in vigilia Nativitatis beate Marie Virginis gloriose. Mater vestra desiderat se visuram T. consanguincum scilicet ante mortem. Si quid maius aut minus congrue scriptum hic fuerit, scribenti imputetur, non mittenti. De difficili reperio scriptorem, et sic ibi est una excusa de me per vestram reverenciam imput[atorum]. Rogat vos compater vester et pater spiritualis Rector de Suthflete quod velletis portare vobiscum de Colonia pectenes eboreos[1] et bene solvetur vobis.

Vestre reverencie licencia

Johanna Swan et servitrix humilis.

[1] *For* eburnos.

Chapter IV
One of Swan's Cases: The Disputed Election at Fountains Abbey, 1410–16

In a paper read to the International Historical Congress at Oslo in 1928 Miss Graham examined some of the difficulties arising from the Great Schism for English monasteries of the Cistercian Order.[1] By 1410 the provisional government of the English Cistercians, which she there described, had come to an end, and the unity of the Order was again in sight; but it was that year that witnessed perhaps the most distressing and contentious of election disputes in the English houses, one that had ultimately to be discussed in the Council of Constance. Paucity of evidence prevents us from following it coherently through all its stages: a brief outline may, however, serve as a postscript to Miss Graham's paper, and illustrate some of the local and more than local disturbances and anxieties to which disputes of this kind gave rise.

During the period of the Great Schism there were two such outstanding contests among the English Cistercians. Both were in Yorkshire convents, a daughter and a mother house, Meaux in Holderness (1396–9) and Fountains (1410–16). The first is recounted by the continuator of the chronicle written by Thomas Burton, the bursar of Meaux, whose election led to the trouble; the second has no chronicler, save the monk who wrote laconic obituary notices of the abbots of Fountains.[2] The case of Meaux was significant, and cannot have passed unremarked at Fountains, whose abbot was deeply concerned in it: it showed how it was possible for a dissident minority to disturb what to all intents and purposes was a valid election, besides pointing to the prominent roles, in the election process, of the patron and the abbot of the mother house.

The facts are not unfamiliar. In 1396 the easy-going abbot, William of Scarborough, succeeded through the intervention of the patron, the duke of Gloucester, in persuading the monks to

---

[1] Printed in *E.H.R.* xliv (1929), pp. 373 f.
[2] *Memorials of the Abbey of St Mary of Fountains*, ed. J. R. Walbran, i (Surtees Soc., vol. 42), 146: 'Rogerus Frank titulo tali quali tempore Henrici Quarti occupavit . . . cujus titulus Romae cassabatur et pro Johanne Rypon, vero abbate, titulus declarabatur.' Cf. ibid., p. 153.

let him resign, and in the ensuing election the bursar, Thomas Burton, was appointed. A fraction, probably consisting of the monks who for some time had feared the threat of reform associated by them with their efficient bursar, made representations to the General Chapter, held owing to the Schism by licence of Boniface IX at St Mary of Graces' Abbey in London, that Burton was an *intrusor*, brought in by the duke of Gloucester and the abbot of Fountains.[1] The chapter appointed a commission of inquiry consisting of the abbots of Furness and Roche, who found, when they reached Meaux, that the abbey was guarded against them by Robert Burley, abbot of Fountains, as well as by the new abbot, Burton, who together had received from Boniface IX a bull annulling all commissions issued by the General Chapter in London. Eventually, after a new commission had been appointed (the abbots of Roche and Garenton) by the intervention of the patron, Edward Plantagenet, duke of Albemarle,[2] the visitors were admitted, and though Burley and Burton could claim that its authority had been set aside, a compromise was arrived at and peace restored on the basis of Burton's recognition by the dissidents and of his promise to admit them to his favour without punitive measures. This concord was broken shortly afterwards by Burley's determination to bring the offenders to justice: the abbot of Fountains visited Meaux and took disciplinary action against the minority party. His conduct provoked them into appealing to Rome, and it was to spare his house from further expenses of litigation that Thomas Burton decided to resign in 1399. Burton lived till 1437, free from cares of office and writing the chronicle of his house. His immediate successor, William of Wendover, had only a short tenure: the next was a monk and cellarer of Fountains, John of Rypon, whose efforts later to return to his mother house form the substance of this paper. It would be going too far to assert that Fountains inherited its election troubles from Meaux; yet it is indisputable that the contest soon to arise at Fountains reproduces certain features in the Meaux case: the plea and counterplea that one or the other competitor was intruded by the secular arm; the use of armed force; the departure of the dissatis-

---

[1] *Chronica Monasterii de Melsa*, ed. Bond (Rolls Ser.), iii. 259.

[2] Ibid., iii. 263. The author of the section on Meaux in *V.C.H. Yorkshire*, iii. 148, ignores the first commission. Gloucester (Thomas of Woodstock) had been replaced as patron, in virtue of Gloucester's posthumous attainder.

fied party from the monastery, and its consequent wanderings; the appeal to the Curia; the eventual displacement of the abbot originally elected. At no point was a Cistercian election in later medieval England more likely to be challenged than on that of intrusion. The Statutes of 1256–7 ordered the elimination from their houses of those who, to secure election, 'potentes adeunt et auxilia eorum implorant'.[1] At the Meaux election in 1396 it was claimed by the minority that the then patron, the Duke of Gloucester, had by his letters commanded his steward and bailiffs in Holderness to take their instructions from the visitor of the monastery and to carry off to his prison at Hedon any refusing assent to the election of Thomas Burton. At Fountains each side charged the other with obtaining secular aid, though the names of the helpers are studiously omitted. But the two cases differ in one important way: in the Meaux dispute the royal jurisdiction was not involved; at Fountains it was prominently engaged, and the king professed himself continually beset with the complaints and representations of both sides.[2] The length and complexity of the Fountains proceedings at the Curia, and finally at the General Council, bring the case into line with some of the more celebrated litigation of the later twelfth and early thirteenth centuries: the Meaux suit was quickly stopped half-way.

When the Fountains case reached the Court of Rome, the elected and confirmed abbot employed as his proctor the English clerk of Rochester diocese, William Swan, whose letter-books are a precious source of information for English litigation in the Curia, as well as for Anglo-Papal relations in general.[3] Swan entered in the letter-book, now preserved in the Bodleian Library, a lengthy memorandum on the case, compiled from information sent him by his client.[4] The first part of the memorandum is in harmony with the official account of the election given in Archbishop Bowet's register and by passages in the petitions which the parties submitted to parliament; the second part supplies information

[1] *Cistercian Statutes, 1256–7*, ed. J. T. Fowler (Yorks. Arch. Soc., 1890), p. 63.

[2] Cf. Appendix, p. 97, no. 2.

[3] In 'To and From the Court of Rome in the Early Fifteenth Century', chap. III above, where I have given a brief account of William Swan's autograph volume [Bodleian Lib., MS. Arch. Seld. B. 23].

[4] I have to thank Dr Dorothy Sarmiento for drawing my attention to certain points arising from the memorandum and for some helpful notes on the proceedings.

essential for the later stages of the suit. Though clearly an *ex parte* statement, containing charges against the opposite side which would be hard to prove, it is of high value as a summarizing of the whole business by a careful and experienced advocate, aware of the tactics of his opponents and alive to the weaknesses of his client's position.

Robert Burley, the abbot of Fountains who had taken so strong a line in support of Thomas Burton, died on 13 May 1410. The election of his successor was fixed for 30 July, and on that day was attended by two commissaries of Matthew, father abbot of Clairvaux, who were the abbots of Jervaulx and Rievaulx,[1] and by the abbot of Kirkstall[2] acting, according to the statutes, as an assessor. Opinion was much divided: there was no clear majority for any of the candidates proposed, and the commissaries, on whom the task of providing an abbot now devolved, quashed all the elections and appointed the monk who received the most 'voices' (votes). He was Roger Frank, called by Swan *nobilis ex utroque latere*, about whom we merely know that he had two brothers, Oliver and Ralph, and a cousin Robert, all laymen; he may have been a kinsman of the Lincolnshire knight, Sir William Frank, who in 1412 held land in the vills of Hole near Grimsby, Utterley, Brigsby, and Ashby.[3] This is Swan's account of the election:

'When the death of the said lord Robert [Burley] had been signified to lord Matthew, abbot of Clairvaux, the father abbot, he commissioned the reverend fathers William, abbot of Rievaulx, and Richard, abbot of Jervaulx, of the same order, to attend the election of the future abbot and to confirm it in his place, or make other provision according to the statutes of the Order.

'In virtue of the said commission, the two abbots caused the convent to proceed in their presence to the said election, as the custom is. The convent elected divers persons in divers ways,[4] and so divided were the electors that their votes (*voces*) fell upon seven elect, of whom Roger Frank had the majority, having thirteen, and brother John Rypon had four; none the less the said brother Roger, though he had thirteen, as was said, did not have the two thirds, which goes to make a valid election.

---

[1] Richard Gower and William X.
[2] Possibly John de Bardsey.
[3] *Feudal Aids*, vi. 612. Cf. *Cal. Close Rolls, Henry IV*, iv. 429; ibid., *Henry V*, i. 426; ii. 198.
[4] *diversos diversimode elegerunt.*

'The said two abbot commissaries, seeing the diversity in the election, and because through that diversity the election or appointment devolved upon them, quashed all the elections as invalid; and by the authority committed to them provided for the said monastery in the person of the same Roger, installing him and inducting him into corporeal and real possession.'[1]

If Swan's information was correct, the proceedings appear to have been in order, and the statutes to have been observed.[2] The father abbot, as Clement IV's constitution ordained, had issued his licence to elect, and had appointed his commissaries to be present.[3] The commissaries attended; the presence, as a third assessor, of the abbot of the daughter house was in accordance with c. XXI of the *Carta Caritatis*;[4] a two-thirds majority was required for a valid election,[5] and this not forthcoming, devolution to the commissaries was the correct course.[6] What followed was also normal. A letter of testimony to the appointment was sent (30 July) under the seals of the two commissaries and of the abbot of Kirkstall, to the archbishop of York, Henry Bowet, with requirement that he should bless the new abbot;[7] and on 3 August 1410 Archbishop Bowet did so in his chapel at Cawood, in the presence of his chancellor, registrar, a notary, and two rectors from the diocese.[8] The record of the proceedings at Fountains was sent forthwith to the chapter-general, which ratified the action of the commissaries and confirmed the father abbot's confirmation.[9] There was only one omission, but that was perhaps technically

---

[1] MS. Arch. Seld. B. 23, fo. 143.

[2] A convenient historical summary of these is given by J. M. Canivez, in *Dict. de droit canonique*, art. 'Cîteaux: Législation de l'Ordre', Fasc. xv. 755–6.

[3] 'Liber Antiquarum Diffinitionum', Art. 7, in *Nomasticon Cisterciense*, ed. Séjalon (Solesmes, 1892), p. 371.

[4] *Statuta Capitulorum Generalium Ordinis Cisterciensis, 1116–1786*, ed. J. M. Canivez, i. xxix.

[5] 'Liber Novellarum Definitionum', Dist. 8, c. 5, in *Nomasticon Cisterciense*, p. 516.

[6] *Memorials*, i. 206: 'juxta regula instituta eiusdem ordinis'.

[7] Ibid., p. 207.

[8] Ibid., loc. cit.

[9] 'Electionem fratris Rogeri in abbatem monasterii de Fontibus in Anglia ac eiusdem confirmationem generale Capitulum confirmat, ratificat et approbat secundum litterarum super hoc confectarum, quibus haec praesens diffinitio annectitur, seriem et tenorem' (*Statuta*, ed. Canivez, iv. 133).

justifiable: under the *Carta Caritatis* the abbot of Meaux, John
Rypon, had the right to be an assessor: but as he was one of the
competitors for the abbacy, his omission from the *litera testimonialis*
to Bowet need cause no surprise.

Rypon, however, had the strongest objection to the election as
it was carried out, and his appeals to the Curia during the next two
and a half years illustrate his persistence and his astuteness. Swan
noted them carefully, for they formed part of his own client's case.
Rypon attacked the election on two grounds: the unsuitability of
Frank's person and the method (*forma*) of his provision by the
commissaries. In the statutes of 1256–7, c. xi of the Seventh
Distinction laid down that the father abbots and the electors must
labour efficaciously to promote as abbots such persons as . . . 'vitae
sunt laudabilis, aetatis legitime, et legitimo matrimonio nati, nisi
cum eis fuerit dispensatum, et competentis literature'.[1] Rypon
charged Frank with *crimina et defectus*, a charge which the abbot-
elect countered by the plea that he was *honeste et laudabilis con-
versationis*, while Rypon was *quamplurimis criminibus notorie diffa-
matus*, a waster of the goods of Meaux, and one who 'frequently
put off his habit and went armed in the sight of all'.[2] But the
other ground of appeal, the procedure followed in the election,
was the more important, and no direct statement made by Frank
or his proctor has survived to record his precise objection. Swan's
memorandum notes that

the said brother John Rypon asserted in the Court of Rome that the
convent or the greater part adhered to him in his process and wished to
have him for abbot, the contrary of which is true, as appears from the
letter of the whole convent who approve the said brother Roger and
hold him for the abbot, as can be seen in writing.

In the report which Cardinal Zabarella made on the case for John
XXIII, mentioned in Swan's memorandum (below), Rypon's
election was found to be 'the better, and made by the *sanior pars*
of the convent'. The final *diffinitio* of the chapter-general (1416)
was based on the discovery that the original account of the election
received by it in 1410 suppressed the facts and was deliberately
misleading.[3] It will be best therefore to assume Rypon to have
pleaded that the assessors disregarded the true state of opinion

[1] *Cistercian Statutes, 1256–7*, ed. Fowler, p. 63.
[2] MS. Arch. Seld. B. 23, fo. 143v.
[3] *Infra*, p. 94.

in the abbey and acted upon a vote that was unrepresentative of it. If this is correct, the question of external influence upon the election is bound to arise, and there is reason to think that this was one of Rypon's main grounds of attack upon the vote.

The first papal judge in the process of appeal, Swan notes, was Francis Uguccione, 'Cardinal of Bordeaux',[1] who gave his verdict for Rypon. Frank appealed on a technical point,[2] and the case went to Cardinal Jordan Orsini, who disagreed with the previous finding, whereupon Rypon appealed again. This time it came before Cardinal Francis Landi,[3] who after full consideration (*mature procedens*) upheld Orsini, and gave costs against Rypon. Undeterred, Rypon made another appeal, and the case was sent to two cardinals, Alfonsi (*Lusitanus*) and Adimari, who reserved judgement: but before it could be delivered, perhaps, as Swan suggests, in order that it should not be delivered, Rypon cleverly contrived that John XXIII should be given a special report on the Fountains dispute. Swan writes:

Brother John Rypon, suspecting that the sentence of the two cardinals would be given against him, surreptitiously secured an oral direction [of the Pope] committing the whole case of the provision of the said monastery—either concealing or not mentioning the verdicts and processes already narrated—to the reverend father the lord Cardinal of Florence in this form, to wit that he should inform himself about the persons of the two competitors, and about the form of the aforesaid election and provision, as well as about the estate of the said monastery, and report on his findings to the Pope. In virtue of this commission the Cardinal of Florence, without summoning or hearing the said brother Roger in aught, without consulting the two Cardinal judges, and utterly ignoring or caring nothing for the processes already undertaken, conducted the case on his own in his private chamber or elsewhere, as he disposed, according to the false suggestions of the opponent. And he reported to the said lord Balthasar entirely against brother Roger, and to the comfort and profit of the said brother John

---

[1] The archbishop of Bordeaux had been in England in 1408 to plead the cause of the cardinals in summoning the Council of Pisa: cf. *The St Albans Chronicle*, ed. V. H. Galbraith, pp. 136–52: E. F. Jacob, *Essays in the Conciliar Epoch*, p. 73.

[2] 'Propter admissionem nonnullorum articulorum quos non debebat admittere' (MS. Arch. Seld. B. 23, fo. 143). Swan evidently regarded them as damaging non-essentials.

[3] 'The Cardinal of Venice', *Veneciarum senior*, to distinguish him from Morosini, *Veneciarum junior*.

Rypon, asserting that he had found the election of brother John Rypon
to be the better and made by the sounder part, although, as we said, he
had no more than four votes, and the said brother Roger thirteen. And
finally by means of that report and fifteen hundred florins he has
secured this, namely that the lord Balthasar, from sure knowledge, *motu
proprio*, and in virtue of the plenitude of power, has confirmed the said
election of John Rypon, has supplemented all and every defect etc.,
extinguished the suit and imposed perpetual silence on the said brother
Roger; and, as far as he was able, has decreed that John should be abbot
of the said monastery of Fountains.[1]

Zabarella made his report to some purpose. On 23 March 1413
John XXIII absolved Rypon, 'to whom the Pope this day intends
to make provision of the abbey of Fountains', from sentences of
excommunication laid upon him in the course of his litigation
against Frank, 'who was intruded by the lay power and is still
in unlawful possession'.[2] The bull of provision cannot be traced:
but that it was received in England, published and acted upon
the clearest possible evidence exists. Rypon evicted Frank immediately. In a petition to parliament, which must have been
lodged in Henry V's first parliament, Frank stated that as the
result of the bull purchased by Rypon, he had been ousted from
his abbacy 'which he had had for three years and more'. The bull
is characterized by Frank as prejudicial to the king, his crown, and
the statutes made on the subject (Provisors), as well as destructive
of the principle of free election; and the petitioner asked that if it
was indeed found contrary to the statute, he might be restored to
his abbacy.[3] The answer given was that a case had already been
begun under a writ 'founded on the Statute of Provisors', which
was now pending in the King's Bench under Hankford C.J. between the parties, and that the result of the trial must be awaited.

The action so begun was under the Great Statute of Praemunire, and the circumstances justifying the issue of the writ are
detailed in some fullness on the Close Roll.[4] In June 1413 information about Rypon's activities in procuring the provision was
laid in Chancery by William Luddyngton, one of the serjeants-at-
law, who was obviously acting for Frank. Rypon was sent for and
examined by Henry Beaufort, the chancellor. It emerged that

[1] MS. Arch. Seld. B. 23, fo. 143v.

[2] *C.P.L.*, vi. 380.

[3] P.R.O., S.C. 8, File 23, no. 1124; *Rot. Parl.* iv. 28–9; *Memorials*, i.
210–12.

[4] *Cal. Close Rolls, Henry V*, i. 112–13.

Robert Watton, who was 'of John Rypon's counsel', had published John XXIII's bull: asked point-blank whether he had sued
for any bulls at the Court of Rome, Rypon denied the charge, at
once to be contradicted by Luddyngton who pointed to Watton's
publication. In the bull, the serjeant maintained, the Pope provided Rypon to the abbey on the grounds: (1) that he had a
majority of votes; (2) that Roger Frank had sought external aid:
'with the support of a great host of esquires he did intrude himself
into the said abbey, did meddle in the rule and administration
thereof, and did secure the confirmation of the chapter [the
chapter-general] for his election or provision'. Beaufort then asked
Rypon whether the bull nominated him as abbot of Fountains.
Cautiously Rypon replied that he was informed that the Pope by
his bulls *confirmed* him as abbot. He did not know, when asked,
who sent for and obtained these bulls at the Court of Rome, or
who had paid for them. He knew that a chaplain called Roger
had brought 'a copy' to England—he was careful not to admit
receiving the original. The chancellor then asked whether Rypon
proposed to hold any benefice on the strength of the bulls mentioned, and Rypon replied that he did, 'if the bulls were of the form
therein contained'. Thereupon the chancellor cautioned him to
renounce and abandon anything in them that might be to the
prejudice of the king or impair the law and statutes of the realm,
and made him and others of his covin enter into a recognizance
in £1,000 not to leave the realm without royal licence or send to
the Court of Rome, 'or if it is proved that papal bulls in the aforesaid form containing anything to the prejudice of the king are
sued for and obtained in the Court of Rome'. Rypon's studied
ignorance of the exact content of the bulls and his refusal to admit
sending for a provision (the suspected bull was really a confirmation, he maintained) can scarcely have deceived the chancellor.

It is possible that an examination of this sort, which appears so
unique, was by this time a matter of common form, and that its
aim was merely to secure a recognizance. Enough, however, had
emerged for Frank to get his writ. The case came on at the beginning of November 1413. The writ of summons to the defendants
(12 July), after rehearsing the penalties provided for those in-
fringing the Statute of Provisors, narrated the circumstances of the
election as given in the Swan version, and directed the sheriff of
York to summon John Rypon, Richard Derham, clerk,[1] Richard

[1] Can this be Richard Dereham, Chancellor of Cambridge University,

Waltham, Major Parys,[1] Simon Northew,[2] and Thomas Darbell, his counsellors and abettors, to appear in the King's Bench on the morrow of All Souls. On the day fixed for the hearing the sheriff made the customary plea for adjournment, and the parties were assigned the morrow of the Purification (3 February 1414).[3] Attorneys were duly appointed in the Hilary term, but on the day for the trial the entry of the case on the Controlment Roll ends with the brief note:

> Ad quem diem per perceptum regis non fit
> inde ulterius processus.[4]

The case had been stopped. And the reason is clear. At the king's order Rypon's bulls had in the meantime been examined by the justices and by 'certain doctors of the clergy', and 'determined to be no provision'.[5] Frank's case against Rypon in the King's Bench was founded on the assumption that they were: in his plea to the court he had stated that Rypon 'quandam provisionem de dicta abbatia sibi fieri procuravit'. A conference of secular and ecclesiastical jurists had decided the question. How Rypon convinced them it will shortly appear.

Before ever the suit was brought, disorder had begun to reign at Fountains. Frank had been ousted, but he and his party of monks continued to act as the lawful authorities of the monastery, entering into bonds *de graundez sommes* and disposing of the abbey's goods and property. Some of the treasure was pledged to John Wyndhill, rector of Arncliffe in the Percy fee of Craven, for 200 marks,[6]

---

whose claims to a bishopric Swan had put forward to the pope? One of the grounds for this claim was that he had always opposed the Statute of Provisors: cf. E. F. Jacob, *Essays in the Conciliar Epoch*, 3rd ed., p. 219.

[1] Not 'Mayor of Parys' as *Memorials*, i. 211, calls Richard Waltham. Paris is a familiar early Lincoln name. See the list of town officials, containing members of that family, in J. W. F. Hill, *Medieval Lincoln*, pp. 379–82, 392.

[2] The curialist, acting for Rypon at the Council of Constance: cf. *infra*, p. 96.

[3] K.B. 27/610, Rex, m. 14: 'Johannes de Etton, vic' Ebor', retornavit quod breve predictum adeo tarde sibi liberatum fuit quod illud exequi non potuit.'

[4] K.B. 29/52/m. 10. Mr H. C. Johnson kindly drew my attention to this ending.

[5] 'Determinez nulle provision': S.C. 8, File 18, no. 885: *Rot. Parl.* iv. 28. The transcript in *Memorials*, i. 209, gives 'determiner nulle provision', which makes nonsense of the passage.

[6] *Memorials*, i. 217.

and, when he left, Frank took the common seal with him. The total amount abstracted Rypon assessed at 2,000 marks.[1] When after Easter 1414 Rypon started for London to sue Frank for restitution, his party was attacked in Welbeck Park by Oliver Frank and Roger's cousin, Robert, and several of Rypon's retainers were wounded.[2] Whether it is to this year or the following that the attack on Rypon's supporters in Craven by the Lancashire esquires John Tunstall and Robert de Worsley[3] belongs seems uncertain; the petition for redress assigns it to 24 October, but in the text the year is obliterated.[4] It appears that a sort of civil war had broken out upon the estates of the abbey, and that a proportion of the tenants in Upper Ribblesdale[5] were loyal to Frank. In the letter which I have attributed to January 1416, printed below,[6] Frank speaks of his drawing rents and farms from certain (unnamed) granges and manors, and recovering possession of others, but the position was anomalous, for on 14 December 1413 the king sequestrated the abbey and committed it to the keeping of Archbishop Bowet and Bishop Thomas Langley of Durham, 'until it is settled to which side the right of the dignity should belong'.[7] After the Praemunire case had been stopped, an official decision in Rypon's favour was taken: on 7 March 1414 John, duke of Bedford, and Ralph Neville, earl of Westmorland, were directed to put him in possession of the abbey.[8] Throughout the summer of 1414 the evicted Frank and thirteen monks—presumably those who had voted for him at the election—were 'wandering from place to place in secular habit'. On 1 June Sir William Tempest and others were commissioned to arrest them and deliver them to Rypon for chastisement 'according to the rule of their order';[9] and in October 1414 a fresh commission was issued to Tempest and colleagues, joined with the sheriff of York,

---

[1] S.C. 8, File 18, no. 885; *Rot. Parl.* iv. 28; *Memorials*, i. 209–10.

[2] S.C. 8, File 23, no. 1125; *Rot. Parl.* iv. 27–8; *Memorials*, i. 208–9.

[3] Ibid., 214–15.

[4] Ibid., 213–14. Tunstall may have been a relation of the William Tunstall, monk of Fountains, who received a dispensation to hold a secular benefice with cure (*Cal. Papal. Lett.* vi. 467), and was a supporter of Frank (*Memorials*, i. 209).

[5] See the list of names, ibid.

[6] pp. 96–7.

[7] *C.P.R., 1413–16*, p. 145.

[8] Ibid., p. 180.

[9] Ibid., p. 223.

G

for their capture: but significantly a *supersedeas* was granted in
favour of Frank himself 'for particular causes laid before the king
in Chancery'.[1]

The king might introduce Rypon into the monastery itself, but
the new-comer had not got possession of the estates, and the
chapter-general of the Cistercians had not yet cancelled its early
confirmation of his opponent's election. In the autumn of 1414
when the Western Church was preparing for the General Council, opinion was setting against John XXIII, and Frank saw his
chance to secure a reversal of the pope's summary determination
of his cause. Robert Appleton, canon of York, appointed one of
Archbishop Chichele's proctors at the Council of Constance,[2]
was ready to lend him assistance, while William Swan was
engaged to prepare a statement of the case. Before precisely what
body at Constance Frank's plea was heard and discussed is very
difficult to say: the point depends on the interpretation of a letter
from Frank to Swan which will be discussed. Of one thing we can
be certain: the case would be powerfully contested by John
Rypon himself, who, with Richard Middleton, abbot of Beaulieu,
was at Constance in 1415–16 to represent the English Cistercians,[3]
having received his protection on 21 November 1415.[4] Though
not a member of the original English delegation, he is described as
being *in obsequio Regis*.

Frank's letter is dated 20 January, without the year. He signs
himself 'the abbot of Fountains, R. Frank, whom you know', and
writes to tell Swan that he has been much disturbed by an inhibition, a copy of which he has sent to master Robert Appleton at
the Council. In virtue of this the archbishop of York has decided
not to execute the bulls issued to him and put him in possession
of the abbey. He has heard, he says, from Master Simon Northew
and Master John Forster at the Council reporting the general
opinion that his bulls were not granted by the ordinary judges of
the Council, but by 'certain private judges not having sufficient
power in these matters', and saying that 'if the verdict given in his
favour had been given by the General Council or at least by the
ordinary judges of the Council, his bulls would undoubtedly
have not been sealed with wax, but with lead, since the General

---

[1] *Cal. Close Rolls, Henry V*, i. 193.

[2] *Reg. Chichele*, iv. 107–8.

[3] Martène et Durand, *Thesaurus novus anecdotorum*, iv. 1563.

[4] *Foedera* (Hague ed.), iv. 2, 150.

Council has a leaden seal especially for the purpose'.[1] Frank's
reference to his bulls and to a verdict given in his favour, which
the archbishop of York was deterred by an inhibition from imple-
menting, may point to one of the far-reaching administrative rifts
which made their appearance in the Council of Constance after
the deposition of John XXIII had raised in an acute form both
the problem of sovereignty in the Church and the nearer and more
concrete problem of how and by whom the acts of the Council
were to be authenticated. The question of the *bulla*, by whom and
on what occasions it was to be used, raised itself in January 1416,
when the nations were becoming jealous of the professional
administrators in the Curia, and were striving their utmost to
control the seal.[2] It is possible that Frank's verdict slipped through,
sealed not with the Council's leaden seal, but with a seal of less
authority, one among many other documents which, as Cardinal
Fillastre complained, were emanating from the Curia while the
Patriarch of Antioch was in control.[3] If this is so, it may help to
determine the date of Frank's letter. He had got *a* verdict, but the
verdict had produced an immediate reaction from his opponent:
Rypon had obtained, at outrageous cost and with his habit of
secrecy (*plurimum exhorbitanter et surreptitie*), a conciliar inhibition
directed to the diocesan authority against putting Frank into
possession. Who then are the *judices privati* whose acts are con-
trasted with the *judices concilii*? It looks very much as if Rypon
knew how to play on an already existing dualism in the Council,
on the tension between the judges of the Curia and the *judices
deputati per Concilium*. From a conciliar point of view, a case taken
to the Council should be settled by the Council's judges and ratified
by the nations. This was not so with Frank's case. Whatever is the
right interpretation here, the fact remains that Frank had got a
verdict and an order for restitution, bulled in a manner which
made certain English proctors suspicious of its source: they

[1] MS. Arch. Seld. B. 23, fos. 64v, 65.

[2] Fillastre's diary, in H. Finke, *Acta Concilii Constanciensis*, ii. 53. See
the pertinent remarks of Martin Souchon, *Die Papstwahlen und die
Kardinäle*, ii. 178.

[3] 'Patriarcha Antiochenus, qui dicebatur illas litteras ad bullam dare et
expedire, multum se excusavit et institit fortiter, quod illa relinquerentur
et nichil mutaretur. Verum naciones prohibuerunt bullatoribus, ne ali-
quam litteram bullarent, nisi esset lector in nacionibus et signata per
quatuor presidentes IIII nacionum et per eosdem data ad bullandum'
(Finke, ibid.).

probably told Rypon, who was determined to stop the order, and did so. The verdict and the order reached Frank, but were followed by the inhibition, and things were back again in their old confusion.

In the October Parliament of 1416 the Commons petitioned for a clear settlement of the issue, one way or the other. They observed that for a long time there had been great debate 'in the court of Rome and in the court Christian at the General Council of Constance' between Frank and Rypon, and asked the king, in view of the harmful nature of the dispute, to direct letters under the Great Seal 'to his ambassadors and all his lieges in the Council', charging them to notify the judges and all the nations assembled there that he desired them to do right to the parties, and so hasten the business to its rightful ending. Henry V promised, in reply, to send letters to his ambassadors, drawn up as he should think best.[1] A letter, probably in pursuance of this promise, was sent by the king to Bishops Nicholas Bubwith and Robert Hallum.[2] Henry states that he was being constantly harassed and assailed by representations from either party, and that the case was becoming the cause of great perplexity and anxiety to him, and to many others. So far he had been neutral (though, as has been mentioned, he ordered Rypon to be put in possession of the abbey in 1414); but he must now ask the bishops to take the opinion of unprejudiced lawyers in the Curia on 'the circumstances and merits of the whole case', and, disregarding the favour of either party, to report to the king which side had the better claim. This is not quite what the Commons asked: it was a request for an authoritative opinion rather than for a further trial and verdict. The king had good reason for this caution, as will presently appear.

At Constance Swan had been watching Rypon closely. He had evidently seen a report made by English Cistercian abbots on the Fountains dispute and had convinced himself that Rypon's account of the election was untrue:

And note that eight abbots visited, over this dissension, the monastery, and drew up a report on the issue, which of the contending parties was the more fit person (*utilis*) and which proceeded in the more just and proper manner: and they report under their eight seals that the

---

[1] *Rot. Parl.* iv. 101; *Memorials*, i. 212–13.
[2] Printed below, p. 97 from MS. Arch. Seld. B. 23, fos. 61v, 62.

said brother Roger has the right [on his side], but that the other is the intruded one; nay, even if he had any right, he has lost it according to the statutes of the Order on account of the methods which he has observed in this business, both by recourse to the secular arm, as in other ways, as they solemnly report.

Then comes a significant passage:

Item, brother John, the intruder, has two bulls from the same lord Balthasar, by one of which he helps his case in England and conceals the other; the other bull helps him in this Council and he conceals the former. In the one it is contained that the Pope *confirmed* the aforesaid election; in the other that he simply *provided* Rypon to the abbey. And because in England they refuse to receive the said provision, he shows there the confirmation of the election;[1] but in this Council, because he cannot maintain the said confirmation to be of any value, he shows the provision; and so it is clear that he proceeds guilefully (*dolose*).

Swan adds a query:

Would it be legitimate to tell in what manner he [Rypon] was intruded with armed force by a certain lord who must not be named (*per aliquem dominum non nominandum*), and how he paid him 500 marks each year, etc.? Brother Roger would not dare to say this, and with reason, save at least when judgement is delivered (*nisi saltem in judicio*).[2]

How much help each side received from secular lords remains a mystery. The Fountains annalist and Rypon himself represented Frank as intruded;[3] Frank in turn charged Rypon with being intruded by some lord whose name could not be revealed. Conjecture is unprofitable, but certain reflections suggest themselves. The patron of Meaux, who as duke of Albemarle after Gloucester's death had taken some part in the dispute over Burton's election in favour of his opponents, was Edward Plantagenet, duke of York: but there is no evidence to suggest that he supported the Meaux candidate for Fountains. One of Frank's helpers may be less difficult to find: there is a certain amount of evidence that Henry Percy, Hotspur's son who was created earl of Northumberland on 16 March 1416, was interested in the election. When Frank was raising money for his campaign against the disseisor Rypon, he pledged, as we noted, a quantity of silver and jewels from the abbey

---

[1] This passage is exactly borne out by the finding of the legal experts that Rypon's bulls were 'no provision'.

[2] MS. Arch. Seld. B 23, fo. 143v.

[3] *Memorials*, i. 146, 208–9.

treasure to John Wyndhill, rector of Arncliffe. Wyndhill had been
presented to this Percy living by the old earl of Northumberland
who had been killed at Bramham Moor. In John Wyndhill's
testament (16 September 1431)[1] the intimate connexion of the
testator with the Percy family appears: the gifts to Henry, earl of
Northumberland, and Ralph Percy, the son, and to the dean and
celebrants in the earl's chapel at Alnwick, his desired burial in the
monastery at Alnwick,[2] suggest that Wyndhill was in early days a
member of the Percy household. If this is the case, the money
advanced by Wyndhill on the security of the goods from Fountains
may have been paid by order of his patron, Henry Percy, and the
document printed by Mr Walbran in his *Memorials of Fountains
Abbey* be capable of receiving the interpretation which that editor
tentatively assigned to it.[3] This document is a bond in 200 marks,
dated 10 April 1424, and payable at midsummer to the prior and
convent of Durham by the abbot and convent of Fountains, but
with the reservation that there should be a defeasance of the bond
if the Crown then or later claimed that the plate and jewels originally pledged to John Wyndhill, and now in the custody of Durham,
belonged to Henry Percy, earl of Northumberland. The defeasance
is headed

Defezancia obligationis cc marcarum facta Priori et Conventui Dunelm'
    pro liberacione jocalium Abbatis de Fontibus, quia Henricus quintus
    Rex Anglie putabat illa jocalia fuisse Henrici Percy Comitis North-
    umbrie.

Henry must have asserted his belief that the jewels and plate were
Percy property on deposit, for safe keeping, at Fountains, and that
the rector's advance to Frank was made by order of young Henry
Percy, the owner. Possibly Percy told him about it. All this, of
course, does not prove that Henry Percy 'intruded' Frank; only
that he was willing to help him.

We leave supposition, and return to the contending parties.
Henry V may have been justified in seeking no more than a legal
opinion on the case, in view of the decision, during 1416, of the
chapter-general of the Order to cancel its earlier confirmation of
Frank's election. It did so on the ground of having clear evidence

---

[1] Rightly termed 'very interesting' by H. W. Morant in his edition (the
third) of Whitaker's *History of Craven*, p. 579.
[2] *Testamenta Eborancensia*, ii. 32–5.
[3] *Memorials*, i. 217–18.

that the facts of the 1410 election had been kept back from it and misrepresented, both orally and in the documents submitted, by a monk who by means of fictitious letters falsely made himself out to be John Rypon's proxy, in order to deceive Rypon and chapter alike. *Suppressa negotii veritate* suggests influences on the election which had not come to light, and the agent who brought the announcement from Fountains is charged with deliberate falsification. This had prevented Rypon from stating his case, as had emerged in the consequent appeal.[1] The *diffinitio* does not proceed to confirm Rypon's election, but the ground was now cut from under Frank's feet, and with this and the refusal of Archbishop Bowet to reinstate him, his case was at an end.

It has difficult and perplexing features. The clash between the evidence now possessed by the chapter-general and the plain and straightforward account given by the assessors at the 1410 election is hard to resolve, because there is nothing to indicate what the *evidentia documenta* disclosed. It is reasonable to suppose that the election was not canonically free, that it was an election either *per abusum saecularis potestatis* or violating in some respect the *Quia propter* of Innocent III. In either case a good many technicalities are involved,[2] of which nothing is heard here. The chapter's *diffinitio* is the first occasion on which anything is known of the fraudulent emissary purporting to represent Rypon. How did such a thing come about? Why were his credentials not more carefully

[1] 'Diffinitionem quae per modum annexae dudum a Capitulo dicitur emanasse, et fratris Rogeri Franck electionem vel provisionem praetensam ad monasterium de Fontibus in Anglia, Eboracensis diocesis, cujus ipse monachus est, confirmasse, dictum capitulum evidentibus certificatum documentis, quod suppressa negotii veritate, multis quoque mendaciorum non tam verbalium quam litteralium commentis subrepta fuerit et obtenta per quemdam monachum litteris factitiis et non veris procurationem domini Johannis Rippon, ut eum et dictum Capitulum deciperet fallaciter se gerentem, quocumque verborum tenore ipsa confirmationis annexio processerit, in praeiudicium dicti Iohannis Rippon, vel juris sui ad monasterium de Fontibus, eo legitime non audito nec vocato, qui ut postea patuit per appellationis remedium dicto Rogero in huiusmodi causa litem moverat, prorsus irritam et nullius roboris aut vigoris esse declarat, notificat et decernit' (*Statuta Ordinis Cisterciensis*, ed. Canivez, iv. 206).

[2] Cf. especially the treatment of these categories in Passerini, *De Electione Canonica* (Cologne, 1694), chs. viii and ix: e.g. 'Electio per abusum saecularis potestatis est si intersit laicus, vel in ea aliquod munus gerat, vel ejus consensus super certis personis expectetur': but each of these conditions is subject to reservations of various kinds.

examined? And how was Rypon able to get, if Swan is right, both a provision to, and a confirmation for, the same benefice? Swan is on the whole a reliable source of information for the affairs of his clients and never unnecessarily blackens his opponents; but he cannot withhold the world *dolosus* from Rypon, and his memorandum is bound to shake confidence in the abbot who was to live in undisputed possession of Fountains till his death on Friday, 12 March 1434.

From William Swan's Letter-book

11 Jan. 1416[1]
Roger Frank to William Swan at Constance

Eximie discrecionis viro magistro Willelmo Swan apud Curiam Romanam. Prestantissime domine et merito singulari, premissa salutatione debita, vobis pro arduis et immensis laboribus et favoribus quos dumtaxat ex gratia gratuita et nequaquam meritis in nostra causa apud Constantiam subire dignabatur vestra elementia compassiva, gratias vobis quas possumus merito referimus[2] cordiales, quamvis non valeamus agere ad condignum. Et prestantissime domine et merito diligende, scire dignemini nos multipliciter perturbari cum quadam inhibicione plurimum exhor[f. 65]bitanter et surreptitie obtenta, ut credimus, cujus quidem inhibicionis copiam misimus nuper cum aliis literis magistro Roberto Appylton'. Et propterea in monasterio de fontibus possessionem nondum recepimus dicta inhibicione nobis obstante, sed in grangiis or maneriis nostris possessionem personaliter recepimus ante presentacionem dicte pretense inhibicionis nobis factam, prout alias vobis scripsimus, et adhuc possessionem dictorum maneriorum et grangiarum et aliarum villarum et locorum debite continuavimus, eorum firmas dietim percipiendo. Insuper sciatis magistrum Simonem Northwe et magistrum Johannem fforster per literas suas publicam famam scripsisse quod bulle nostre non fuerunt concesse per judices ordinarios consilii generalis sed per quosdam judices privatos, sufficientem potestatem in hujusmodi non habentes, asserentes quod si processisset sentencia nostra per dictum generale concilium vel saltem per judices ordinarios ipsius concilii, quod bulle nostre nequaquam cum cera sed cum plumbo fuissent indubie sigilate, eo quod ipsum generale concilium habeat sigillum plumbeum ad hoc specialiter deputatum. Quibus nobis sic, ut prefertur, obstantibus, dominus Archiepiscopus Eboracensis ad executionem dictarum bullarum nostrarum amplius

---

[1] Bodl. Lib., MS. Arch. Seld. B. 23, fo. 64v.
[2] MS. referrimus.

procedere non intendit. Quia [ante] presentacionem dicte inhibicionis nos decrevit per commissionem suam in possessionem mittendos[1] et post hujusmodi exhibitam inhibicionem mandavit commissariis suis quod supersederent. Et sic, prout aliis vobis scripsimus, in dies indebite molestamur. Idcirco in premissis omnibus et singulis per vestrum discretum concilium et bonum avisiamentum magistri Roberti Appylton' sic invigilare dignemini, ut nostra causa in hujusmodi gravaminibus enormiter perturbata absque competenti remedio nullomodo relinquatur. Vestram prestantissimam et precarissimam personam ad sui laudem conservet feliciter Altissimus in honore. Scriptum in manerio de Merkyngfeld xx^{to} die mensis Januarii.

Abbas de ffontibus R. ffrank
quem novistis.

Undated, probably late 1416.[2] *Henry V to Nicholas Bubwith, Bishop of Bath and Wells, and Robert Hallum, Bishop of Salisbury, at the Council of Constance*

Reverendi in Christo patres et nobis sincere dilecti intima cordis salutacione premissa. Fidelitatibus vestris, reverendi patres, providimus intimare quod cotidianis querimoniis et importunis instanciis pro parte religiosorum virorum Rogeri Frank et Johannis Rypon' super jure abbatie de Fontibus contendentium afficimur incessanter, et est nobis continuo de justicia supplicatum pro qua nos reputamus cuilibet debitores; cujus namque contentionis negotium cum sit in opinione varium, obscurum in jure, et periculosum in exemplo, concitat mentes et animos pulsat plurimorum, multis hinc inde deductis nobis suggestionibus et fortissimis argumentis. Qua de causa neutrales adhuc, donec ubi justicia vigeat veraciter informemur, fidelitates vestras exhortamur attente et nichilominus sanas conscientias vestras oneramus in domino, quod de controversie hujusmodi circumstanciis et meritis universis a jurisperitis in Curia, qui indifferenti favore et equa libra negotium complectuntur, curetis animo solicito indagare, et subsequenter postpositis favoribus utriusque contendentium, quis eorum justiciam foveat, quantum investigare poteritis, cum celeritate accommoda certitudinaliter et plenarie nobis rescribere studeatis: ut ab inquietudine, qua cotidianis [diebus] superinde lacessimur, vestris fidelibus [f. 62] et bene regulatis conscientiis respiremus, dum de vestris circumspeccionibus et fidelitatibus plurimum confidentes debitum in ea parte, quo ad nos attinet, exhibere valeamus secura conscientia justicie complementum; in eo pregratam nobis complacentiam facientes, et majorem animi nostri quietudinem procurantes, qui solicitudinem continuam profitemur. Dat' etc. Henricus dei gracia Rex Anglie.

---

[1] MS. nos in possessionem mittend'.
[2] MS. Arch. Seld. B. 23, fo. 61v–62.

Chapter V
The Conciliar Movement in Recent Study

At the International Historical Congress in Rome (1955), a well-known professor referred contentedly to the Conciliar Movement as 'un petit nuage sur l'horizon'. A little cloud the size of a man's hand, one remembers, sent Elijah running before Ahab's chariot to the entrance of Jezreel. King and prophet had to make their best paces before the oncoming storm.

It was the king, not the priest, who came off best as the result of the councils. Such is the opinion of Mgr Hubert Jedin, writing the introductory chapter to a celebrated work. The ultimate beneficiary of the Church councils of the fifteenth century was the modern state.[1] The failure of the councils to secure any general measure of reform left it to the local monarchs to make, through their own churches, bargains or compacts with the Holy See. The councils, therefore, Dr Jedin regards as helping to establish the Renaissance monarchy. There are plenty of examples: the concordats made by the Papacy with the several nations at the end of the Council of Constance; the memoranda and discussions at the Diet of Nuremberg in 1444 showing the bargains which the German princes proposed to strike through their policy of neutrality;[2] the Pragmatic Sanction of Bourges and the later Concordat of Bologna between Leo X and Francis I (1516);[3] the Concordat of Vienna between Pope Nicholas V and the Emperor Frederick III in 1448.[4] Yet to view thus in perspective the concordats and agreements made by the various secular powers with the Holy See should not be allowed to belittle the achievement of re-establishing unity in the Church, when it seemed so difficult to convene a council at all, nor the great and prolonged effort at producing measures of reform. The councils, whether they are judged to have failed or not, at least provided a European sounding-board for grievances felt within the Church, while the treatises and

[1] *A History of the Council of Trent*, trans. A. Graf, i (1957), 21.
[2] See especially *Reichstagsakten*, VII, 2, i, nos. 165, 168, 175.
[3] A. Mercati, *Raccolta di Concordate tra la Santa Sede e le autorità civili* (1919), p. 233
[4] Text in Altmann-Bernheim, *Urkunden zur Verfassungsgeschichte Deutschlands*, p. 142. An English version is given in S. Z. Ehler and J. B. Morrall, *Church and State through the Centuries* (1954), pp. 125–31.

schemes they evoked have taken a permanent place in the literature of reforming thought.

Over twenty-five years ago I attempted to review some of those efforts and treatises from the English point of view.[1] It had long been the custom to undervalue this country's effort in the councils and to misjudge their importance on the grounds that they were a venture of the academic spirit in politics. Certainly, in so far as personnel is concerned, this view finds little support in recent studies. The dissertations of Dr Christopher Crowder (Oxford, 1953) and Dr A. N. E. D. Schofield (London, 1957) on the English delegations at Constance and Basel respectively have shown that in the two carefully balanced and highly distinguished representative groups attending, academics by no means predominated, and that, as far as policy was concerned, the influence of the Crown, when exercised, and of the secular church at large was of much more significance. One may add that university representatives throughout the councils, however important individually, were in a minority in their nations. Active and vocal Paris professors, men like Simon Cramaud, Pierre d'Ailly or Jean Courtecuisse, leaders in the national councils of 1398 and 1406, were churchmen first and foremost, and if they expressed themselves in the terms of the schools, this was because such language was the normal vehicle of serious argument. If, however, it is meant that conciliarism failed because the thinkers of the movement lacked the experience enabling them to understand how powerful was the weight of custom and vested interest both in the Roman Curia, in the exempt houses and the greater cathedral chapters, there is something in the contention; so is there for the view long ago expressed by Dr Neville Figgis, when he thought that the failure of the Conciliar Movement to restrain the Pope permanently or to further the growth of federalism in the Church provided a justification at once of the reformation and of ultramontanism:

of ultramontanism on one side, for there must apparently have been some grounds for absolute monarchy either in the nature of political society or in the condition of the Christian Church, for the Papal monarchy to triumph in so overwhelming a fashion over a movement so

---

[1] 'Some English Documents of the Conciliar Movement', *Bulletin of the John Rylands Library*, xv (1931), 358 f. Dr Ullmann added important testimony on the attitude of Cambridge University to the Schism, *Journal of Theological Studies*, new ser., ix. i (April, 1958).

reasonable and so respectable, supported by men of such learning as
Gerson and Zabarella . . .

We now know more of the theoretical 'grounds';[1] and more about
the weakness and the strength of curial administration which the
clergy were always criticizing but could not do without.

What Figgis perhaps did not fully realize was the complexity of
the diplomatic situation within which the councils had to work, its
far too inveterate character; account has to be taken of the strength
of the alliances formed by the two sides in the Anglo-French war;
the determination of the French kings to support the adventures
of their cadets and relations in Italy, and the resolution with which
the German monarchy under Sigismund set about asserting its
function as advocate and protector of the Church, determined to
put the word *sacrum* into *imperium* again.[2] Given these diplomatic
constants, now more familiar through the work of French scholars
like Noel Valois, Victor Martin, Canon Delaruelle and Professor
Ourliac, we have now a more proportioned picture of these international Councils established to restore the unity of the Head, the
purity of the Faith and the reform of the Curia and the Church
alike.

First, if they were not always inflamed by charity, the leaders of
the council had both faith and hope. They believed that the
Church had within itself the power to restore its own life and that
that restoration came through an act of sovereignty derived from
the consent of the faithful as a whole: and that that consent was
conveyed through representatives meeting in a General Council.
Of late a Cambridge graduate, Professor Brian Tierny, has made a
notable contribution to the history of Conciliar ideas by arguing

[1] W. Ullmann, *Medieval Papalism* (1949), ch. iv, deals in particular
with the plenitude of power. For a realistic assessment of its growth, cf.
essays of Fr Stickler and Mgr Maccarrone in *Sacerdozio e Regno da
Gregorio VII a Bonifacio VIII*, ed. F. Kempf (Misc. Hist. Pont. xviii,
Rome, 1954). For the canonist contribution, see especially Brian Tierney,
'Ockham, the Conciliar Theory and the Canonists', *Journal of the History
of Ideas*, xv (1954), 40–70 and bibliography.

[2] Egged on by publicists like Dietrich of Niem, whose *Viridarium
Imperatorum et Regum Romanorum* (ed. Lhotsky and Pivec, Stuttgart
1956) glorifies on historical grounds the position of the Emperor vis-à-vis
the Church. For Dietrich's use of sources, cf. K. Pivec, 'Das imperium in
den Privilegien und im *Viridarium*', *Neue Forschungen zu Dietrich von
Niem* (with H. Heimpel), (Nachrichten der Akad. d. Wiss. in Göttingen),
1957.

that they sprang as much from the lawyers of the Church as from the professed theological publicists.[1] The emergence of the Schism, its long duration and the necessity for ending it, raised fundamental questions about the nature of the Church. Much of this speculation had been anticipated in the twelfth and thirteenth centuries, as Professor Tierney shows from the glosses on the *Decretum* from Huguccio to Johannes Teutonicus and Bernard of Parma. Was the 'Roman Church' to be identified with the whole body of the faithful? Was it *ecclesia totius mundi*? Or was it a particular local church having primacy over the others? To Huguccio for instance it was clear that the Roman Church, understood as the Pope and the Curia, could not be the Church that was to endure for ever 'unwavering in faith and unstained by sin'. The distinction can be found in Dietrich of Niem's first (1410) edition of his *De modis uniendi et reformandi ecclesiam in concilio universali.*[2] On the relations of Pope and Council, heresy is the one crime mentioned in the text of the *Decretum* justifying the punishment of the Pope by the Universal Church; but notorious crimes might also go into the category of heresy, and the canonists of the last generation before the Councils treated many crimes as such. But the most interesting problem concerned the Pope and Cardinals; for, as Huguccio concluded, during the vacancy of the Holy See the Cardinals might act as one, in place of a head.

In certain cases, when the Papacy was vacant, it was maintained that the Cardinals might summon a general council, and the *Glossa Palatina* goes as far as to assert that the Pope alone was actually incompetent to establish a general law for the whole Church, and that such enactments were valid only when approved by the Cardinals. It is important, as Professor Tierney reminds his readers, to regard the speculations of the early canonists as speculations and as suggested principles for this or that case, not as authoritative opinions altering or modifying the law. And there are times when, perhaps, he may not himself have fully recognized the rather experimental, even exceptional, nature of the glosses. The most characteristic speculation, however, concerned the structure

---

[1] *Foundations of the Conciliar Theory*, Cambridge, 1956. For the early decretist period, cf. John Watt, 'The Early Medieval Canonists and the Formation of Conciliar Theory', *Irish Theological Review*, xxiv (January 1957), 1.

[2] Dietrich von Niem, *Dialog über und Reform der Kirche, 1410*, ed. H. Heimpel (1933), p. 6.

of a medieval ecclesiastical corporation.[1] Can corporations act when the rectors (as in the case of universities) are missing? Or where they are present, have the members as well the right to consent? With an ecclesiastical chapter, should the consent of the canons be required when any vital interest of the whole corporation was involved? Hostiensis thought so: in the matter of alienations, for instance, he pointed out that their special consent was necessary even in the case of property pertaining specially to a bishop, since bishop and chapter together formed a single corporate body which suffered as a whole from any loss.[2] Naturally the theory of the corporate unity of bishop and chapter raised difficulties. How was the consent to be expressed? Did it require the consent of all or of the *maior et sanior pars*—and so forth. From the chapter, it was possible to advance to the theory of the whole Church as a corporation, and indeed the concept of the Church as the Mystical Body of Christ did not frighten the canonists, since the idea of the *Corpus mysticum* had been associated with the definition of the Church as a *universitas fidelium*. In such a body, what should the position of the Pope be? Here one may recollect the view of Hostiensis (Henry of Suso) that the head of a corporation was its principal part, enjoying an authority greater than that of any single member of the corporation, but not greater than that of all the members together.

In the fourteenth century the conflict of figures in Church and State, Boniface VIII and Philip the Fair, Lewis of Bavaria and John XXII aroused speculation about the doctrine of the plenitude of power and the jurisdiction of the supreme pontiff. One subtle and far-seeing publicist, John of Paris, maintained that the jurisdiction of a Pope was conferred by the whole Church, and several times asserted that the Cardinals acted on behalf of the Church. In general, his work, as Professor Tierney rightly states, 'provides by far the most consistent and complete formulation of Conciliar doctrine before the outbreak of the Great Schism'.[3]

This conclusion and many of the theories found in the Decretalists formed part of a corpus of liberal or 'progressive' thought on the subject of authority in the Church which had been built up as the result of study or controversy. It was entirely loyal to the Papacy as an institution, but it was critical and 'constitutional', in-

[1] Tierney, ch. ii.
[2] Ibid., pp. 122–3.
[3] Ibid., p. 177.

clined, where reform was concerned, to start everything at the Curia itself, instead of with the chapters and corporations. That it should be used effectively and decisively when the Great Schism, dragging itself out, provided the occasion and the opportunity, is in great part due to the brilliant synthesizing mind of Cardinal Zabarella. It is the achievement of Professor Walter Ullmann (for which all conciliar historians should be grateful) to have pointed in his book on the *Origins of the Great Schism* (1948), precisely to those passages in Zabarella which seem to have stressed the fundamental point that the Schism is a matter of faith, and that in dealing with such a context, the synod is greater than the Pope. He also calls attention to Zabarella's definition of the Roman Church as *non solus Papa sed ipse Papa cum cardinalibus, qui sunt partes corporis Papae*:[1] 'Not only the Pope, but the Pope with the Cardinals who are part of the Pope's body.' And, says Zabarella, 'if there arises discord between Pope and Cardinals, it is necessary to convene the Church, i.e. the whole congregation of catholics and the principal ministers of the faith, the prelates, who represent the whole congregation'.[2] Zabarella, Professor Tierney concludes, 'was able to unite the discordant theories of the earlier canonists by applying the concepts of corporation law not only to the relations between Pope and Cardinal but between Pope and Council, and also to the status of the Cardinals themselves in relation to the Universal Church'. Inspired by the urgent necessities of his own day, Zabarella had clothed the bare framework of Decretalist corporation theory with all the complex details of an integrated theory of Church government.[3]

Let us turn to the councils themselves. The printed authorities for the Council of Pisa are normally studied in the large volumes of Mansi (XXVII) and Martène and Durand. They are drawn mainly from epistolary sources and semi-official *Acta*. On the eve of the last war a friend and pupil of Heinrich Finke who like his master had worked long and fruitfully in the Crown archives of Aragon put the study of the council on a secure footing by re-editing, with new source material added, the hitherto unpublished version of the *Acta* made by three scholars, Erler, Finke himself and Schmitz-Kallenberg; and by an analysis of letter-books and registers hitherto unused. Dr Johannes Vincke's extracts from the

[1] Ullmann, op. cit., p. 203.
[2] Ibid., p. 210.
[3] Tierney, pp. 236–7.

letters mainly concern the preliminaries of the Council.[1] A register
of 'out' letters was kept by the seceding cardinals of Gregory XII,
ever since the time when, wearied with the delays and procrastin-
ation of their master, they separated themselves from him and set
up their headquarters, first at Livorno and later, with Florentine
assent, at Pisa. Besides this register they kept another containing
their letters of summons to the European powers and high church
dignitaries; a selection of the answers received from the summoned, and of the letters accrediting representatives to the forthcoming council at Pisa; and a group of documents emanating from
the Council itself, including a collection of proofs made for the
process against Gregory and Benedict. These registers are for the
most part preserved in three manuscripts in the Vatican library:
Ottobono Codex III, Vatican Codex Latinus 4172 and its deriva-
tive 4171. In addition there are newly examined registers nearly
contemporary, preserved at Berlin, Danzig and at Eichstadt, and
the very important contemporary register of 'out' letters from the
Signory of Florence preserved in the *Archivio di Stato* there.[2]

These documents enable us to trace more clearly than before
the resistance of both Gregory XII and Benedict XIII in 1408–9
to the proposed council and their determination, in response to
the summons to Pisa issued by the Cardinals, each to hold a
General Council on his own, Benedict at Perpignan, Gregory
somewhere (though this was left vague) in the Exarchate of
Rauenna. Both pontiffs had considerable support, Gregory in King
Rupert of Germany, in Hungary, in Venice and in Charles
Malatesta at Rimini: Benedict in the kingdoms of Aragon and
Castile and among certain sections in France; as well as in Scotland. The letters show the cardinals striving to the utmost to convince the European powers that the council was necessary. They
even asked the local collectors to finance the representatives of the
ecclesiastical provinces in their district who were going to the
forthcoming council: *provideatis de necessariis in suis expensis*,[3] for
which sums, they blandly say, when unity has been achieved, we
will make the new undoubted pontiff or his chamberlain or other
relevant officials responsible. In other words, the local collectors
were to put up the money for travelling expenses until the new

[1] 'Acta Concilii Pisani', *Römische Quartalschrift*, 46 (1941), 1–331.
[2] Johannes Vincke, *Briefe zum Pisanerkonzil* (*Beiträge zur Kirchen-und
Rechtsgeschichte*, i, Bonn, 1940), pp. 8–10, 239, and nos. 18, 19.
[3] Vincke, pp. 95–6.

régime had taken over. Florence, however, when asked to put up a
thousand guilders replied that 'considering we are in the obedience
of Pope Gregory it does not appear honorable to make this inno-
vation at present'.[1] Meanwhile Cardinal Peter Philargi of Milan
pressed the university of Paris to urge upon the French king that
Gregory XII must resign. Letters also went out to the doge telling
him of the cardinal's vain endeavours to secure an audience with
Gregory XII.[2]

Fresh accounts are to be found of the approach to both the
Popes by supporters of the Council. Benedict, surrounded by his
cardinals, was interviewed at Perpignan on 6 November 1408.
Four of the cardinals who had since seceded had originally
written to him from Livorno, on 14 July, but no direct reply had
been forthcoming. He gave his answer now on a paper document,
replying that the letters just presented to him by William Sanhete
on the cardinals' behalf contained much that was otherwise in fact.
Benedict said that he proposed to answer the cardinals' missive
and to deal with 'other things pertaining to the unity of the Church'
in a general council to be celebrated immediately.[3] The council
was, in fact, celebrated. Gregory XII was more polite, but no less
obstinate. The register records the visit to him at Rimini on
28 February 1409 of three envoys of Henry IV who were the king's
accredited representatives at the Council of Pisa: they were the
Abbot of Westminster; Sir John Colville, a king's knight already
possessed of considerable diplomatic experience; and the papal
auditor, Nicholas Ryssheton, a Lancashire diplomat much employed by Henry IV. Ryssheton was a product of Wykeham's
school at Winchester, whence he passed to New College. He had
been employed on difficult negotiations in the Low Countries in
1400–1.[4] The envoys were to persuade Gregory to come to the
Council of Pisa and there resign. Colville began with an eloquent
speech in Italian, a point specially noted by the Pope in his reply.
The abbot then taking as his text *coadunate senes et congregate
parvulos*, and 'proceeding very deliberately and elegantly on the
matter of union, exhorted the Lord Gregory to condescend to
come to Pisa'; then the auditor, on the text *Audi nos domine*, 'used

[1] Ibid., p. 97.
[2] Ibid., pp. 101–2.
[3] Ibid., p. 117.
[4] For Ryssheton and Colville, see J. H. Wylie, *History of England under
Henry IV*, iii. 369–73, Emden, *Biog. Register Univ. of Oxford*, iii. 1619–20.

H

many varieties of persuasive arguments in asking the lord Gregory
to come to Pisa to the General Council and there renounce his
right as the letters of Henry IV had urged him to do'. Gregory
thanked the ambassadors for the speeches; after which he gave a
long account of what had happened: how he had laboured for
union and how he was originally disposed to go to Pisa: but his
final resolve was that he would not go, 'and this for several reasons
which he professed himself ready to expound to the ambassadors
orally or in writing'. And as regards his resignation or renunciation, he replied that all his intention was to reunite the Church of
Christendom; 'but because, as he said, God knows that it was not
his responsibility that union had not been effected, he therefore
declared that a council must be celebrated which should contain
all ways in itself (consider all methods of securing unity) and that
the ambassadors should deem it a special grace given by God, if
the general council to be lawfully summoned by him should take
account of all expedients for union'.[1] Details of Henry IV's intervention have hitherto been lacking. It would be interesting to know
if he or his ambassadors were acquainted with Gregory's discredit-
able sale of Papal lands to King Ladislas.

The ambassadors, not content with this, pressed him to answer
Henry's inquiry: would he go to Pisa and resign? He replied that
when he had read the king's letter, he would readily reply. In fact
he stalled, just like Benedict. He still had hopes of arousing sympathy. He wrote a letter to Bishops Hallum and Chichele, representatives of the province of Canterbury to the Council of Pisa,[2]
to be received by them on the way. He had heard that they were
going to the council, to prevent the Church of God being trodden
underfoot by the iniquities of those already gathered at Pisa (i.e.
the cardinals who had forsaken him). He asked them to inform
themselves of the attitude taken up by the envoys of the king of
Hungary, the doge of Venice, the orators of the king Rupert and by
Charles Malatesta.[3] At the same time Gregory did not cease providing to sees and religious houses, and the cardinals had to inform
the chapter of Ratisbon, for instance, that the see must not be filled
for the time being.[4] The register shows that the Viennese repre-

---

[1] Vincke, pp. 175–6.
[2] For their commission, cf. ibid., pp. 135–8, which includes the Prior of
Christ Church, Canterbury.
[3] Vincke, p. 193.
[4] Ibid., p. 199.

sentatives at Pisa were assiduous in reporting back to the university: in the end, after Alexander V had been elected, their letter to the University finished by describing

how the said supreme pontiff and the cardinals displayed favour towards the said university. And therefore our representatives have advised that as quickly as possible a roll (of graduates for promotion) should be sent to the Pope.[1]

Back to the old system of rolls and papal provisions! All that can emerge from a council partly dedicated to reform is a return to the practice of petitioning the Curia which Dietrich of Niem was to criticize so severely at Constance.

The publication of a text of the *Acta* from the earliest notaries' materials has given the Council of Pisa a clearer orientation. The Council can now be seen for what it was, a legal process conducted against the *contendentes* for the crime of schism which, because of its long duration, had passed into heresy. It is *causa scismatis et fidei*. In the early stages the advocates, the promoters and the notaries are formally nominated and approved for the case. The parties are *legitime requisiti, vocati et provocati ad causam*. The chief advocate, Simon of Perugia, asks, perhaps a little prematurely, *Deest igitur materia heresum?*[2] The promoters get all preliminaries and the documentary evidence together, produce evidence that the parties had been summoned: the envoy who had to present the summons to Gregory XII at Siena alleged that he could not serve it himself for fear of death, so deposited the letter on the high altar of the cathedral church.[3] At the third session the cardinals who had left Gregory at Lucca and had gone to Pisa presented a report (*relatio*) which was read by the Cardinal of Aquileia.[4] Thrice the contending parties were summoned at the entrance of the cathedral of Pisa, and after the third time the certificate of contumacy was affixed to the doors. Meanwhile the Cardinals adhering to the contenddents were summoned and proceeded against, as contumacious also. At the fifth session the *libellus* containing an account of the measures taken by the contendents to hinder union was read in the Council.[5] Already a dissident element had appeared

[1] Ibid., p. 208.

[2] *Römische Quartalschrift*, 46, p. 99. The other conciliar advocate appointed was Ardicino de Novara.

[3] Ibid., p. 107.

[4] Ibid., p. 119.

[5] Ibid., pp. 134–5.

in the persons of the envoys of King Rupert of Germany, who presented a *memoriale* giving a pro-Gregory view, but did not urge that it should be immediately discussed.

It is clear that with the sixth session (30 April 1409) the main phase of the Council opened, introduced by the 'notable sermon' of Robert Hallum in the pulpit of the cathedral, on the theme *Justicia et judicium praeparacio sedis eius.* The text was carefully chosen, Hallum said that he had come

nomine et pro parte dicti domini regis [Henry IV] et eciam dominorum prelatorum denique regni illius [England] et tocius ecclesie Anglicane cum sufficienti et necessaria potestate ad omnia concernentia factum desiderate unionis et hoc presens concilium.

to do what it or the greater part of it should define and ordain

and that the supreme desire of the said lord king is that in this sacred business the council should proceed justly and lawfully and by practical means.[1]

Iuste et legitime ac modis utilibus. The next stage (24 April) accordingly was the examination of witnesses, and a large part of the notaries' accounts is given up to the *informaciones et probaciones super hiis que proposita et allegata fuerunt.* Various clerks with legal training were appointed for receiving the testimony and examining the witnesses, who are all carefully named. The English envoy of Henry IV, Dr Nicholas Ryssheton, was one of those appointed.[2] He is here described as auditor of the sacred palace, canon of Salisbury. As a witness to the misdeeds of Gregory, Richard Dereham, chancellor of Cambridge, played a considerable part.[3] Each of the witnesses was questioned on the thirty-seven articles charged against the two contending popes, to which further articles were added, on 18 May and later.[4] Dereham testified to the charge of collusion between the two popes in refusing to repair to a common meeting-place: he was also present in the church of Lucca when Gregory created cardinals, but they, Dereham said, *a paucis ut cardinales reputabantur.* The names of the examining and examined are given

[1] *Römische Quartalschrift*, p. 137.

[2] Ibid., pp. 142, 169. He sat with the abbot of Poggibonsi and fr Thomas de Firmo, O.P. He was then Archbishop Arundel's auditory, Reg. Arundel i, fo. 66.

[3] Ibid., pp. 231, 248, 257, 262. Ryssheton examined him on articles 10–17, 19, 20, 22–8.

[4] Ibid., pp. 184–5.

with great care and only two other Englishmen can be traced as participating in the inquiry; the Abbot of Westminster and Sir John Colville both gave evidence about Gregory's refusal to obey the summons.

The *Acta* are notarial minutes, business-like, with few attempts to judge the actors. Rupert's chief emissary, Ulrich, bishop of Verden, is however alleged to have stated in his address to the Council

aliqua minus vera in facto et in verbo capciosa, frivola, dolosa et scandalosa ad turbandum, impediendum et infamandum, quantum in eo fuit, sacrum concilium.

The bishop, without waiting for the answer which the canonist Petrus de Anchorano was about to give on behalf of the Council, 'illicentiatus cum suis recessit'. The minutes are first and foremost concerned with propounding the legal procedure followed by the Council. Thus the amalgamation of the two colleges and the withdrawal of obedience from either pope had to be declared 'canonical and legitimate'[1] (8th session), by the Patriarch of Alexandria (Simon Cramaud) and Bishop Robert Hallum, standing together in the same pulpit, before the Council could proceed to final verdict and sentence. Reform was relegated to the very end, and the only information given about it here is private and unofficial, from the 21st session on 27 July 1409. This amounted to very little: and it is possible that Henry IV's anxiety on this account may have been perfectly genuine.

The light cast upon the Council of Pisa by these registers is frontal and direct. More oblique a beam, though no less revealing, is thrown from central and eastern Europe upon the great assembly met at Constance from the late autumn of 1414 until the spring of 1418. Constance, famed for its decrees *Haec Sancta* and *Frequens*, was the most populous and the most effective of the General Councils: effective not for what was finally concluded, but for the ventilation of grievances as well as of celebrated causes. That a really comprehensive programme of reform was not forthcoming, that in the end most of the *avisamenta* or recommendations of the reforming Committee had to be abbreviated and battened down into the concordats of the individual nations with the newly unified Papacy, are familiar facts: what is less known and hitherto has been less studied is the relation of the Council of Constance to the

[1] *Römische Quartalschrift*, 46, p. 150.

problems of central and eastern Europe, to the reforming movement which covered more than Bohemia, to the desire of the
excluded for closer community with the West. The older Christendom is being looked at with critical eyes from a new angle. This is
the position emerging from more recent studies of the intellectual
and political agitation in central Europe in the first half of the
fifteenth century.

The diplomatic scene is dominated by two great influences,
the one familiar, though it has not been fully studied in its
general European bearings, the other little known, but of the
highest importance; the Anglo-French war and the ferment in
central and eastern Europe, all the country within or just without
the Slavonic border-land. Political changes here are startling
enough. The union of Poland and Lithuania under the Jagiellonian
dynasty, the resistance offered by Poland to the Teutonic knights,
the Hussite movement, the beginnings of the Muscovite kingdom
after the defeat of the Tartars, all show that, in spite of internal
disagreements between these Slavonic kingdoms, east-central
Europe was consolidating itself and arresting the German pressure
to the East. Poland and Bohemia were being lost to the Reich.
Partly racial, partly religious causes were at work behind these
assertions of Slavonic independence. Poland, though in no way
disposed to unite with Bohemia, had similar grievances, social,
economic and moral, against her existing régime. The administration of governmental affairs by the king and nobles became increasingly difficult as more and more taxes and services were pre-
empted by wealthy monasteries and other Church foundations,
and in Poland, as elsewhere, the problem of the apportionment of
tithe was of great importance.[1] The ferment was not only political.
It was a writer originating from Polish Cracow who voiced some
of the sharpest criticisms of conditions within the Church before
Hus arose in Bohemia. This was Matthew of Cracow who died
in 1410; a prominent member of the University of Prague, an
eminent preacher before Church synods, who wrote a discussion
anticipating in certain respects the position of Hus, called *A Conflict of Reason and Conscience*, about the nature and use of the sac-
rament of the eucharist. More important was his pre-reformation
tract (if indeed it was his) *De Squaloribus Romanae Curiae*, which
castigates the abuses of simony, laxity of morals, and the intro-

[1] Margaret Slauch, 'A Polish Vernacular Eulogy of Wyclif', *Journal of
Ecclesiastical History*, viii, no. 1 (April, 1957), 55.

duction of unworthy candidates into the priesthood, raising doubts about the validity of their function as priests. Poland was much affected by the precursor of Hus in Bohemia, Mathias of Janow, who argued for the more frequent communion of the laity and more general direct study of the Bible. The orthodox theologians of Prague who were later to attack Hus were also known in Poland, especially at the University of Cracow where the famous Czech theologian Stefan Palecz ended his life in 1422 as professor. Palecz had originally been an adherent of Hus, but was to pursue him fiercely after 1408. Wyclif's philosophy had a considerable influence in Cracow, especially the *De Universalibus*, which was a counter-blast to the nominalism of Ockham. Two manuscripts of the Wyclif text were preserved in the University library at Cracow.[1]

Professor Margaret Slauch of the University of Warsaw has printed a Polish vernacular eulogy of Wyclif by Master Andreas Galka of Dobczyn, an out-and-out Wycliffite, in the middle of the fifteenth century. Cracow, Professor Slauch thinks, was the spot auspicious in the fostering of an iconoclastic thinker. On the one hand there was the knowledge of a successful egalitarian revolution, social and religious, in a neighbouring country by Hus's followers, which had strong ties of kinship with the Wycliffite Lollards and the poor priests; on the other hand consciousness of the division within the Church, the struggle of Pope against Councils. The grievances and the projects for reform discussed at Basel all favoured latitude of criticism in Cracow and elsewhere.[2] At the Jagiellonian court there was quite exceptional tolerance of religious opinions, yet it is not such influences to which it is worth drawing attention here, but rather a theological plea made in the interests of the Polish people for the struggle of that country against the Teutonic knights.

Among the Polish delegation, incorporated in the German nation at the Council of Constance, were men charged with the duty of presenting the case of Poland against the Teutonic order. The main duty fell upon Paul Włodkowic of Brudzewo, rector of Cracow University, who came to the Council as envoy of the king and representative of the Jagiellonian University.[3] Włodkowic,

[1] Slauch, op. cit., p. 57.
[2] Ibid., p. 60. Cf. K. Morawski, *Histoire de l'Université de Cracovie* (Paris, 1905), especially pp. 135 f., for the Canon Law at Cracow.
[3] He has been specially studied by Mrs U. Goble, 'The Case of Poland

originally educated at the University of Prague, Master of Arts in
1393, went with his colleague, the theologian Lascaris (also to
appear at the Council), to the University of Padua (1404) where he
studied law under Zabarella, who had been teaching there since
1391. From Zabarella Włodkowic must have heard the doctrines
of toleration which he applied later to the Polish problem in his
own work. Włodkowic could not afford to be promoted to the
Doctorate of Law at Padua and had to return to his own country
and take the degree at Cracow. The conflict between Poland and
the Teutonic knights involved fundamental questions of principle.
Włodkowic was engaged in the problem from 1411 onwards. When
King Jagiello decided to take his protest against the Order to
Constance, he sent the rector of Cracow to prepare a rational
exposition of Poland's case before the nation, and the result was
his first pamphlet *De potestate Papae et imperatoris respectu
infidelium* which he offered to the German nation (of which he was
a member) on 5 July 1415.[1]

Two courses, he said, were open to him; either a judicial process,
the decision to be given after the facts had been reported by witnesses, or a doctrinal, where general principles are discussed in the
natural light of reason. Włodkowic chose the latter and showed his
keen mind in focusing the attention of his audience on the question: do pagans possess intrinsic rights or are they deprived of all
claims to humane treatment, and have Christians the right to
pillage them and convert them by fire and blood? Włodkowic
shows that the papal and imperial privileges to which the Order
appealed are by their very nature invalid. He then gives a short
summary of the history and origin of the conflict, outlining the
coming of the Order to Poland and the growth and power of the
knights. Even once the subjugated Prussians were quiet, the
expeditions of the knights continued. Meanwhile God gave the
faith to two pagan princes, one of whom became the ruler of

---

against the Teutonic Knights at the Council of Constance' (University of
Oxford thesis, 1957), ch. 3, to which I am much indebted. The main
monographs are those of T. Brzostowski, *Paweł Włodkowic* (Warsaw,
1954), and L. Ehrlich, *Paweł Włodkowic i Stanisław ze Skarbimierza*
[Warsaw, 1954]. A useful summary is in Marian Biskup, 'The Role of the
Order and State of the Teutonic Knights in Prussia in the History of
Poland', *Polish Western Affairs*, Vol. VH, no. 2 [Poznan 1966] 337 f.

[1] Text in *Starodawne Prawa Polskiego Pomniki*, v. 161–85. For the date,
cf. H. von der Hardt, *Magnum Oecumenicum Constantiense Concilium*
(1697–1700), vi. 388.

Poland, the other of Lithuania, and the pagans who had once been the terror of Christian people now flocked to be baptized. Yet the knights attacked them even more fiercely, burning their new churches and killing Christians in their fury.[1] Włodkowic ends his summary with the defeat of the knights at Grünwald. He now proceeds to the first part of his treatise, examining the power of the Pope in regard to the infidel in the form of eleven questions. The first of these is whether, without sin, princes can expel Saracens and Jews from their kingdom and from their goods, which he answers by saying that if they are willing to live quietly with Christians they should not be molested. Especially should Jews be tolerated, since from their writings we establish the truth of our own faith.[2]

Such reasoning is not unlike that of St Bernard in his letter to Eugenius III. Włodkowic brings his argument into relation with the actual problem of the Teutonic knights, when in the second question he asks whether it is lawful for Christians to make war on infidels living peaceably in their own lands and under their own jurisdiction. In answer he quotes the discrepant opinions of Innocent IV and Hostiensis cited above, the latter of whom denied pagans any right of ownership or jurisdiction. Innocent, however, would concede such rights, since, after the creation of man, God gave the whole world to him and the Bible contains many instances of the division of land. Jurisdiction may also arise from the law of nature, by which, for instance, a father has jurisdiction over his own family. Innocent held that possession and jurisdiction can lawfully and without sin belong to infidels since such rights are destined not only for the faithful, but for all rational creatures. In consequence it is not lawful for Christians to take these away: 'because infidels possess them without sin and by the authority of God'.

What then is the Pope's power over unbelievers? Following Innocent, Włodkowic asserts that the Pope has power over all men, pagans as well as faithful; but for the occasions on which he can use this power the writer turns to the conditions established by Zabarella: if the Gentiles sin against the law of nature or if they worship idols, or in the case of the Jews, if they raise heresies against their own law, the Pope has power to inflict penalties, and the Pope also may have power over the infidel

---

[1] *Starodawne Prawa Polskiego Pomniki*, v. 162.

[2] Ibid., p. 164.

ruler of a Christian people: he may command him to treat Christians under his rule well. But infidels 'must not be brought by compulsion to the faith', since all men must be left in such free will and 'only the grace of God avails in this vocation'. Even infidels may have free will and Włodkowic insists that it must be respected. What then is the extent of the imperial power? Włodkowic shows that the Pope alone has the power of both swords, while the Emperor is only his minister in temporal matters. Włodkowic reveals his familiarity with the imperial theory of Dante and of Marsilius of Padua. But the Emperor has no right to claim dominion over infidels. He has no power to occupy the lands of infidels who do not recognize his authority. One therefore infers that the privileges granted by the Emperor to the Order are null and void in so far as they relate to the occupation of the lands of the infidel. Włodkowic then considers whether the war waged by the Teutonic knights against the heathen can be considered just. He takes the five categories set out by St Thomas for consideration: the person, the matter, the cause, the intention and the authority involved. The person waging war should be a secular not a clerk, the matter of dispute the recovery of his own goods or the defence of his own country; the cause should be one of necessity to win peace; the intention should be one of desire for correction and justice. Having set out the theory of 'just' war, Włodkowic examines the practice of the Teutonic knights in their campaign against the heathen. Such a war he condemns on three grounds, as being contrary to civil law by which one should not molest those living in peace, to natural law according to which a man should not do to another what he would not wish to have done to himself and finally to divine law, by which one is forbidden to kill. The matter of the war is unjust since to compel infidels to accept faith by arms is against reason and against the teaching of the General Council of Toledo, and in the time chosen for their campaigns the Knights sin, for they are in the habit of beginning an expedition on the feast of Our Lady, whereas one should sanctify the Sabbath by good deeds and abstention from servile work. The interesting point about this treatise presented to the Council on 6 July, along with fifty-two conclusions by which the audience could the more easily recognize the main principles of the case, is the use Włodkowic makes of Innocent IV and the teaching of Zabarella.[1] The positive side he developed in the proposition that it is not lawful to

[1] Goble, op. cit., p. 23.

attack or subjugate pagans unless for an absolute and immediate cause of faith. Letters supporting a contrary way of preaching the faith contain heresy and are void. They can give no general or special power to attack the infidels; even a religious order founded to fight against the infidel cannot do so for any special reason unless a superior power authorizes them and none appears to offer itself in the present case, nor has any special apostolic permission been given. It may be added that Zabarella was a member of the commission appointed by the Council to examine the Polish case against the Teutonic knights, and must have recognized his own doctrines of toleration presented to him by Włodkowic. The rector's work in clarifying the position of Poland in north-west Europe was recognized by the expression of the king himself who called him *regni zelator supremus*, while the Teutonic knights themselves regarded him as their main adversary. But the Emperor had already made his decision before the parties arrived in Constance. Not only did he recognize the Order's right to retain Pomerania, but even enjoined the immediate restitution of Samogitia—King Jagiello was correspondingly indignant and abandoned the hopes hitherto placed in the Emperor, concentrating now on a reversal of Sigismund's sentence. For this the Poles appealed to Martin V, *tanquam ad arbitrium viri boni*.[1]

This is the voice of an orthodox Pole, trained in the arguments of western thought. The Polish protest against the Teutonic knights is at bottom the claim of a nation to be regarded as part of the European family. In much the same way during 1956 Hungarian intellectuals, asserting their right to believe or disbelieve the official statistics and pronouncements of the Communist party, decided to defy the bureaucratic censorship and compulsion to obey the party rules. In the following passage from Tamas Aczel's poem *Ode to Europe*, published in early September 1956, the idea is expressed:

> This little nation would also like to live:
> I know that it depends on us—but believe me
> We are now doing what we must.
> Europe, our common mother, we return to Thee.
> Set an example, show us how,
> As you have done for centuries,
> We are one, no matter what the sages preach
> Or the priests, whose dark touch caused souls to stiffen.

---

[1] A. Prochaska, *Na Soborz w Konstancji* (Cracow, 1898), p. 77.

Not they but we are living,
Europe, before whom the barriers are lifted,
The gates are opened for millions of simple people;
Oh, homeland, humanity, creative restless life,
Stay with me and Thee, be with us, Europe,
Common fate, love, work, future,
Oh, beating heart, pure truth
To plough, to sow, to harvest, to die and rise again a thousand times.[1]

Alongside Włodkowic we may set a very different character, a
Bohemian visionary, the product of the Czech claim to be allowed
to obey the divine law embodied in the original Four Articles of
Prague, which, in a watered-down form, were proclaimed at
Iglau in 1436. About the life of Peter Chelčický very little is
known. He was probably born about 1390 in Chelčice, a southern
Bohemian village near the small country town of Vodnany,
and Professor Bartoš has identified him with a certain Peter
Záhorka, a well-to-do squire from nearby Zahorsi who was
born about 1379–81. It is most likely, Mr Brock thinks, that
Chelčický was for most of his life a working farmer.[2] He does
not appear till 1419, four years after the burning of Hus, and he
may have come to Prague as an adherent of some of the tenets of
the Waldensian heresy, widespread in that area. When the Czechs
took arms under Žižka and the minor gentry took an important
rôle in the direction of the movement he remained a non-militant,
a Taborite before Tabor, disbelieving in force and asking even the
utraquist theologian Jakoubek of Stříbro what sanction he had in
the scriptures for warfare among the Christians. He was a young
countryman standing out alone against the opinion universally
accepted by his own party, even condemning the revered leader
of the whole Hussite movement for his militant attitude. In
southern Bohemia he was to stand in a succession of preachers who
had already re-established a tradition of moral protest against
social injustice, a fellow feeling for the oppressed, in exaltation of
the humble and meek against the proud and rulers of the world.
The cult of the little man, of the peasant, reminding one of the
English Piers Plowman, was connected, in the thought of Hus's
predecessors, with the attempt to renew the practice of Christian
moral principles. They were primarily moral reformers involved

---

[1] The poem is printed in *Soviet Survey*, No. 11 (January 1957), p. 18.
[2] Peter Brock, *The Political and Social Doctrines of the Unity of Czech
Brethren* ('s-Gravenhage, 1957), p. 26.

in political questions only incidentally. Konrad Waldhauser (1326–69) inveighing against those lords who oppressed their tenants had proclaimed the moral superiority of the simple peasant; so too Mathias of Janow (1350–94), to whom reference has already been made, carried on this tradition by pointing to the early Church with its community of goods and rule by love alone as a model for contemporaries to follow. Chelčický found Wyclif himself the strongest direct influence: 'none of the first doctors', he writes, 'did so zealously speak or write against the poison poured into the Holy Church. . . . Wyclif has routed the hosts of Anti-Christ as well as those doctors who introduced cunning rules in the place of the law of Christ.'[1] When Tabor took a militant line he broke decisively with the party, but lived on some thirty years in his little village, writing continually and preserving his independence both of Hus and of other Bohemian leaders, though he would quote Hus or Wyclif to illustrate some of his points. How a layman or a working farmer could have evolved a startlingly original social philosophy and have expressed those ideas in a literary style it is difficult to see. As Mr Brock thinks, it was his comparative ignorance of the theological systems of the past which enabled him to draw directly from the Bible, unencumbered with the philosophical and other conceptions of his contemporaries, and endowed him with independence of thought. The kernel of Christ's teaching, Chelčický wrote, the secret of His power, was His law of love; and he proceeded to describe a political Utopia placed on a historic background.[2] This was the foundation of the movement known as the Unity of the Czech Brethren. Its bases were voluntary and anarchical. All government for Chelčický would seem an instrument of oppression and legalized robbery. Authority, he says, cannot exist without cruelty. If it ceases to be cruel it will at once perish of itself since none will fear it: therefore authority is far removed from love. Warfare between Christians, too, is an inseparable concomitant to the participations of Christians in the state. For Chelčický the Tolstoyan gospel of non-resistance to evil was the guiding motive. He was the opposite to a direct revolutionary. For the Christian he advised obedience to the civil authority as a matter of conscience, not merely out of fear of the consequences of disobedience; at the same time as he condemned the whole existing social

[1] Cited by Brock, op. cit., p. 34.
[2] Described in Brock, op. cit., pp. 44 f.

order, he preached throughout his life its conditional justification. This seeming paradox was, however, a logical development of his first principle. Orthodox medieval political theorists had granted that the institution of the State was a result of sin. Without the Fall, civil government would lose its justification. Chelčický also was ready to assent to the existence of the State, but slightly modifying the accepted view, he restricted its validity to the community of the non-Christians and the false Christians, 'the foolish people who neither know God nor are under His yoke'. If, however, the non-Christians and the false Christians all truly followed in Christ's footsteps it would wither away. In the meantime the remnant of true Christians must hold to their principles.[1]

These relativist views of the State have been interestingly compared to those propounded by Karl Marx. Closely linked with Chelčický's rejection of civil authority was his demand for the complete separation of Church and State. He opposed the whole use of force in spiritual matters and did not agree with the action prescribed for the laity in the Articles of Prague. He was at one with the Hussites in attacking the temporal wealth of the clergy of the mendicant orders, but for him priests should only concern themselves with preaching the Gospel, relying for their safety on the example of a pure life and never calling in the aid of the secular arm. The sort of compulsory virtue which the Prague articles envisaged was worse than useless. The Geneva Constitution of John Calvin would have been an abomination to him. He approved conditionally the maintenance of public order by the ruler, but he is most emphatic that no Christian could himself become king. His reason should be against it, his conscience would recoil from doing many things condemned by God, but inseparable from the exercise of kingly power. The Christian has the law of love inscribed in the Gospels as his guide and that is sufficient for all branches of life.

It is not difficult to see how within a sect maintaining these principles a testing time would come. By the end of the 1480's serious disunity appeared under the influence of men like Lukas of Prague who urged compromise in the relations of the Brethren to the civil authorities and the Hussite Church, particularly over the attitude of the Unity to the acceptance of authority by its members. Were men who were trying to live out the Christian gospel to permit worldly power among themselves whether actively

[1] Brock, p. 48.

or passively? This question became more important as the humble and unlettered men, mostly peasants with a sprinkling of artisans, who had at first formed the overwhelming majority of the rank and file brethren, were giving way to the burgess brethren, some of whom had amassed considerable wealth, and to the University-bred leaders like Lukas of Prague.

These two figures, Włodkowic and Chelčický—and there were others less outstanding—offer some illustration of the ideas liberated in the course of the intellectual ferment in Central Europe during the fifteenth century. The study of the Conciliar movement is incomplete without an understanding of the dynamic forces face to face with the Church from a new quarter. An intellectual and spiritual central, nay even eastern, Europe was in process of formation based on the *studia* of Cracow, Vienna and Prague. Vienna, for example, was the university of Nicholas of Dinkelsbühl, the reformer, and of Peter of Pulka, the conciliar zealot and master of another notable conciliar, Thomas Ebendorfer, of whose career Alphons Lhotsky has recently given an account.[1]

The Bohemian visionaries and warriors, the reformers and Cromwellian saints who came to the Councils of Constance and Basel were a problem of a kind that had not occurred in the Church since the patristic centuries. At Constance the fate of Jan Hus and Jerome of Prague raised only faint interest in the French and Italian nations, though to the English the linking of Hus and Wyclif was both a necessity and a point of national humiliation. It is not surprising therefore to find Hus gaoled in the castle which was the seat of Robert Hallum, the best of the English reforming bishops. Hus was condemned largely on the strength of his *De Ecclesia*. But this treatise, as the new edition by Professor Harrison Thomson makes clear, only recapitulates Wyclif in chapters i-xi, and in chapters xii-xiii constitutes a running commentary on the position put forward by eight doctors of the Faculty of Theology in Prague on 6 February 1413. 'The Pope is head of the Roman Church and the Cardinals its body' was the *Concilium*, or theological verdict; this was 'a serious and cleverly written manifesto of the curial party'.[2] If the basic

---

[1] *Thomas Ebendorfer: ein österreichischer Geschichtsschreiber, Theologe und Diplomat des 15. Jahrhunderts* (Schriften der Monumenta Germaniae Historica XV, Stuttgart, 1957).

[2] *Magistri Johannis Hus Tractatus de Ecclesia* (1956), pp. xiv–xv.

lines of Hus's thought had been determined by 1410, his opinions
were now becoming sharpened and clear cut, when, in the later
phase after 1413 he was writing, at Kozí Hrádek in southern
Bohemia, the treatise read in the Bethlehem Chapel in June 1413.
For the Pope and Cardinals who must be obeyed Hus substituted
the law of God.[1] This was the prologue to the military revivalism
which after the martyrdom of Hus took the Czech armies into the
imperial territory and threatened the structure of the whole Empire. If the Church, after the victories of Prokop and Žižka, had
continued to rely upon force and had declined to argue with the
Hussites, the West would have suffered the greatest military
disaster of the Middle Ages. But Cardinal Cesarini saw to it that
the good sense and solidarity of the Council prevailed over the
alarmism of Eugenius IV. The Bohemians were admitted to
Basel and allowed to argue their four articles, 'evangelical verities'
as they called them, on the understanding that the Council would
not be the judge, but holy scripture, the practice of Christ and of
the early Church, along with the councils and doctors which
based themselves thereupon.

The investigation by Professor Bartoš, working in the chapter
library of Prague cathedral on the collection of speeches and
debates at the Council which Matej of Chlumčany, the Taborite
commandant of Pisck, made for his own use, has provided new
and more complete texts of the Hussite arguments and replies to
their opponents. In certain cases, the version corrects or supplements those printed by Martène and Durand, or by Mansi. In the
case of Peter Payne, the Oxford academic, then chief foreign
minister of the revolutionary Czech government, it is the only
source which has so far come to light.[2] The speeches can now be
judged as a whole, and the impression they make is noteworthy:
for at Basel four men of very different background, Rockyčaný an
academic, a Taborite bishop Mikulas, the Taborite commander
Prokop and the orphan Ulrich of Znojmo were sinking their
differences in an effort to propound a formula which should represent the essential elements of the Bohemian position. These
men were inspired by an idea of the Church which, deriving alike
from primitive practice and from the more modern treatises of

---

[1] *Magistri Johannis Hus Tractatus de Ecclesia* (1956), pp. 127 f.
[2] The speeches and the sources for them are discussed by me in *Prague
Essays*, ed. R. W. Seton-Watson (1949), p. 92 f. A recent treatment of the
subject is in ch. 6 of F. M. Bartoš, *Husitská Revoluce*, ii, (Prague, 1966).

Ockham and Marsilius, departed from the hierarchical conceptions of the last five centuries and sought to restore the laity to
their place in the community of the faithful. To Rockyčaný and
his colleagues *universitas fidelium* was no cant phrase. All these
debates were in 1433. Though the Council had defied the Pope
and continued in existence against papal prohibition, the testing
time came when Eugenius IV had recognized its existence, but
was regarded with so much suspicion for his attitude in the past
and for sending papal presidents to replace Cesarini, that the anti-
papalists got out of hand and passed the decree abolishing Annates
(1435); as a result of which, moderate conciliars like Nicholas of
Cues (who had published the *De Concordantia Catholica* in 1433)
found that they would have to reconsider their position. What most
of all made them do so was the split among the Fathers over the
meeting place of an imminent Council of Union between Greeks
and Latins. In the course of this, Cusanus became convinced that
the Holy Spirit had deserted the assembly.

The work and scholarship of the last thirty years upon the life,
writings and sermons of this great philosopher and churchman
have contributed greatly to an understanding of the Council he
attended from 1433-8. This study, associated with the Heidel-
berg edition of Cusanus and the work of Gerhard Kallen, Ernst
Hofmann and Josef Koch, centres upon Cusanus's letters, sermons
and treatises bearing upon the Council of Basel and his reforming
legation in Germany. Both aspects of Nicholas's statesmanship
find expression: the early phase, when he was still a 'conciliar',
writing a guarded treatise on the admission of the papal presidents
at Basel;[1] and the later period (1437 onwards) when, outraged
by the extremists, he was becoming the 'Hercules of the Euge-
nians'. The first instalment of the letters, published in 1942-4,
includes a welcome to Cusanus from Francesco Piccolpasso,
Archbishop of Milan, in 1438, just after Nicholas had returned
from a Papal embassy at Constantinople. The Archbishop, after
deploring the tactics of the majority at Basel, congratulates
Cusanus on having put up 200 ducats for the expenses of the
Greeks going to the Council.[2] Here also can be read the striking

---

[1] The 'De auctoritate presidendi in Concilio Generali', ed. G Kallen
(*Sitzungs. d. Heidelberger Akad. d. Wiss., phil. hist. Kl.*, Jg. 1935/6, 3).

[2] Ed. J. Koch, *Cusanus-Texte IV*, Briefe, erste Sammlung, p. 27. The
letter mentions the zeal of Filippo Maria Visconti of Milan for union
with the Greeks.

I

defence by Nicholas of his having forsaken the conciliar majority
and having sided with Eugenius, against the politely expressed
but subtle and relevant questions put to him by a Carthusian
house unspecified.[1] This was towards the end of 1439, showing
that the Carthusians were still working upon what they took to
be the doctrines expressed in the *De Concordantia Catholica.*
Nicholas had to extricate himself. He did so by emphasizing
unity and general interest as the sign of a true council, whereas
schism indicated that the Holy Spirit has departed from it. Representatives might indeed be there, but no council so divided could
be truly representative of the Church which is one and undivided.
By 1439 he was writing to correspondents about the *fatuitas
Basiliensium* and, if Dr Koch is right in his identification, he was
composing the treatise *Contra Amedistarum errorem,* his reply to
the elevation of Amedaeus of Savoy by the conciliar majority as
anti-pope.[2]

The debates with the Hussites at Basel raised in an acute form
the problem of communication: of understanding the arguments
put forward by opponents and critics outside the Church. The
question was how to meet them on their own ground. Scholastic
methods of argument were not everywhere appreciated. Not only
was there a gulf in method but one in terminology, between the
thinker trained in western *studia* and (to use Bishop Pecock's
phrase) the 'bible-men' of central Europe. Both difficulties were
experienced in the Council of Ferrara-Florence. It is from this
Council that the most important recent addition to conciliar
study is derived. The publication by the Pontifical Institute of
Oriental Studies, under the editorship of Dr Joseph Gill, S.J., of
the Greek Acta of the Council of Florence[3] comprised in the thirty-
four manuscripts submitted for examination is too lengthy and
complicated a matter adequately to be noticed here. The complete
revaluation of the sources of which I have given a summary
account elsewhere[4] enables the main body of the discussions at

[1] Letter 4. Ibid., pp. 37–8.
[2] 'Über eine aus der nächsten Umgebung des Nikolaus von Kues
stammende Handschrift der Trierer Stadtbibliothek (1927/1426)', *Aus
Mittelalter und Neuzeit* (Festschrift G. Kallen, Bonn, 1957), pp. 117–35.
[3] *Quae Supersunt Actorum Graecorum Concilii Florentini,* 2 parts
(Concilium Florentinum, Documenta et Scriptores, Rome, 1953). All
previous accounts of the Canons are superseded by Fr Gill's *The Council
of Florence* (Cambridge, 1959).
[4] *Journal of Theological Studies, New Series,* VII, i (April 1956), 160.

Ferrara and Florence to be seen in the right perspective. It has now become clear of what great importance were the sessions at Ferrara for revealing the fundamental differences of method employed by the two sides. If there was an atmosphere of common study in which the debates between the Greeks and the Latins were conducted, the significance attached by the Emperor's party to traditional theological terms must have been found very difficult by the Latins. On the Greek side much was taken for granted which Latin theologians, with Ockhamist training, versed in nice distinctions of theology, could not willingly accept. Latin canonists and theologians had become accustomed to commenting and glossing the acts of their own General Councils in terms that corresponded with the advance of grammatical scholarship and philosophical thought. They looked to their Eastern colleagues for a similar understanding, but they found conservatism of an extreme kind. Even in recording the texts of discussions, the Greek notaries did not always understand the Latin argument and must have had great difficulty in reporting the theological discussions.

This is only one of many new points revealed by the publication of the Greek text. Even more clearly than before the predominant position of the Patriarch who died during the Council makes itself apparent and without his leadership it is doubtful whether the discussions would have reached any result.

Chapter VI
Theory and Fact in the General Councils of the Fifteenth Century

The twentieth General Council of the Roman Church may provide a sufficient excuse for reflecting on some earlier assemblies of this kind, particularly those of the fifteenth century.[1] One may well inquire what the twin-headed Church of 1409 has to do with the unified body of today. Historical parallels and analyses may be stretched too far, and the Church has indeed turned its back upon the events of the period 1378–1449; but there is always a connexion between unity and reform, and we have been reminded recently that they go hand in hand. If the recent Council has no longer the task of reconciling a divided body, it had in front of it, just as in those fifteenth-century councils, the problem of internal reorganization and of presenting the result to the outside world.

In the period of the councils with which we deal there was for many years no unity of the head and the utmost discrepancy of view upon the methods of achieving reform. Christendom had received in the Schism a shock from which no one seemed able to recover. But it was a shock that aroused an extraordinary effort, a determination to tolerate weary years of absence in lands far from home on the part of those participating in the council and, moreover, one that brought about a period of self-examination in which not only professional theologians but also the moderate wayfaring man took part. It is common now to see conciliar activity against the background of law and administration: it must also be seen in the light of contemporary Christian humanism and Christian spirituality; and the leaders of the movement, whether from Paris, Salisbury, Deventer, Windesheim or the universities of Vienna and Cracow, to name only a few centres, were people who put the individual, and the bearing of his life upon the society of the Church, into a new context. It is this bent which altered the contemporary attitude towards positive

[1] Since this was written, Mgr Jedin has published an admirable discussion of Conciliarism (H. Jedin, *Bischöfliches Konzil oder Kirchenparlament?* Vorträge der Aeneas Silvius Stiftung an der Universität Basel, ii, 1963) with bibliographical notes to which readers may be referred.

law and ceremony, and ranked the humbler academics with the professional administrators. The new attitude is well stated by Gerson in his *De Unitate Ecclesiastica*:

The Fifth Consideration:
The unity of the Church in one vicar of Christ does not for its attainment at the present time require a literal observance of the outward terms of positive law, or of ordinary processes in summonses, accusations, denunciations, or similar matters. This General Council may proceed summarily, and with the good and important [principle] of equity. It shall have sufficient judicial authority to use ἐπιείκεια, i.e. the power to interpret all positive law, to adapt it for the sake of accomplishing the union more speedily and more advantageously, and, if need be, to abandon it [positive law, including the canon laws] because it was instituted for the peace and well-being of the Church. If it had been instituted properly and not by any tyrannical malignity, it should not militate against the Church, lest the power that has been conferred on human institutions bring about the destruction rather than the edification of the Church. In fact the power of using ἐπιείκεια with regard to a matter of doctrine [*doctrinaliter*] belongs principally to those learned in theology, which in relation to other (sciences) is architectonic (*architectoria*) and thereafter to those skilled in the science of canon and civil law, as they have to take their basic ideas from the principles of divine and natural law.[1]

This attitude is, needless to say, derived from Aquinas[2] and was taken up by other conciliar thinkers when they were considering how to break through the canonical rule that it is the pope alone who summons the general council. The initiative, they argue, under existing circumstances, comes from the Church at large.

The assemblies for which the historian's sources are most abundant are Constance and Basle along with Ferrara-Florence (1438–9). For Pisa in 1409, the publication of the *Acta* by Dr Vincke in *Römische Quartalschrift*[3] brought that Council into line with the other three and demonstrated its character as a great legal process against Gregory XII and Benedict XIII. As the

[1] In the translation of J. K. Cameron, *Advocates of Reform*, ed. M. Spinka, S.C.M. Library of Christian Classics, xiv (1953), 143.
[2] See W. Ullmann, *The Origins of the Great Schism* (London, 1948), 198 f.; and his *Principles of Government and Politics in the Middle Ages* (London, 1961), 293–4.
[3] XLVI (1938), 81–331.

process was, with minor exceptions, practically the only serious work undertaken by the Council, Pisa stands apart from the other ecumenical councils of the fifteenth century.[1] Its interest lies more in the wealth of preliminary treatise rather than in the results (which were unhappy) or in its day-to-day progress. A possible further exception is Siena where the protocol is largely missing and only the Sienese archives can supply the gaps. For Constance, Basle and Ferrara-Florence, both official *Acta* and personal narratives have survived, for the latter in a Greek version as well as in the Latin, while there is a Greek historian's commentary of high importance. Each council presents its own documentary problems, but perhaps only for Ferrara-Florence can they be said to be scientifically exposed from a documentary point of view.[2] For Constance the way onward was brilliantly pointed by Finke, working on the basis of von der Hardt, but even his magisterial works—the *Quellen und Forschungen zur Geschichte des Konstanzer Konzils* (Paderborn 1889) and the introductions prefixed to the various sections of the *Acta Concilii Constanciensis*— mark only the beginnings of modern manuscript study[3] and no Jedin can arise to write fully the history of this Council before further discovery and examination of manuscript sources has taken place. In the case of Basle it was fortunate that a scholar like Johannes Haller was available to begin the edition of the notaries' manuals, and even more to give in the masterly first volume of the edition (1896) an introduction to the historians of the Council and to the available correspondence in the papal archives and elsewhere. It is the relation between the official *Acta* and the narrative historians which presents some of the best opportunities for study. Thus, in the case of Constance, for example, a close study of Cardinal Guillaume Fillastre's diary, which, as Finke pointed out, is in many respects more accurate

---

[1] It is omitted from *Conciliorum Oecumenicorum Decreta*, compiled by the Centro di Documentazione, Istituto per le Scienze Religiose (Bologna, 1962).

[2] Cf. the series edited by G. Hofman, *Concilium Florentinum: Documenta et Scriptores* (Orientalia Christiana) which contains the *Acta Graeca* of the Council, ed. Fr Joseph Gill, S.J. There is an excellent bibliography of sources in J. Gill, *The Council of Florence* (Cambridge, 1959), 416–20.

[3] Some of these problems are discussed by C. M. D. Crowder, 'Le Concile de Constance et l'édition de Von der Hardt', *R.H.E.* lvii (1962), 409–45.

than the protocol itself[1] and is now available for English readers in the excellent version of Dr Loomis,[2] is much to be desired.

Fillastre, who gave practical shape and form to the ideas of his colleague at Constance, Pierre d'Ailly, cardinal of Cambrai, was an observer as well as one of the main actors during the whole of the Council's existence, and nothing is more illuminating than his account of the confusions and complications of February and March 1415 and of the period June to October 1417. The dean of Rheims, cardinal of St Mark, is a particularly interesting figure because he was both a French ecclesiastic and a curialist, foreseeing in some of the reforming measures presented to the Council's commissions of reform the decline in authority of the Sacred College, and because he himself became practically the author of its resurrection. In him, the patriotic anti-Lancastrian and far-seeing administrator are found combined, and it is natural that he should view any attempt to control the policy of a Roman Church apart from the Sacred College with the gravest suspicion. He believed in the corporate direction of events by the College. He was not opposed to reform and he had a high sense of the duty of *reformatio capitis*, but he was determined that the process should be directed from the top, and, whatever he may have thought about the members, it was there that the change must start. In the election of Martin V he played a leading part, for in the end it was only his accession and that of Foix to Cardinal Odo Colonna that made Martin V's election secure. The passage in which he narrates this is one to be remembered:

Note that when the accession occurred, a procession of the General Council and City Clergy, among whom were some two hundred innocent children of the city wearing their surplices, was passing in front of the conclave chanting the hymn 'Veni Creator'. It was heard clearly from the conclave. The electors were praying on their knees and many were stirred to tears. Afterwards the transfer of votes was completed and the election held according to rule. All who had left the chapel were recalled and the election resumed, the candidate elect standing on the altar and the electors in their seats. All and everyone, cardinals as well as the rest, voted in turn for him. He was asked to consent and did so humbly. Then all in order of their rank came forward to kiss his foot,

---

[1] *Acta Concilii Constanciensis* (Münster, 1923), ii. 8.
[2] In *The Council of Constance: the Unification of the Church*, ed. J. H. Mundy and K. M. Woody, Records of Civilization (Columbia, 1961), lxii. 200–447.

his hand and his mouth and thus accepted him as Roman and Supreme Pontiff and in honour of St Martin (for it was St Martin's Day) he was advised to take the name of Martin and he agreed.[1]

Fillastre realizes that this was the most notable moment in the long process of *unio capitis* which had been sought since the cardinals came to Pisa. Viewing the election of John XXIII after Alexander V had died at Bologna, he merely observed, 'it is said that the election was corrupt, and certainly was so as regards the merits of the man elected'.[2] Here he followed the opinion of his time. Recent research on the relations of John to Ladislas of Naples and the condottiere regime in northern Italy has shown how difficult it is to pass clear and categorical judgements upon John XXIII.[3]

To Fillastre we owe the story of the deepening distrust of the French, Italians and Aragonese for the tactics of the Anglo-German bloc that had come to formal existence after the Treaty of Canterbury in 1416: a difference cleverly exploited by himself and the majority of the Sacred College to prevent the emperor from carrying out his projects of reform. It is impossible that with all this significant observation Fillastre's constitutional day-book can ever be neglected. But Ulrich of Richental, from whose chronicle Finke drew so much colour in his famous but too little known *Pictures from the Council of Constance*, deserves just as much comment, and to write him down, as has commonly been done, as a superficial observer of the ceremonial side of the Council and of local detail in the markets and streets of Constance is short-sighted and unhistorical. The extraordinary honour accorded to the emperor which is reflected upon throughout the whole narrative is a practical illustration of the position of the emperor as given in Dietrich of Niem's *Viridarium* and requires pondering, if his imperial journey for peacemaking in Europe is to be understood.[4]

---

[1] *Council of Constance*, 428, from *Acta Concilii Constanciensis*, ii, 159.

[2] Finke, *Acta*, ii, 14.

[3] Fillastre is reporting current views about John XXIII's character, but as P. D. Partner, *The Papal State under Martin V* (London, 1958), 20 f., points out, John, while legate in the Romagna, had proved himself an administrator of character and ability in contrast to Gregory XII who had become the creature of Ladislas of Naples.

[4] Recent work on this important curialist is noticed in E. F. Jacob, *Essays in the Conciliar Epoch*, 3rd ed. Manchester, 1963, appendix to ch. 2, 'Dietrich of Niem'.

It is to the Council of Basle that one must rather look for modern studies of the relationship of chronicle to record. For this Council there are a number of narrative accounts by contemporaries. The historian who commands greatest acclaim is John of Segovia, the Salamanca graduate, whom we know in two capacities: as an advocate of peaceful understanding with Islam, and as the composer of a chronicle less partisan and more generously conceived than Fillastre's account. The first of these aspects has been dealt with by Dr Cabanelas Rodríguez in his *Juan di Segovia y el problemo Islamico*, published at Madrid in 1952, and recently by Professor R. W. Southern;[1] the second, though with frequent references to Cabanelas Rodríguez, by Uta Fromherz (Basle 1960). The latter is an important treatise upon a man who steadily grew in stature as the Council of Basle proceeded. In 1440 he was made cardinal St Calixtus by Felix V whose election he supported, and he remained an ardent conciliar to the end of the Council. That he had a clear and accurate recording mind can be seen from the fact that in 1440 he was given, along with certain others, the task of editing the acts of the Council of Constance; and after Felix's departure from the Council he was made overseer for the papal finances at Basle, a post of which, because of its difficulties, he was to complain bitterly.

The chronicle of John of Segovia is drawn from his own experience as well as from the official *Acta*. He was incorporated on 8 April 1433 under his own hand, since the embassy of the king of Castile did not arrive till August 1434, delayed because the king wanted to see which side, the pope or the Council, was going to win in the debate over the papal dissolution. In the first year of his stay he belonged to the household of the Spanish Cardinal Cervantes, and was assigned to the Deputation of the Faith. That is why in his chronicle such stress is laid upon the *reduccio Bohemorum* and later upon the dogma of the Immaculate Conception. In the famous debate in general congregation of 5 December 1436 over the place for the prospective council of Greeks and Latins, he recorded a vote for the cautious formula: Vienna; if the Greeks wish, Avignon; Pavia, Florence, Udine, Savoy and Siena or a place on which the two sides agree—as Dr Fromherz remarks, *ein sehr vorsichtige Formulierung*.[2] Aeneas Sylvius in one

[1] R. W. Southern, *Western Views of Islam in the Middle Ages* (Cambridge, Mass., 1962).
[2] Uta Fromherz, *Johannes von Segovia als Geschichtsschreiber des Konzils von Basel* (Basle 1960), 29.

of his letters remarked that Segovia belonged to the party of the
legate (Cesarini) who was already voting in the papal interest,
but this, as Haller showed, was most unlikely: he certainly voted
with the majority led by Cardinal Aleman, who proposed Avignon
as the meeting place and it was after this that he began to appreciate Cesarini's progressive alienation from the conciliar majority.
He took no active part in the second process of the Council
against the pope in 1437: he still had too great an admiration for
the remarkable president, Cesarini, to join in the conciliar hue
and cry,[1] and one of the most touching things in the chronicle
is the delicacy and skill with which he delineates the legate's
attempts to mediate, even at an advanced stage in the dispute,
between the Council and Eugenius IV. The subtlety of spirit
which Voigt attributed to Cesarini,[2] here was illustrated at its
best. But it was of no avail. Cesarini left a deeply regretful—not a
resentful—Council in January 1438, and a new phase in the proceedings of Basle had begun.

Segovia had to throw in his lot with the radicals and to state the
case, moderately, for the deposition of Eugenius IV. Aeneas
Sylvius in his historical commentary on the Council of Basle has
depicted a scene from the discussion, after Cesarini had gone, over
the eight conclusions why the pope should be deposed as a
heretic:

> Inter tot tamen strepitus turbulentasque vociferationes non defuit
> spectato et optimo viro Johanni Segovia ex gymnasio Salamantino
> Theologo, audientia, quoniam et illum conciliares avidi audiebant, quasi
> ex suis unum, et alii virtutem hominis, summamque bonitatem etiam
> inviti venerabantur. Tanta est enim virtuti innata authoritas, ut etiam
> in hoste colatur; verumque illud Vergilianum in eo fuit:
>> Tum pietate gravem, ac meritis si forte virum quem
>> Conspexere, silent arrectisque auribus adstant.
> Omnes namque (ut assurrexit Johannes) silentium tenuerunt.[3]

In voting for a new election after the deposition of Eugenius IV,
Segovia insisted on a sixty-day delay, which he said was prescribed
by *honestas*, rather than on the quick election suggested by *utilitas*
(sectional interests). It is natural therefore that after the election of
Count Amadeus of Savoy as Felix V, a man of his authority and
standing should play a part in the attempt to win the German

[1] Fromherz, op. cit., pp. 101 ff.
[2] *Aenco Silvio de' Piccolomini* (Berlin, 1856), i, 216.
[3] Fromherz, op. cit., p. 31.

electors from their neutrality. To be an advocate of the Council to the end required more than a sense of opportunism. Aeneas Sylvius had the opportunist's *flair* for judging the exact moment. Segovia had stood firm from 1445 on, trying to bring about a new council so as to effect the reform repeatedly put off. The faith which sustained him was a belief that the Church itself was the competent authority with power derived immediately from God and Christ. It is itself the *suprema potestas*; it is *illimitata, nullis circumclusa terminis*; what is unlimited can of its very nature only be one. *Plurificacio omnino sibi repugnat.*

... quod ecclesia universalis sit primum et unicum eius supreme potestatis adequatum subiectum, ad ipsum demonstrante irrefragabiliter necessarie evidencia racionis, non minoris entitatis fore subiectum pre accidente, quod in illo fundatur. Cum igitur suprema potestas ecclesie accidens sit, subiectum profecto, a quo dependet, maioris erit entitatis. Est autem potestas ecclesie, sicut et regimen ipsius, continua permanens, invariabilis seu immobilis, eterne sibi competens et usque ad seculi consummacionem, propter quod assignari illi opportet subiectum eiusmodi condiciones habens; non vero tale est papa aut generale concilium, neutro eorum continuo permanente. Erit igitur ecclesia primum per se ac principale subiectum et adequatum supreme ecclesiastice potestatis.[1]

Segovia ascribes to the Church and its power a fundamental unity; he sees in it more than the *congregatio fidelium*; unity belongs to the concept and the very being of the Church; it is involved in its existence and does not arise as a secondary effect from the multitude of individual believers. Here one might compare Nicholas of Cues who thinks of the *unitas concordantiae* as an end to be striven for by all believers, and one without which the Church has no authority.[2] To Segovia unity is a reality inherent in the concept of the Church and he makes no distinction between *mater ecclesia* and *populus fidelis*. To the *fideles* belong the bishops and the hierarchy as well as the lower ranks.

Did not this doctrine of the Church as supreme ecclesiastical power fail to take into account the very patent facts of division from 1437 onwards?[3] Segovia would only imply that it is *the Church as a whole*, not the hierarchy or any section of it, which must

---

[1] The quotation is in Fromherz, pp. 131–2.
[2] Fromherz, op. cit., p. 50.
[3] Ibid., p. 149.

display its unity in action, and, if the present Council is failing, contrive a fresh assembly under an undoubted pontiff. Confronted with the fact of the success of the transferred Council at Ferrara-Florence he could claim that these were the tactics of a minority: the true council suffers a *passio*, it is assailed by the papal dissolution, yet among the Fathers there is *persistencia*, princes in number adhere to it, and marks of confidence give it genuine *consolacio* or *comfortatio*.[1] To him Basle is a suffering body, patient as the physical body of Christ was and now, as his *corpus mysticum*, had to be.

One other aspect of Segovia which has been the subject of recent research is his attitude towards Islam. Here Darío Cabanelas Rodríguez has emphasized Segovia's deep interest in bringing about harmony between the Church and Mohammedanism: converting if possible the Moorish princes of Spain, and if that was impossible, showing the fundamental resemblances between the two religions. In 1431, after a successful campaign of John II of Castile against the Moors, he held a disputation at Medina del Campo, John's headquarters, on the Moorish charge against the Christians that they had two gods, father and son, and that God had abandoned his son to die rather than rescuing him. Segovia's reply to the charge constitutes the first of his treatises dealing with the persons of the Trinity. In 1453, when he had become bishop of St Jean de Maurienne, he wrote for the priory of Aiton a number of works on Islam, especially a translation of the Koran and the treatise *De gladio spiritus*. It is in this that he gave the story of his disputation at Medina del Campo, followed by twelve *intelligentiae* on the doctrine of the Trinity and seven *questiones* or *animadvertentiae* on the doctrine of the Incarnation. The treatise belongs to the latter part of 1453.[2] In September that year, to Segovia's deep disillusionment, Nicholas V proclaimed a new crusade; Segovia had been hoping to send the new treatise to the pope but clearly this was now useless; he tried in 1458 to influence Aeneas Sylvius (Pius II), but without avail, by sending some of his treatises.

In the *De gladio spiritus* Segovia recognizes that the Crusades were a mistake: it is true that the capture of Jerusalem was important but its maintenance imposed a severe strain, and after its capture the attempts to recover the Holy Places did nothing but

[1] Fromherz, op. cit., p. 21.
[2] Ibid., pp. 42 ff.

harm. This seems to echo the complaints made at Constance of Christian incursions into Slavonic territories.

How were the Mohammedans to be brought to a knowledge of the Trinity and the Incarnation? At bottom lay a problem of the sources, and while many passages in the Koran could be interpreted in the Christian sense, the Bible and the Koran are so fundamentally different that only an appeal to reason could convince the Mohammedans. Segovia has to show that the Word of God became Man and to produce a rational proof for the existence of the Trinity. These arguments bring to mind the vision of Cusanus, *De pace fidei*, where, in a disputation conducted by the Word, St Peter and St Paul, representatives of the various religions were brought to a knowledge of the truth and professed that they were not aware of it previously: they discover *religio una in rituum varietate*.[1] Unlike Segovia, Cusanus in his later days held that in the end such a unification can only come through the immediate intervention of God. He does not think that he can make out a strong rational case, but his Christian disputants, St Peter and St Paul, ask for the Divine help to influence the conflicting sects. The dialogue is deeply interesting because the aim is to bring the parties to a single religion,[2] whereas Segovia is in the end content with a *convivencia humana*, perhaps somewhat on the model of the World Council of Churches at Delhi, that is, an understanding to live and work and perhaps pray together, rather than a formal unity. Here I must quote the observation of Uta Fromherz: 'Ideas like his could only arise at that time in the mind of a Spaniard who from his experience knew the possibility of friendly intercourse with the Mohammedans and in whose world Islam was far from dangerous and to be regarded as a philosophical problem.'[3] It is to be noted that both Segovia and Cusanus regard Mohammedans as tinged with Nestorian heresy and Cusanus declares in the Introduction to his *Cibratio Alchoran* that 'the sect of the Mohammedans arose in the same spirit as the Nestorians, with like mind and with equally potent eloquence'.[4] Cusanus knew Segovia and corresponded with him and, like Cusanus, Segovia was aware that an accurate establishment and

---

[1] *De pace fidei*, ed. R. Klibansky and H. Bascour, *Medieval and Renaissance Studies*, Supplement iii (London, 1956), 7.

[2] 'Veritas veri cultus,' ibid., p. 62.

[3] Fromherz, op. cit., pp. 50–1.

[4] Ibid., p. 51.

full understanding of the text of the Koran must precede any attempts to argue against the sectaries.

One turns back to Constance to discover an important fact, based on principle. At Basle dialectic had become the supreme test. In Constance the work of the reforming commissions was discussed and argued, but little attempt was made to talk with those who held views different from the Church. The process against Hus and Jerome was conducted by dogmatic statements and although we know that Bishop Robert Hallum did his best to convince the Bohemian, it was statement rather than argument which was employed. The great difference at Basle and at Ferrara-Florence was that the Church had consented to discuss and defend, on a carefully delimited basis, tenets which for centuries had been regarded by her as essential and fundamental. These were not only matters of belief but also of administrative and judicial order, and attention was coming to be focussed on the significance of this change and of the place taken in the disputes by the ordinary academics, by the doctors and masters incorporated in the deputations.[1] The fact of their being able to influence the discussions was an important advance for the middle and lower ranks of the clergy.

[1] P. Ourliac, 'Sociologie du Concile de Bâle', *R.H.E.*, lvi (1961), 19 ff. The influence of a university 'middle' element can be seen, for instance, in the career at Basle and elsewhere of Dr Thomas Ebendorfer, a theological professor, one of the representatives of the university of Vienna at the Council. Ebendorfer's diary was printed in 'Monumenta Conciliorum Generalium', ed. E. Birk, i (1857), 701 ff. His life is studied by Alphons Lhotsky, *Thomas Ebendorfer, Ein österreichischer Geschichtsschreiber, Theologe und Diplomat des 15 Jahrhunderts*, Schriften der Monumenta Germanica Historica, xv (Stuttgart, 1957). The strong support of the Council (and of the earlier fifteenth-century councils) given by the academics derived largely from their conviction of the need for reform. It was specially evident among the Germans at the time of Basle, and can be heard in the famous document known as the 'Reformatio Sigismundi' and the concomitant literature: cf. Lothar Graf zu Dohna, *Reformatio Sigismundi, Beiträge zum Verstandnis einer Reformschrift des funfzehnten Jahrhunderts* (Veröffentlichen des Max-Planck Instituts für Geschichte, Göttingen, 1960). Vienna, as the letters of Peter of Pulka show, was urging this strongly at Constance. The function of academics as ambassadors in conciliar diplomacy (though varying in their support according to national instructions) is well illustrated in R. H. Trame, S.J., *Rodrigo Sanchez de Arévalo, 1404-1470*, Catholic Univ. of America (Washington, 1958), 16-62, a study of the Salamanca theologian, and, of course, by the career of Ebendorfer himself, especially at the diets of Nuremberg and Frankfurt, 1444-5.

This change was reflected in, and made possible by, the passage from the 'nation' to the 'deputation' system. A 'nation' system was one of administrative convenience and political necessity, forced upon the Council by the need for counteracting the numerous votes of Italian prelates supporting John XXIII. Fillastre's diary shows that it was not easily accepted. The impatience of Sigismund for a favourable French vote in favour of John XXIII, giving adequate guarantees of resignation, led to an atmosphere of doubt and distrust and alienated the cardinals, who, like d'Ailly, were convinced of the need to uphold the central control and direction of the Council by themselves. But it is interesting to note that in his memorandum *De Ecclesiae et cardinalium auctoritate*, read in one of the churches in Constance on 1 October 1416, d'Ailly maintained that the government of the Church should not be regarded as an unmixed monarchy: that it had elements of aristocracy and of democracy, and that, in Aristotelian style, a mixture of the two, or 'polity', is best. Now at the Council of Constance polity, on the whole, went under; the predominant authority of leaders of Church and State in the 'nation' delegations and their liability to be directed by their own monarchs ruled out in many cases the more democratic discussions which we know to have taken place at Basle; and with the Bohemians who appeared at Constance there could be no other method than the genuine give and take of opinion. There was wrangling in the general sessions at Constance over procedural points, but there was no one there like Cesarini to steer the argument.

A principal advance made by modern conciliar history is to be found in the study of debates and treatises, read or published, and positions advocated in the Basle Assembly. The Council had deserted the way of dogma and admitted the way of argument. It is this change which, combined with the contemporary political situation in France, made inevitable the failure of the English representatives at Basle to influence the course of the proceedings or to lend themselves to the pacification of Europe at which the Council was aiming. A significant attestation is found in Dr Schofield's discussion of the reception of the Basle envoy Gerardo Landriani, bishop of Lodi, who came in June 1432 to secure Henry VI's adherence to the Council and the subsequent failure of the English delegation to make any impression.[1] Landriani, on the

[1] 'The First English Delegation to the Council of Basel', *J.E.H.*, xii (1961), 167–95.

whole, found both the English Council and the bishops friendly, and arragements were made for the departure of a powerful delegation, but on 28 January 1433, Henry VI wrote a letter to his ambassadors, while they were still on the way, showing how meagre and inaccurate was the information about the Council that was available in England and how slow were the movements of the English delegation compared with those of the Bohemians, who had been in the Council since 4 January. 'Still more astonishing', remarks Dr Schofield, 'is the evidence contained in this letter (it is from Emmanuel College MS. 142) that the King had heard for the first time of the Council's adoption of "deputations" instead of "nations" only after his ambassadors had left England.' He therefore sent them fresh instructions:

We remember having instructed you at your departure from our realm of England that, on coming to the place of the Council, you should there participate and co-operate with others, especially in the cause of the faith and for bringing back the Bohemians. However, since we have heard that the same Council has decided to proceed not by nations but deputations, we perceive in such case it is to be feared the decrees of the said Council must proceed from and be enacted by a majority not of nations but of persons. And as the Bohemians, for whose reunion you have principally been sent, have not yet come to the place of the Council—so it is said—we wish you in the absence of the same Bohemians from the aforesaid place, also to absent yourselves and to remain in some convenient place until our orators come to join you and can arrive simultaneously at the same place [i.e., of the Council].[1]

They were sent to the Council and very nearly in the same breath told to absent themselves! In the summer of 1433 Henry VI protested against the oath of incorporation by which the entrants undertook to work for the Council's honour, to give good advice, not to disclose individual votes, and, this is most important, to maintain and defend the Council's decrees. Henry VI on 17 July wrote to the Council complaining of this oath and described it as unprecedented, contrary to the teaching of Christ and degrading to the temporal rulers whose ambassadors were expected to submit to it. Now this oath had been adopted by the Council at the beginning of February 1432, which was the month in which the system of the four deputations had been accepted. These deputations and incorporation became the two main obstacles to English

[1] Schofield, art. cit., pp. 180–1.

participation in the Council. Only in the debates on the four articles of Prague was the first English delegation to share in the Council's work. Despite the ineffectiveness of their stand against the Hussites the English were deeply interested in the Council's offer of mediation in France and had made it the basis of provisional plans for diplomatic work at Basle by a later section of the delegation. These plans were ultimately frustrated. Generally speaking, if the first English delegation had been allowed to accept the deputation system and be incorporated,[1] the influence of this country in the peace negotiations of the Council would have been substantially greater than, in fact, it turned out to be.

The attitude of this delegation may in the end have been determined by the fact that representatives of Charles VII of France had already been incorporated before the English arrived. The Council was anxious for the adhesion of any power that could help it. It had to compete against papal efforts in the same direction and the struggle with Eugenius was the whole time in the background. The English Council was interested in Basle as a method of refuting the Hussites and perhaps of procuring the extradition of one of their leaders, the renegade Peter Payne, and it was envisaging the Council as possible mediator for a satisfactory settlement in France. On reform it does not appear to have described or uttered any observation. Recent work on the diplomatic history of the three years has pointed to the failure at Basle as an important factor in the depression suffered by the English cause in France.

The study of conciliar thought has been invigorated and to some extent revolutionized by modern work on the impact which the canon lawyers made upon contemporary political theory, in particular the theory of the *plenitudo potestatis*. The canon lawyer is not by definition a political theorist: he is essentially a commentator on texts and cases; and these, for their elucidation, depend in part upon the opinions of his canonist predecessors and in part upon concrete instances within his own range of view. It is not his business to embark upon general questions which are matters for the theologian; but in the later Middle Ages the canonist was continually concerned with the practical problem of authority, most of all of what the pope could or could not do by reason of the

---

[1] 'No member of the English delegation was incorporated—a point that has not been sufficiently stressed': Schofield, art. cit., p. 183.

plentitude of his power. Here I may be allowed to quote a passage written elsewhere:

The canonists could deal with this by two different methods. On the one hand, and here they act strictly within their own field, they could insist with Huguccio that any reasonable theory of Church government must be founded on a clear distinction between the authority inherent in the whole *congregatio fidelium* and the powers that could be exercised by the institutional *ecclesia Romana* which he identified with the Pope and cardinals. Secondly, the canonist could subscribe to a theory put forward by Hostiensis of the distribution of authority within an ecclesiastical corporation in the same way as the bishop is part of the corporation of his cathedral church, sharing with the canons the responsibility for guiding its affairs and possessing practical powers to act on its behalf; so that the Pope is part of the college of cardinals, and in turn pope and cardinals stand in a like relationship to the *universitas fidelium* in which ultimate sovereignty resides. To establish this it was necessary to show that the *universitas fidelium* was a *universitas* in the most legally precise sense of the term, and this was demonstrated by Huguccio when he asserted that the Church as a whole was subject to the same rules of corporation structure as any lesser chapter or college.[1]

But there was another, an extra-legal way of combating the *plenitudo potestatis*: to set against it the need for moral action and moral restraint and to maintain that the pope is bound by the faith that he owes to the Catholic religion and to the Church as its organ, to uphold the example of Christ. His ideal in fact must be the *imitatio Christi*. How characteristic of the Christian humanism of the fifteenth century! If the pope falls away from this, action can be taken against him by the whole body of the Church. It is in pursuit of these moral ends, recently summed up by Ludwig Buisson as *caritas*, that process can be undertaken.[2] Thus certain great fifteenth-century canonists departed from the cautious distinctions made by their predecessors and subscribed to what is practically a subjective doctrine justifying resistance to the papal plenitude.

These extra-legal, almost 'nature-rightly', doctrines are found embodied in the work of men like Petrus de Anchorano, prominent at Pisa, who died in 1416, Antonius de Butrio (d. 1408) and, need

[1] Jacob, *Essays in the Conciliar Epoch*, 3rd ed., 1963, pp. 240–1. This is based upon B. Tierney, *Foundations of the Conciliar Theory* (Cambridge, 1953), chs. 2 and 3.

[2] Ludwig Buisson, *Potestas und Caritas* (Cologne, 1958), chs. 4 and 5 (especially p. 269).

we say, in the great Zabarella (d. 1417) whose gloss on the Schism in his commentary on the Clementines is known to all conciliar scholars. Zabarella, of course, knew all the strictly legal arguments for the control of papal plentitude. These jurists set the standard for their noteworthy successors, John of Imola and Nicholas de Tudeschis, better known as Panormitanus. Zabarella taught both of these men and it may be remembered that Nicholas was auditor-general of accounts in the Apostolic Camera at the beginning of the Council of Basle. He stood for Eugenius IV in the Council when he (Nicholas) had joined it, then followed the conciliar majority and passed over to the side of Felix V, who made him cardinal. He is a most important canonist, not only for his mastery of the sources, but also because he thinks out familiar problems in a fresh way and carries them a stage further.

In the early stages of this development it is action against the pope on the ground of his heresy which is demanded and argued. This goes back to a gloss of Huguccio on the words *nisi depre-hendatur a fide devius* (*Dist.* 40, 1, 6) as Professor Tierney has shown.[1] The concept of heresy widens in Conrad of Gelnhausen, Petrus de Anchorano and Zabarella. The pope is heretical if he remains long in schism; if, in fact, there is *error et pertinacia*, then as Anchorano stresses, action against him is justified because of the *crimen periurii fraccionis voti*. Panormitanus delivered a very clear opinion. If the pope sins he can be warned according to the evangelical rule, 'If thy brother sin against thee', etc. Supposing his sin is public and the Church sustains scandal therefrom, if despite warning he will not abstain, it must be told to the Church, i.e. to the council representing it, and by it he can be punished, particularly if he refuses to reform. This charge of scandal can be applied to the pope not merely for persisting in the schism and so incurring the charge of heresy, but for persistent refusal to reform his administration: thus the papal system of reservations came in question at Constance. In 1415, the French nation in a special *Deliberatio* made *annates* the subject of their complaint. Excesses in administration, evil administration of the spiritualities and temporalities of the Church were joined together in the document deposing John XXIII for dishonourable life and morals, scandalizing the Church of God and the people of Christ. John had persisted in this conduct 'after due and caritative admonition and so had rendered himself notoriously incorrigible'. Here is the moral

[1] Tierney, op. cit., pp. 57–8, and Appendix 1.

rather than the legal revolt against the plentitude of power.[1] But it was all the more difficult to bring the charge of scandal against a pope of upright life like Eugenius IV when he declined to reform the curial system. This was a matter of finance and technique, and John of Torquemada could very well stand out against the conciliar majority when such extra-legal sanctions were applied. Once Eugenius IV had been led, his hand forced by the Council, to sanction Cesarini's method of securing the *reduccio Bohemorum*, what strictly legal justification had the Council for their action against, and eventual deposition of, Eugenius? The papal lawyer could argue that even if *maior pars concilii* resisted a papal transfer of the Council of Basle to Ferrara-Florence, and voted for the continuance of the Council in a meeting place chosen by them, it was not necessarily the *sanior pars* that did so. The history of the passage of Cesarini and others including Cusanus to the papal side in 1437–8 illustrates the fears of men who saw the dangers in these subjective criteria that were sweeping the Council.

For some this has a certain paradoxical interest when it is recollected that in England Archbishop Henry Chichele who in 1431–2 had held firm by Eugenius and persuaded his Convocation to follow that pontiff, Chichele, who had refused to apply in England the *annates* decree of the Council (1435), sent down to Oxford among his first present of legal books to the library of his new college (All Souls) the Commentaries of Anchorano, de Butrio, Zabarella and Panormitanus. Perhaps the fact is that in many leading canonists one can find material wherewith to build a theory of resistance to the papal power. But whether this theory should pass from a series of isolated comments and glosses into political action, and Christendom be torn on such an issue, is not for a historian, least of all for the writer of this chapter, to say. One statement of opinion may perhaps be put in the form of a question: Is not the Church at its finest (*optime se habet*, as the *Monarchia* puts it), not when it is presenting an ironclad unity to its critics, but when it is applying its dialectic to the choice between conflicting ideas and cannot yet clarify its mind in its internal differences? In other words, when the possible intellect is being exercised to the utmost in a supremely spiritual cause?

[1] Buisson, op. cit. p. 209.

Chapter VII
Huizinga and the Autumn of the Middle Ages

Not till comparatively late did I come to know Johan Huizinga. It was three years so so after the publication of his best-known book in its English form, *The Waning of the Middle Ages* (1924). He looked then like a solid Dutch business man, the only outstanding feature being eyes that were alert and interesting, sometimes melancholy. I had read the book and been deeply engaged by it, but was then too inexperienced to review it adequately.

Only when other works of his appeared in an English form—especially the little book on Erasmus—could one fully realize what sort of a visitor this was. Spiritually Huizinga was a Burgundian: he drew his inspiration from both sides of the Middle Kingdom, the French and the German: he himself was firmly median, like the great international Dutchmen of the seventeenth-eighteenth century.[1] He must be one of the few twentieth-century scholars to have had a collected edition made of his works. The nine volumes published by Willink at Haarlem are an impressive testimony to one whose intellectual life was centered in the age of Erasmus, but who was at the same time a barometer sensitive to the decline of European politics between the two World Wars. In a country of deeply educated men Huizinga stood out as a scholar wholly dedicated to the humanities, while himself not a specialist in any discipline but one, and that the history of civilization.

He was born at Groningen in 1872, took his doctor's degree in 1897, having studied mainly in the field of Indo-Aryan philosophy. He was, as he said in his autobiography, a 'Sanskritist'. After teaching for eight years at Haarlem he was recommended by his teacher the Dutch historian P. J. Blok for the Groningen chair of history which he held till 1915, when he was promoted to Leiden. At Leiden he taught till 1942 when the University was closed by the Nazis. His own independent views brought him relegation to the Concentration Camp at S. Michielsgestel and he was only released from the camp by Swedish intervention: but he

---

[1] This seems a legitimate inference from ch. vii ('Niederlandisches Nationalbewusstsein'), of *Wege der Kulturgeschichte* (Munich, 1930), p. 208 f. and *Die Mittlerstellung der Niederlände zwischen West-und Mittel Europa* (Teubner, 1933).

was not allowed to return to Leiden. During the rigours of the
winter 1944–5, when there was an acute shortage of food in
Holland, Huizinga became ill and died (1 February 1945), some
weeks before the liberation of his country.

At Groningen he gave a two years' course of lectures on the
outline of history. He never thought of himself as a historical
specialist. As he observes, 'I never was a historical researcher
pur sang.' He worked for long on the constitutional history of
Haarlem which he approached through the City archives, and he
wrote a particularly interesting history of Groningen University,
1814–1914. It was at Groningen that he conceived the idea of his
Waning of the Middle Ages, probably in 1907. He came to see that
the later Middle Ages were not so much the precursor of the
Renaissance but a period with a character of its own—this 'abster-
ben' as he calls it, was the period of high activity even in decline.
In other words, he did not see the culture of the Burgundian
Netherlands as a forerunner of the Northern Renaissance but as
the culmination and decline of medieval civilization. With this
idea in mind he began to read Burgundian and French historians,
especially Chastellain. He immersed himself in Burgundian art,
chiefly the art of Van Eyck, and the Van Eyck illustrations given
in his *Waning* are more than illustrations to the text: they are a
glimpse into his mind and his emotions, where he seizes for a
moment the barely tangible spirit of such an age. Such moments of
illumination he has described in one of the best known of his essays
recently printed in Men and Ideas:[1]

There is a very important element in historical understanding which
might best be indicated by the term 'historical sensation'. One might
also speak of 'historical contact'. 'Historical imagination' says too much,
and so does 'historical vision', since the description as a visual conception is too restrictive. The German term *Ahnung*, 'presentiment',
which was already used by William von Humboldt in this connection,
would express it almost completely, if it were not worn too threadbare
in other contexts. This not completely reduceable contact with the past
is an entry into an atmosphere, it is one of the many forms of reaching
beyond oneself, of experiencing truth, which are given to man. It is not
an aesthetic enjoyment, a religious emotion, an awe of nature, a meta-
physical recognition—and yet it is a figure in this series. The object
of the sensation is not human figures in their individual form, not
human lives or human thoughts one thinks one can disentangle. What

---

[1] J. Huizinga, *Men and Ideas*, p. 53.

the mind creates or experiences in this connection can hardly be called
an image. If and in so far as it assumes a form, it is one that remains
complex and vague: an *Ahnung* just as much of roads and houses and
fields, of sounds and colours, as of stimulated and stimulating people.
This contact with the past, which is accompanied by an utter conviction
of genuineness and truth, can be evoked by a line from a Document
or a chronicle, by a print, by a few notes of an old song. It is not an
element that the writer infuses in his work by using certain words. It
lies beyond the book of history, not in it. The reader brings it to the
writer, in his response to the writer's call.

In reality this sensation, vision, contact, *Ahnung* is limited to moments
of special intellectual clarity, moments of a sudden penetration of the
spirit.

This historical sensation is apparently so essential that it is felt again
and again on the true moment of historical cognition. Inscribed on
Michelet's grave are his own words: '*L'histoire c'est une résurrection*'.
Taine said '*L'histoire c'est à peu près voir les hommes d'autrefois*'. In their
vagueness these two statements are more usable than careful definitions
in the theory of knowledge. It is the *à peu près*, the more or less, that
matters. It is a resurrection that takes place in the sphere of the dream,
a series of intangible figures, a hearing of half-understood words.

Implicit in the value of the historical sensation, is its quality of a
necessary of life (a quality befitting that urge towards contact with the
fact), is also the rehabilitation of the antiquarian interest that Nietzsche
in his day cast aside disdainfully. The most modest historical research,
that of the genealogist and student of heraldry, that of the local
dilettante, can be exalted and ennobled by this intellectual preoccupa-
tion. Their work has its own fully-fledged goal if the scholar or the
reader experience that sensation from it.

The fastidious phrasing, the insight into the nature of genuine
scholarship can be better appreciated when some words of his in
The Shadow of Tomorrow are remembered. They were written in
1936, three years before the great débâcle:

We are living in a demented world. And we know it. It would not
come as a surprise to anyone if tomorrow the madness gave way to a
frenzy which would leave our poor Europe in a state of distracted
stupor with engines still turning and flags streaming in the breeze but
with the spirit gone.[1]

The contrast between this scene and the exquisite jewelled world
of the Flemish painters pressed home upon him so that he felt a

---

[1] P. 1. The first words of the book.

kind of hopeless nostalgia for a past of light and quietude, the silence of the Adoration of the Lamb.

This then was the Huizinga whose nature was unknown to the young scholar who met him in 1927. He had never been, as he says, 'ein richtiger geschichtsforscher' and perhaps I was looking for the wrong thing from him; but now after forty years his *Waning of the Middle Ages* seems more significant than it did when it appeared. This book was not meant to be a history of the later Middle Ages but the portrayal of a chapter in the story of civilization; a work that interpreted through its study of letters and art the spirit of a period. Huizinga used his literary and artistic texts to enucleate the mental habits and assumptions of the fourteenth and fifteenth centuries. We are doing it today only with a less conscious sense of the peculiar character of a cultural period; none the less we are following Huizinga's method, linking medieval legend, art, chivalry and taste as in the brilliant recent address 'Form and Meaning in Medieval Romance' of Professor Vinaver to the Modern Humanities Research Association (1966), which throws light upon the structure of the Arthurian legend by reference to manuscript decoration and the detail of sculpture. In Huizinga two chapters are called 'Verbal and Plastic Expression compared'. It is Huizinga who has taught us the method of analogy and comparison and has helped to make iconography an ally of the historian.

However we may translate Huizinga's title 'Herfsttij' which means the plenitude of autumn with its suggestion of end and decay, his intention was clear. He was depicting a civilization which had reached its zenith and could not remain dominant. It is therefore pertinent to ask in what respects civilization had reached the summit of its efforts: but—first—it will not do to follow certain critics in thinking that the *Waning* is a study in elegant negation, a treatise on a society now devoid of creative initiative where prejudice outweighed promise and the spirit of discovery was asleep. Before cavilling starts it is well to remember even to the extent of repetition what the achievements of the book are. It is essentially an essay on later medieval mentality: on tendencies in thought and behaviour as they expressed themselves *per sensibilia*, in religious ceremony and ritual, in competition, in fine arts and literature of the mannered folk. At this point it is proper to recall Huizinga's training in Eastern language and custom. He was a bit of an anthropologist. He makes all kinds of incursions into Folk custom and behaviour. There is in his book *Homo Ludens* a notable description of a judicial duel among the Eskimos where he catches exactly the love of play and gesture that characterize primitive peoples.[1] His theory was that even the most civilized people show in their behaviour to one another the spirit of play and gesture. He essays in *Homo Ludens* 'to ascertain how far culture itself bears the character of play':[2] thus for example the whole functioning of the medieval universe was profoundly agonistic and 'ludic'. This accounts for the polemical nature of knowledge. All knowledge, he says, is polemical by nature and polemics cannot be divorced from agonistics. Epochs in which great new treasures of the mind come to light are generally epochs of great and violent controversy. Such was the seventeenth century when Natural science underwent a glorious efflorescence coinciding with the weakening of authority and antiquity and the decay of faith.[3] Towards the end of the book he observes:

it has not been difficult to show that a certain play factor was extremely active all through the cultural process and that it produces many of the fundamental forms of social life. The spirit of playful competition is, as a social impulse, older than culture itself and pervades all life like a veritable ferment. Ritual grew up in sacred play, poetry was born in play and nourished on play. Music and dancing were pure play. Wisdom and philosophy found expression in words and forms derived from religious contests. The rules of warfare, the conventions of noble living were built up on play patterns. We have to conclude therefore that civilization is in its earliest phases play. It does not come *from* play, like a babe detaching itself from the womb. It arises in and *as* play and never leaves it.

'We find it difficult', he writes, 'to fancy the mind cultivating the ancient forms of medieval thought and expression, while aspiring at the same time to antique wisdom and beauty, yet this is just what we have to picture to ourselves.' 'Classicism did not come as a sudden revelation. It grew up among the luxurious vegetation of medieval thought. Humanism was a form before it was an inspiration.' From this Huizinga develops the idea that the 'waning' period is one of gesture rather than of realism; and of this gesture in religious observance, in courtly love and in many

---

[1] Op cit., p. 85.
[2] Op. cit., Foreword.
[3] *Homo Ludens*, p. 156.

other activities an abundance of examples is given. The age of courtly etiquette is thus described

after the young Count of Charolais, out of modesty, has obstinately refused to use the wash basin before a meal at the same time as the Queen of England, the court talks the whole day of the incident: the Duke to whom the case is submitted charges two noblemen to argue it on both sides. Humble refusals to take precedence of another last upwards of a quarter of an hour: the longer one resists, the more one is praised. People hide their hands to avoid the honour of a hand kiss: The Queen of Spain does so on meeting the young Archduke Philip le Beau. The latter waits patiently for a moment of inattentiveness on the part of the Queen to seize her hand and kiss it. For once Spanish gravity was at fault: the court laughed.[1]

With gesture goes rule or protocol. As there are rules of daily politesse, so there is a code of conventions for love and loving, behaviour that is both *curiale et aulicum*, though another standard raises its head:

In the erotic conceptions of the Middle Ages two diverging currents are to be distinguished. Extreme indecency showing itself freely in customs as in literature contrasts with an excessive formalism bordering on prudery.[2]

Such customs, writes Huizinga, seem to be absolutely opposed to the constraint and the modesty imposed by courtesy. His explanation is that two layers of civilization are superimposed, coexisting, though contradictory: side by side with the courtly style of literary and rather recent origin, the primitive forms of erotic life kept all their force.

This coexistence in which both elements seem to have reached a state of exaggeration is according to Huizinga a principal characteristic of the declining Middle Ages; and this, he implies, gives the period an ethos of its own. It is a period of a high degree of self-consciousness with an acute religious sensibility expressing itself in artistic images of all kinds[3] and marked by a revival of chivalry and courtly accomplishments. But—and here we may make a vital reservation—it is not a period of deep internal pessimism, however cynical are the men who play the game correctly. There are, as I shall suggest, both in later medieval philosophy as well as in

[1] *Waning of the Middle Ages*, pp. 35–6.
[2] Ibid., pp. 96–7.
[3] Ibid., ch. xii *passim.*

political life all sorts of tensions that may even seem revolutionary and making for the decline of society, but they are marks not of decay but of evolution, where competing forces threaten, but do not actually undermine contemporary society.

But first the contradictory element. To the antagonisms Huizinga devotes much space. Life was violent and high-strung, cruelty and compassion alternated:

> Tortures and executions are enjoyed by the spectators like an entertainment at a fair. The citizens of Mons bought a brigand, at far too high a price, for the pleasure of seeing him quartered 'at which the people rejoiced more than if a new holy body had risen from the dead'. The people of Bruges in 1488 during the captivity of Maximilian, King of the Romans, cannot get their fill of seeing the tortures inflicted, on a high platform in the middle of the market-place, on the magistrates suspected of treason. The unfortunates are refused the death-blow which they implore, that the people may feast again upon their torments.[1]

But Huizinga can speak of the very strong and direct feeling of pity and forgiveness which alternated with extreme severity. Instead of lenient penalties, inflicted with hesitation, the Middle Ages knew but two extremes: the fullness of cruel punishment and mercy. The contrast of cruelty and pity occurs at every turn in the manners and customs of the Middle Ages.

On the one hand, the sick, the poor, the insane are objects of that deeply moved pity, born of a feeling of fraternity akin to that which is so strikingly expressed in modern Russian literature; on the other hand they are treated with incredible harshness or cruelly mocked. The chronicler Pierre de Fenin having described the death of a gang of brigands, winds up naïvely: 'and people laughed a good deal, because they were all poor men'. In 1425 an 'esbatement' takes place in Paris, of 4 blind beggars, armed with sticks, with which they hit each other in trying to kill a pig, which is the prize of the combat. On the evening before, they were led through the town 'all armed, with a great banner in front, on which was pictured a pig, and preceded by a man beating a drum'.[2]

Judicially, cruelty and mercy alternate, as can be seen in the practice of the judicial pardon. The fourteenth and fifteenth centuries were a period of such pardons whereby the courts could be told to remit the penalties for lawless crimes, even those

[1] Waning, p. 15.
[2] Ibid., p. 17.

committed against a whole countryside. For an appropriate sum of money the King averted his 'indignation'. All students of the period of civil strife in England 1450–85 will have encountered these pardons, which are not always in fact the product of merciful-ness but were granted in return for cash and as a means of averting further disturbance. The later Middle Ages might indeed mingle cruelty with kindness, but were they any worse than the century depicted by the satirical Hogarth or, further back, the anti-Jewish first century of the Crusades?

And now, pessimism. Taken wrongly, Huizinga's book may well exalt the cult of the corpse. The image of death is ubiquitous but is it any more prevailing than in the later Tudor period, e.g. in *Christian Prayers and Meditations* (John Day, 1569)? Pessimism however is at bottom a philosophical problem. It does not mean a general feeling of hopelessness about the future but a deeply rooted scepticism about the scope of human rationality and on this subject Huizinga in the preface to his *In the Shadow of Tomorrow* has specifically to deny the charge of pessimism which his critics made. By pessimism we understand the despair of reaching through the ordinary powers of discursive reason a solution of the ultimate philosophical problem of reality—what really is.

This philosophical pessimism, which I have described else-where in outlining the thesis of Stadelmann,[1] is not really the type discussed by Huizinga. He has a chapter 'pessimism and the idea of the sublime', but what he describes is not pessimism but a belief in the static, predetermined order of society: the graded hierarchy, each part of which has its rules and standards which respond to the whole social unit. He is thinking of the impossibility to the later Middle Ages of conceiving any sort of radical change in human society. By the voyages of discovery the known world may become larger, but the cosmic organization does not move or change till the seventeenth century. It is curious that Huizinga should almost entirely have avoided treating the various forms of reaction against this hierarchical order. The only attention he pays to it is a short chapter headed 'Religious Thought beyond the Limits of Imagination' in which he deals not with criticism of the prevailing order, but with mystics like Denys the Carthusian or, very superficially, Ruysbroek. There is not a single reference to Wyclif and his revolt against symbolism and images. No doubt

[1] 'The Fifeenth Century: some recent interpretations', *Bulletin of the John Rylands Library*, vol. 14, No. 2 (July 1930), pp. 8–10.

this is because Huizinga was determined to avoid academic theology, but to omit the studied iconoclasm of English Lollardy is
seriously to weaken any treatment of the relations between art and
imagination, particularly religious imagination. About England
there is so much in his *Erasmus* and, needless to say, his *Philip
Sydney*, that one marvels at the omission of the English religious
revolution which we can now trace in its local and diocesan as
well as its University setting: a movement which ran like a flame
into central Europe, nearly overthrew the Empire, and itself led,
in part, to the Tridentine reformation.

Dr Huizinga did not set out to be a historian of religious
Europe, but it should be remembered that the period whose mind
he is interpreting saw the crisis of the Great Schism and the
Conciliar Movement. With the causes of the Schism and its long
duration he naturally could have no concern, but behind the
Councils there lies a great deal of thinking and utterance about the
nature of the Church which, for all the failure of the movement in
practice to achieve reform, must be regarded as constructive
political thought.[1] Dr Figgis considered this thought to be a
precursor of European liberal ideas; none the less, as Professor
Tierney shows, it is closely linked with canonist speculation from
the period of the early thirteenth century: it discusses the importance of representation in the Church government, the need for
communities and societies within the Church to make their voices
heard and with the fundamental problem of the authority of the
Vicar of Christ in the Church. The discussion of the papal plenitude
of power with its bearing upon the position of the Sacred College
on the one hand and the episcopate on the other set in motion
ideas which have remained active till the present age. With the
growth of absolutism the ideas represented were often suppressed
but were never destroyed and in modern times they have broken
out again with renewed vigour. These tremendous currents can
hardly be represented as compatible with the notion of a declining
Church: the expression only suits the conservatives who misunderstood or opposed them.

[1] Not merely constructive by way of elucidating concepts that are
genuinely 'conciliar', but of reformulating the theory of the papal plenitude of power and so contributing to the Renaissance doctrine of absolutism: two opposites represented, in the middle of the fifteenth century,
by John of Segovia on the one hand and John de Turrecremata (Torquemada) on the other.

The difficulty one feels about the *Waning of the Middle Ages* is
not its effective (though largely unannotated) marshalling of fact
and instance, but a failure in structure. This is largely one of
feeling and emotion. The book ignores the pressures of public
life, the routines of the courts, the manipulation of opinion by the
administrators, the influence of politics. We are given instead an
essay in subjectivism: yet in the cultural movement which
Huizinga describes, one of the most formative facts is the en-
hanced position of the prince. The states system of modern Europe
was emerging. Very little is said in the *Waning* about the new
Messiah or his enlightened court or system of patronage. Perhaps
Huizinga left the Burgundian aspect of this movement to Cartel-
lieri to describe in one of the most enjoyable of histories of culture.[1] Anyhow, the curial structure of civilized society cannot be
disregarded; for at the courts of the nobility were repeated the
characteristics of the royal organization and the royal organization is the civil service of the country. The central judicial and
financial institutions were naturally more complicated than
those of a single magnate: but royal and financial administra-
tions were significantly alike for their personnel to be at times
interchangeable.

Thus, whether in France, England or Burgundy, a pattern of
government, a way of doing business, runs with comparative
uniformity throughout the country. It does not take a learned
political historian to know that in the later Middle Ages the art of
government is the art of keeping the smaller seignorial units
responsive to the prince's organization. The political body sets the
tune and the pace. However much they grumble, the magnates
find it in their interest to comply. The courtier civil servant is the
important man, and the growth of this class the key to the history
of the later Middle Ages. These men were by no means always
submissive to authority over them, and if they were lawyers they
could be, and were, sometimes retained against the Crown by
patrons and others. They might still retain some independence
of both patron and crown; and they had to find friends and retain
their position. Mr Peter Lewis has admirably portrayed the personal position of the medieval administrator vis-à-vis the court.

Guillaume Juvenel des Ursins was advised when he became chan-

[1] *Am Hofe der Herzöge von Burgund: kulturhistorische Bilde* (Basel,
1926).

cellor by his brother Jean 'not to think you can resist the will of those who will be at court: because that will only have you suppressed and thrown out. It's much better to have patience and dissemble and be the cause of making less trouble, since one can't profit by being too firm and losing one's job: Messire Arnault de Corbie used to. . . .' To deplore the nervous strain of being a courtier was an established literary affectation. 'The court', wrote Alain Chartier, 'is an assembly of people who under the pretence of acting for the good of all come together to diddle each other: for there's scarcely anyone there who isn't engaged in buying and selling and exchanging sometimes their income, sometimes their old clothes—for we of the court are high-class merchants, we buy other people—and sometimes for their money we sell *them* our own precious humanity.' The corruption of the court was deplorable. 'The abuses of the court and the habits of the courtiers are such that no one lasts there without being corrupted and no one succeeds there without being corruptible.' But corrupt, nerve-wracking, or not, the court was nevertheless the source *par excellence* of political power.[1]

To a system which both Mr Armstrong and M. Jean Bartier have described in their writings,[2] M. Bartier in his *Légistes et gens de finance au XV siècle* has illustrated many of his biographical sketches of ducal officials with Van der Weyden portraits which bring them so clearly to life. One of the most vivid representations is Dirk Bout's Hippolyte de Berthoz the chief fiscal official of Charles the Bold in 1473, who in 1477 became treasurer for the duchess Margaret of York.[3] He and his wife Elizabeth de Keverwyck presented the church of St Saviour at Bruges with a triptych commemorating the martyrdom of St Hippolytus, the patron of Berthoz—a work in which Hugo van der Goes had some part: then there are bishop Jean Chevrot, a university figure who in 1433 became president of the ducal court and in 1440 was engaged in diplomatic work with England and France and in reconciling certain of the Flemish barons to the policy of Philip the Good;[4] Pierre de Goux, the ideal bailli, sought after by many noble families, became Philip's chancellor and founded a small administrative dynasty;[5] Jean III Gros, auditor of Charles the Bold, painted

[1] 'France in the Fifteenth Century', *Europe in the later Middle Ages*, ed. Hale, Highfield and Smalley, pp. 285–9.

[2] E.g. C. A. J. Armstrong, 'The Burgundian Netherlands 1477–1551', *The New Cambridge Modern History*, i. 230.

[3] *Légistes et gens de finances aux XVe siècle*, 1957, 300 and n. Dirk Bout's portrait of them is opposite p. 296.

[4] Ibid., pp. 310–24.

[5] Ibid., *passim*.

by Van der Weyden; the family of Plaine, quite a dynasty, a rich, efficient, devoted set of men, who if their masters had been able to avoid the hostility of France could have set the ducal throne clear of dangers.[1]

How far do we find English administrative families establishing their masters in the same way? Here we do not possess an 'official' class. There is an old noblesse, young cadets of which are seeking to enter the royal household and to serve in expeditions when necessary (the great force assembled by Edward IV for the invasion of France in 1475 contained a good number); but the highest governmental unit, the Council is, under Edward IV and Henry VII, a mixed body whose criterion is ability and loyalty as much as hereditary position; it contains men of law as well as of arms. It is an aristocratic unit in the broad sense. Still, the dangers lurked: even under Yorkist rule, the system of indentured retainers, very different from that of the peaceful Burgundian administrator family, spread, and the military power of the lords who had made these indentures became the principal danger to peaceful government. To them the Crown might send licences to retain men; thus on 23 July 1454, when Henry VI was *non compos mentis*, Richard of York, protector and defender of England got the Council to grant that the duke

should have power and authority to give the king's livery of colours to 80 gentlemen after his discretion, they and every one of them sworn to be agreed with no man but the king, without his special licence; and that hereupon letters under the privy and great seal be made in due form.[2]

But alas! in many cases when indenture took place, there is no word of any permit: the most prominent of these cases being William lord Hastings, Edward IV's chamberlain, who controlled large forces in the Midlands: suspicion of such power may have been the reason why, as a precaution, Richard III had Hastings put to death. Another example of such indenturing is that of the Duke of Buckingham who turned round upon Richard, and in consequence suffered a like penalty.

This was not the atmosphere for works of art like the portraits

---

[1] *Légistes et gens de finances aux XVᵉ siècle*, p. 367.

[2] W. H. Dunham Jr., *Lord Hastings's Indentured Retainers*, Connecticut, 1955, p. 81, citing Nicolas, *Proc. and Ordinances of Privy Council*, vi. 209.

of Rogier Van der Weyden or, more suitable for the days of the victorious prince, of the younger Holbein. Yet for all the description, by writers from Mr Kingsford onwards, of the fifteenth century in England as a period of ferment, I would scruple to call that period one of waning or decline. Enormously vigorous, at times desperately misguided, the country was none the less working out a system of control over the big families which led it to put its faith in the sovereign and his administrators, an institution which neither the French nor the Burgundian estates could match: this came through the establishment of the notion of the Crown in parliament as the sole unchallenged secular authority. It took a long while and much family extinction (not through bloodshed, but by natural death) to arrive at this concept of public authority but Sir John Fortescue, in the middle of the fifteenth century, himself a county and a borough lord, had arrived at something like this idea, when he proclaimed England to be a *dominium politicum et regale*, and he himself derived politicum from *polus*— a plurality, many contributing: a rule based upon the lords and the commons.

Another more peaceful point comes to mind. The later Middle Ages is the great period of foundation in the universities. At Oxford, one need not recall William of Wykeham, Richard Fleming, Henry Chichele, William Waynflete. The universities were working out new plans of collegiate organization, building new lecture theatres (e.g. the Oxford Divinity Schools), bringing in for the first time the undergraduate, as at King's or at Magdalen. This is the time in which logic reaches the peak of its development: architecture the summit of proportion; while heraldry becomes the artistic expression of chivalry. Are these signs of waning or decline?

L

Chapter VIII
Founders and Foundations in the Later Middle Ages

Many have benefited, some continue to benefit, from the munificence of founders and benefactors who at certain seasons are
commemorated both in religious services and *in escis et poculentis*
by their gratified children. Their obits, in the life of the societies
they founded, demand more than a passing memorial, so many
actual records of their foundation survive in muniment rooms and
repositories; yet interest in the early process of bringing together
a corporation, of endowing it with an income and of making it
act as a collectivity, is scanty and tends to be left to the antiquarian
bursar or to the occasional Fellow who can read medieval script.
The publication of the two university volumes of the *Victoria
County History* may have done something to redress the balance,
even if few college writers have the chance to emulate the descrip-
tions found there of the beginnings of King's College, Cambridge,
or of Merton College, Oxford.

These foundings and donations were characteristic of a great
period in European religious and academic history, 1300–1500,
which has been called 'the age of the pious founder'. Conformably,
it is the period of a rich community life unequalled save by the age
of monastic settlement, when kings and noblemen were prominent
in aiding the process. From distinguished foundations like St
George's, Windsor, or the Yorkist college of Fotheringhay, from
the colleges at the English universities and at Paris, down to the
smallest chantry, the endowment of perpetual intercession and the
common life of study was in active progress, and the concept of
the 'poor and indigent scholar' had, to our lasting advantage,
fastened itself upon the minds of those qualified to help. The
purpose here is to use foundation documents to show something
of what the process involves, the tensions and the disappointments,
so that the patience as much as the piety of the founders may be
more fully appreciated. With archival help it may be possible to
explore their minds and understand some of the difficulties that
confronted them.

As we are dealing very largely with collegiate foundations it may
be well to explain how certain types of document are here des-

cribed. By 'licence' we refer (*a*) to a royal licence granted to the founder to hold the land he is acquiring in mortmain, approving his intention of creating the new community and permitting others to make grants to the new foundation, the existence of which is now officially sanctioned; (*b*) to the privileges granted by pope, king or diocesan bishop, such as freedom from taxation, freedom from the jurisdiction of the ordinary, permission to have a chapel and hold services there. By the 'charter' is meant the founder's charter defining the purpose of the foundation, the number of persons it contains, and the area which it is to occupy, besides giving a statement of the licences already obtained. This mentions in a good many cases the name of the first provost or warden. It binds the personnel to obey the statutes, constitutes the body a community with perpetual succession and with the right to make legislation, and defines the relationship of the corporation to the founder. In certain cases, as we shall see, the charter is in the form of royal letters patent ratifying what has already been done by the founder and confirming his act of incorporation. It may thus found the society *de novo*, re-granting to it the estates already accumulated and for this purpose handed over to the Crown. Lastly, by the 'statutes' we allude to the rules or rubrics, sealed and notarially attested, made by the founder or his successors, that govern the admission of members, their religious services and the studies pursued, as well as provide for the election of the members, and for their daily life and discipline. It is not possible here to deal at length with the deeds of property and estate documents which are the main territorial and economic evidence for the foundations. Where these exist, they constitute a large part of a college's early archives and are specially important for the process of acquiring its territorial rights and its income.[1]

It is easy to acquire the seventeenth or eighteenth century view of the founder which represents him in an architectural or artistic context in the manner of Roubiliac or Thornhill, as a figure of classical mien and noble features, filling just the right place in a hall or building for which his portrait or bust was ordered, one hand grasping the cross of his arch-diocese, the other held aloft in benediction. There is a striking example of this in the hall of

---

[1] An excellent example, in brief, of a list is that of J. G. Milne, 'The muniments of Corpus Christi College, Oxford', *Oxoniensia*, ii (1937), 129–33. Cf. the same writer, *The Early History of Corpus Christi College, Oxford* (1946), ch. v.

All Souls College, Oxford. Over the fireplace also there is a charming picture representing the founder sitting upon a throne and
surrounded by the legal members of his staff, while in front of
him is the plan of his college, for which the architect is seeking his
approval. In the background are seen the warden and the newly
appointed Fellows. Look more closely, and the figure on the right
would be seen to bear, and the date of its painting would make this
appropriate, a curious resemblance to a portrait at the further end
of the hall. This is of none other than Sir George Clark[1] who
pressed upon the college, and secured the adoption of, Nicholas
Hawksmoor's designs for the Great Quadrangle. The picture is
over the fireplace in one of Hawksmoor's best buildings and the
dual implication is obvious. Morally the founder is approving the
new, as well as the old, work. The plans of his building are here
before him, presented by the craftsmen; and surrounded by his
advisers, Archbishop Chichele indicates his assent with a princely
gesture.

A founder was certainly fortunate, if, at any given moment, he
(or she) was able to approve, in one comprehensive blessing, any
such building planned, still more to formulate precisely the legal
structure of the college or institution now coming into being.
Foundation is a lengthy and developing process which has to be
sustained both by the flow of ready money and by an administrative dexterity which in many cases arouses admiration for the
tenacity and application shown. Lack of that dexterity, sometimes
arising from the absence of a single driving will, might spell the
failure of the project in hand. The story of University Hall, Cambridge, is a good example. In 1326 Edward II granted by letters
patent licence to the chancellor and university to found a college
and to assign two messuages which they had in Milne Street for
the habitation of the scholars. Nothing happened for twelve years,
and at the end of this time Richard de Badew, chancellor of the
university when the college was founded, by a deed dated 6 April
1338 in which he styled himself 'Founder, Patron and Advocate
of the House called the Hall of the University of Cambridge'
granted all his rights and titles therein to Lady Elizabeth de Burgo,

---

[1] See, besides *D.N.B.*, the account of him in M. Burrows, *Worthies of
All Souls* (1874), pp. 315–18, 364–5, 384–6. A sturdy bachelor: 'I have
no great joy in hearing of your conjugal proceedings, for I think Colleges
were not designed for women. . . . If all my friends marry, I shall have
little encouragement to come to Oxford.'

daughter of Gilbert de Clare, who refounded it as Clare Hall and supplied the endowments previously lacking.[1]

In most cases 'the main motive underlying the private munificence of college founders in the middle ages was the priority enjoyed by them in the daily prayers and celebrations of such institutions'.[2] As Henry VI said in his licence to William Byngham for the foundation of Godshouse, Cambridge:

Observing by divine inspiration that the founders of sacred places are most faithfully commended by the prayers and intercessions of the same before all the other benefactors and enjoy the same intercessions almost as first fruits for ever and resolving to alleviate by prayers and devotions the great dangers . . . for ourselves and the realm. . . . Know ye that we graciously assenting to the prayers and supplication of the said William Byngham . . . design to found a certain perpetual college of a proctor and certain scholars in grammar and the other liberal faculties in our said town of Cambridge to study and to pray for our healthful state and that of William Byngham himself while we live and for our souls when we shall have departed from this light and for the souls of our most illustrious parents and progenitors sometime Kings and Queens of England and for the souls of the parents of the said William Byngham and of the other benefactors of the same College and of all the faithful departed.[3]

There must be the determination to complete the work and before all else there must be the money; and, one may add, a complete co-operation between the founder and feoffees employed to accumulate the estates or the rents, as well as between the founder and first master, proctor, warden or other head of the developing community. Sometimes the new head appointed is an administrator with a knowledge of law rather than an intellectual of academic standing.

The finance of these early stages and the acquisition of the land for the endowment may be handled by feoffees of whom the founder may himself be one, though this is not always the case, for, standing outside, he may employ his own lawyers and friends (sometimes also benefactors) to hold the newly acquired estates, and may utilize, if he has no special treasurer, the first warden as

[1] W. J. Harrison in *V.C.H. Cambridge*, iii. 340. 'It seems clear that for several years he (Richard de Badew) supplemented the scanty endowments of the College from his own resources.'
[2] A. H. Lloyd, *The Early History of Christ's College* (1934), p. 30.
[3] Ibid.

receiver for the new society. The deed under which these groups acted is the familiar form of conveyance known as 'feoffment to use'. The feoffees were joint tenants, not tenants in common: they held, i.e. each of them, the whole estate, so that when one died his interest passed not to his heirs but to the surviving feoffees. At the appropriate time the feoffees to use might convey the properties in their hands to the new society, i.e. the president or head, and Fellows, after the society had, in the act of foundation, been made a corporate body. Foundation and incorporation expressed in a formal document may be the prelude to the making over of the whole corpus of estates to the king, who in a solemn instrument of re-grant founds the college. Other circumstances, for instance a change of site, may cause the king to re-found, as happened when Henry VI wanted the original site of Godshouse for his own college. In this case the original founder, William Byngham, asked the king to be called founder, and Henry in reply designated William Byngham and his heirs as co-founders.[1] Thus a foundation may be a dual process, of acts by founder and co-founder, in an order that varies. Royal intervention is of importance, for in the middle of the fifteenth century, especially in the case of King's College, Cambridge, and All Souls College, Oxford, alien priories constituted no small part of the wealth of the new colleges and it was necessary to protect them against the possibility of resumption. Naturally a change of dynasty involved the royal corporate body in very serious danger. King's College, Cambridge, had in 1460 an income of over £1,000 a year. After the deposition of the founder, in spite of the fact that the parliament of November 1461 confirmed the foundations of the Lancastrian kings, the income of the college was reduced to £500 a year, the estates not having been exempted from the general resumption. As Mr Saltmarsh has observed, a great part of the founder's endowment was lost for ever and it was not until the middle of the sixteenth century that the full complement of Fellows and scholars was again achieved.[2]

The founder may be an individual or a collectivity such as a guild or a municipality. The unique university instance of a founder guild is that of Corpus Christi College, Cambridge, founded jointly by the Corpus Christi guild and the guild of the Blessed Virgin Mary. Both at Bristol and at York there were foundations

---

[1] *Early Statutes of Christ's College, Cambridge*, ed. H. Rackham (1927), pp. 1–3.

[2] *V.C.H. Cambridge*, iii. 379.

by groups of citizens, by the parishioners or by the municipality itself, in the form of chantries; at York notably in St William's chapel on Ousebridge which was the city chapel *par excellence*. The priests were chosen, as Miss Wood-Legh has pointed out, by the founder's heirs and by representatives of the parish which they were to serve, or by the incumbent of the parish church along with the churchwardens or a specified number of parishioners; and they were also presented to the mayor or mayor and burgesses for admission.[1] It may not be irrelevant to add that the civic authorities took their duties very seriously. Some of them were themselves founders of chantries: thus Nicholas Blackburn, citizen of York, who was interested in at least four chantries, one of them founded by himself in St Anne's, Fossgate; and the wealthy merchant Richard Russell, founder of another in St John the Baptist, Hungate.[2] The mayor of Bristol

annually summoned the chantry priests before him to swear faithfully to comply with the regulations laid down by their founders and every year he went to the church of St Mary Redcliff to attend the anniversary of William Cannynges and to audit the accounts of the two chantries Cannynges had founded in that church.[3]

At York, when Archbishop Thoresby tried to visit the chantries in St William's chapel, Ousebridge, resistance was offered by the mayor and burgesses of York claiming immunity for their own municipal chapel: resistance, however, which did not in the end overcome the tenacity of the archbishop.[4]

Foundation is often a matter of years. The stages of a larger example may be very roughly described, but the chronological order is by no means uniform and there is much overlapping. The first is to acquire, either by direct purchase or by a perpetual annual rent, a site for the projected building. The second, which may precede and frepuently is coeval with the first, is the process of accumulating the main sources of revenue for the college in the shape of churches, alien priories and manors or territorial rights, and of procuring the royal licence to amortize such property. The actual building may by now have started. Normally it is begun as

[1] Kathleen Wood-Legh, 'The Chantries in some Medieval English Towns', in *Festschrift E. E. Stengel*, ed. E. Kunz (Cologne, 1952), p. 433.
[2] *Testamenta Eboracensia* (Surtees Soc., 1836–1902), ii. 17–18, 55; cf. A. Raine, *Medieval York* (1955), p. 83.
[3] Wood-Legh, p. 436.
[4] Borthwick Institute, York, Reg. Thoresby, fos. 105, 105v.

soon as possession of the site can be guaranteed, and often before completion the first *custos* or guardian, together with a limited number of the corporators, have already been chosen and occupy temporary quarters.

In Scotland where the civil law prevailed, the actual acquisition of the land might be marked by a formal *bailment* or *traditio*, like the one portrayed in the deeds of St Salvator's College. In a notarial instrument of 27 August 1450 two citizens of St Andrews make over to the founder, Bishop James Kennedy, the tenements they own by surrendering them symbolically to the local bailiff *per tradicionem terre et lapidis*. The clod and pebble are by him handed over to the bishop and with them Kennedy is inducted and personally invested. The bishop, then, in founding the college, mortified the lands and by the common consent of his chapter, gave them purely and freely into the dead hand. This done and with no obligations remaining, he founded 'in honour of God omnipotent and the most glorious Mother of God and All Saints the College of the Holy Saviour' upon the area of land specified, and with his own hands at the four extremities placed 'corner stones', *lapides angulares*, and in sign and title of the foundation erected upon it an altar sprinkled with holy water in the name of the Trinity. His next step was to make John Altmare provost and to commit to him the administration of the college and all its rights.[1]

Sites could seldom be purchased as a whole. In a built-up area of small tenements their acquisition was a matter of a number of elaborate small-scale transactions both with the parishes out of which they were taken and with the individual occupiers. When Richard Fleming founded Lincoln College in 1427 he began by a union of benefices, securing from Henry VI permission, which he confirmed by the archbishop's authority, to unite the three Oxford parishes of All Saints, St Mildred and St Michael at the North Gate, all in the patronage of the bishops of Lincoln since 1326, and there to establish a college under the patronage of Our Lady and

---

[1] The notarial instrument is printed by R. G. Cant, *The College of St Salvator* (Edinburgh, 1950), pp. 49–53, cf. pp. 81–2. Notarially attested instruments of this sort that survive are not very common. One occurs in the detailed account of the foundation by Cardinal Nicholas of Cues of his hospital of St Nicholas but without the detail of the actual taking of the land. Printed by J. Marx, *Nikolaus von Cues und seine Stiftungen zu Cues und Deventer* (Trier, 1906), appendix. For England, what more frequently has the notary's attestation is the grant of the statutes, the final and culminating act in the history of a foundation.

All Saints.[1] The charter was issued in December 1429 but the acquisition of the properties came the year after. First St Mildred's Church was pulled down and part of the college buildings erected on the site of the church and the churchyard. Then a toft, or garden, a narrow strip of land forty-one yards long, reaching to Turl Street, was acquired and the south-west corner of the quadrangle erected on this site. Then the house called 'Deep Hall' belonging to the hospital of St John Baptist (afterwards Magdalen College) was sold by its master to Fleming's agents, to be the site on which the college buttery and hall were later built. Fourthly, Brend Hall belonging to St Frideswide, a tenement of twelve and a half by thirty-one yards between St Mildred's on the north and the toft purchased on the south, was secured. Fifthly a tenement of St Frideswide called Winton Hall, sixty-two feet wide by a hundred and fifty feet long in one place, situated between Deep Hall to the west and a tenement of University College to the east, was purchased. This hall stood on the site of the college kitchen.[2] This was what Fleming had acquired when he died, in January 1431. But after that the city authorities in 1435 granted in fee farm a wedge-shaped piece of land a hundred and three feet long and thirteen feet wide, lying between Brasenose lane on the north and Winton Hall and Deep Hall on the south. Afterwards there was a pause for thirty years, then in 1463 further additions were made. The college's original endowments were the revenues of All Saints and St Michael at the North Gate. The lands did not come until 1445 and were acquired very spasmodically, partly in Iffley, partly in Northamptonshire and Buckinghamshire.[3] Lincoln is a good instance of the founder's direct interest and initial care.

Fourteenth-century Paris also offers examples of the gradual acquisition of messuages and tenements in a congested area for the expansion of a college. There were, for instance, many stages in the establishment of Ave Maria College, the society founded by John of Hubant, the Nivernais administrator. He fixed the first dwelling for his warden, chaplain and six *pueri*, in the cloister of Sainte-Geneviève, and then expanded into houses in the Rue des Amandiers, while various revenues or rents were acquired in the fief of the monastery and outside. The title deeds and amortizations show how the rent-bearing properties were established about the

[1] *The Register of Henry Chichele*, iv. 92–5.
[2] M. R. Toynbee, 'Lincoln College', in *V.C.H. Oxon.*, iii. 163.
[3] Ibid., p. 164.

quartier.[1] The instance of the Ave Maria College happens to be instructive because the whole community which Hubant, helped by his friend John Beatus, was bringing into existence consisted not only of the boys (below sixteen), but of older students (*beneficarii*), poor women and retired workmen, all of whom took part in the regular services in commemoration of the founder.[2]

It is the taking of physical possession which the St Andrews' narrative of a foundation emphasizes. An English account, belonging to 1427, of the foundation of a college by the archbishop of Canterbury in his own birth-place, Higham Ferrers, lays stress on the consent of all parties to the act and seems in marked contrast to the Scottish story. Having secured the properties necessary, the St Ouen manor of West Mersea, Essex, and the castle and manor of Higham, the archbishop held a ceremony on 28 August 1425 at which the rectors of Higham Ferrers (the dean and chapter of St Mary, Leicester) represented by their proctors, and the vicar and parishioners in large numbers being present, 'the letters of the pope and the king were read and declared and those present were asked to express dissent or consent for their interests in common or severally'. Nobody dissenting, the archbishop proceeded to found the college and to appoint the first Master or warden, but reserved to himself 'the right of introducing chaplains, clerks and choristers to the appointed number'. The document giving effect to this was sealed with the seal of St Thomas the Martyr and with the archbishop's own signet and the seal of the redacting notary.[3]

In Paris Hubant obviously acquired for his college houses that were in working order. Where, as is more usual, the founder has to erect something new, the question arises: to what extent did he determine the nature of the work in progress? He was, of course, seldom an expert on the technical side of building, but was naturally more concerned with the provision of a site, and with the accumulation of resources in ready cash or in lands. At King's College, Cambridge, in March 1448, when the work had been going on for two years, the founder, Henry VI, gave very detailed instructions in the document known erroneously as the 'Will of King Henry VI'. In a considered statement that dealt both with 'the demensions of the chirche of my said College of oure lady and

---

[1] A L. Gabriel, *Student Life in Ave Maria College, Medieval Paris* (Notre Dame, Indiana, 1955), ch. iii, pp. 50 ff.

[2] Ibid., pp. 110–16.

[3] *C.P.R., 1422–29*, pp. 472–4.

saint Nicholas of Cambrige' and 'the demensions of the housynge of the said College',[1] the king certainly succeeded in impressing on his agents in Cambridge his idea of collegiate architecture: 'large fourme clene and substancial, settyng a parte superfluite of too gret curious work of entaille and besy moldyng'.[2] Before he started to build Eton, Henry made the most careful preparations. He sent to Winchester for information about the subsoil of the site, and had samples of earth sent to him 'pro noticiis terre fundamenti collegii',[3] evidently thinking that the geological evidence from one river site would do for another. Two founders with more than ordinary administrative capacity for building were William of Wykeham and Richard Fox, both bishops of Winchester. Wykeham, needless to say, had been clerk of the king's works, and, as his household roll of 1393 shows, was on terms of friendship with his building executives Simon Membury, clerk of works, William Wynford, chief mason, and Hugh Harland, the king's carpenter, who dined not infrequently at his table.[4] To them he could communicate his idea for the closed quadrangle and the hugely dominant chapel, realized in both his colleges.[5] Of Fox, Francis Bacon wrote that he was not only a grave counsellor for war or peace, but also a good surveyor of works. In a letter to Wolsey in 1522 Fox spoke of 'the scluse (sluice) that I caused to be made' at Calais by command of Henry VIII.[6]

But to return to the fifteenth century: the inference can certainly be drawn that while the chapel and the (Old) library were in construction at All Souls, Chichele determined the selection of many of the figures to be placed in the window lights of both. In

[1] R. Willis and J. W. Clark, *The Architectural History of the University of Cambridge and of the Colleges of Cambridge and Eton* (4 vols., Cambridge, 1886), i. 368–9.

[2] T. D. Atkinson and J. W. Clark, *Cambridge Described and Illustrated* (1897), p. 359.

[3] See the extract from the Winchester College accounts in T. F. Kirby, *Annals of Winchester College* (1892), p. 193.

[4] Winchester College Muniments, household roll of Bishop William of Wykeham. I owe my knowledge of this exceptional document to Mr John Harvey.

[5] 'In Wykeham's strongly marked character the strongest stream of all (though it is clearly connected with the rest) is an absorbing devotion to beauty in architecture and in all works of art.' A. H. Smith, *New College, Oxford, and its buildings* (1952), p. 11.

[6] F. Bacon, *Works* (1765), iii. 96; *Original Letters illustrative of English History*, ed. Sir H. Ellis, 2nd ser. (1827), ii. 7.

the King's window of the Old Library, removed during the
nineteenth century from the Wharton building to the chapel,
there are no kings after the Anglo-Saxons, until Edward II; then
come John of Gaunt (Rex Hispanie), Henry IV, probably wrongly
labelled by the restorers, Messrs Clayton and Bell, as 'Canute Rex',
Henry V and Henry VI.[1] Here is the vindication of the Lancastrian descent from the Edwards (*via* John of Gaunt, Edward
III's son). In the window portraying the four doctors of the Church,
stands the figure of John Stratford,[2] who lifted up his voice against
royal administrative tyranny, while in the windows of the northern
and southern transept (the 'nave' of the chapel) are the apostles
and holy women that bear unmistakable traits of contemporary
pietism.[3]

The same sort of relationship between founder and craftsmen
must have existed between Andrew Doket, founder of Queens'
College, Cambridge, described in an early list of benefactors as the
'first president and most worthy founder of the college', and
Reginald Ely, master mason.[4] While this was, of course, Queen
Margaret of Anjou's college (her charter of foundation, the third
in the series, is dated 15 April 1448), Doket through his friendship
with wealthy parishioners of St Botolph's like Richard Andrew
and John Morris, was responsible for the acquisition of the lands
and tenements which enabled the college, as stated in its second
charter of 21 August 1447, to be re-founded on a new site. The
mason himself, Reginald Ely, left a house to the college of (as it was
popularly called) St Margaret.[5] Ely, who was the chief mason of
Henry VI's college of St Mary and St Nicholas from 1444 until
work was, as will be seen, stopped shortly after Edward IV's
accession, was frequently entertained at the Fellows' table, *in
prandio* or *in cena* or both.[6] The close touch established between
the founders themselves and their senior executives is to be noted.

Fortunately we are able, through surviving documents, to explore to a small extent the minds of two founders, one of whom
was both master and surveyor of the works in his own college, the
other a celebrated bishop and statesman. The one was Robert

[1] F. E. Hutchinson, *Medieval Glass at All Souls College* (1949), pl. xxiv.
[2] Ibid., pl. xxx.
[3] Ibid., pp. 22 ff., for the description of the individual figures.
[4] A. Oswald, 'Andrew Doket and his architect', *Cambridge Antiq. Soc.
Proc.*, xlii. 8 f.
[5] Ibid., p. 15.
[6] Ibid., p. 21.

Woodlark, founder of St Catharine's College, Cambridge, the other the already cited bishop Richard Fox, the founder of Corpus Christi College, Oxford, and of a number of schools. Woodlark left in a manuscript notebook, called the *Memoriale Nigrum*, the record of his somewhat disillusioning experiences when financing the works.[1] Part of Fox's correspondence is available in the edition of Dr Percy Allen.[2]

Woodlark was made provost of the college of St Mary and St Nicholas (King's College), Cambridge, in May 1452 and in December of that year succeeded Close, another of the original Fellows, as master of the works. In 1459 he was chosen to be chancellor, as again in 1462. He had the royal licence to erect Catharine Hall on a site fronting Milne Street (now Queen's Lane) on one side; and during the acquisition of the site and the building of his second college he kept his accounts strictly separated from those of King's, remarking in his *Memoriale* 'there is nothing to the charge of or owing to the King's College to the last farthing'. As master of the works at King's he had the spending of large sums of Henry VI's money and access to as much timber and stone as he needed. He begins his *Memoriale* with his account of the *funda* or properties that enabled him to build St Catharine's Hall. He held office as master of the works at St Catharine's from 1452 until the date of their completion, but complications set in at the revolution of the earls. When first Henry VI, he says, was captured by the earl of Salisbury and the earl of Warwick (at Northampton),

to please the King, the earls promised and willed that in all haste possible I should be able to acquire stone masons and all other workers by a royal letter to hasten the work, and that they should come quickly, promising to pay without delay and contradiction £1000 a year and that they would not fail in continuing to pay the money, with which promise they asserted that the king was highly gratified. To their honour the said earls intended to keep their promise faithfully and were very friendly to the project; and the Receiver of the Duchy of Lancaster came into the transactions, being commanded by royal mandate that from the monies and proceeds of his office he should pay the sum of

---

[1] I am indebted to the Master and to Dr MacDonagh, Librarian of St Catharine's College, for permission to study the *Memoriale* and their early charters relating to Cambridge in the college muniments.

[2] *Letters of Richard Fox, 1486-1527*, ed. P. S. and H. M. Allen (Oxford, 1929).

£1000 and give it first priority, and that the business should be expedited in every way; indentured bills were to pass between the Master of the Works and the Receiver General of the Duchy.

At intervals, says Woodlark, money came to hand, but not very much, and in time,

when new evil arose in the kingdom after the money was in the hands of the Receiver, in order to allay and resist the trouble, royal letters were sent to all Receivers of the Duchy under strict commands and pain of losing office, to send all the sums they had received to the king and his Council in London, and thus the Receiver General was unable to pay the sum specified in the indentures; and so the burden of paying the wages of the stonemasons and other labourers, and even of the carpenters, one and all, was thrown upon me, Robert Woodlark, and seeing that I could not satisfy them all I pledged my goods and other possessions for payment. Most of the payments I was able to make from my own goods and property, as can be judged from my own statement of sales and costs, and I shall be ready at all times to give it. Seeing that no remedy would be forthcoming, I sent for Thomas Betts, auditor both of the College and of the works kept in a separate account, and, as it appeared by a detailed statement, I was found, and by the Auditor adjudged, to have overspent £328 10s. 4d. which will have to be restored to me.[1]

The original *funda* of St Catharine's, the Milne Street tenements in the parish of St Edward and St Botulph belonging to John Botwright and others (bought 10 September 1459), the house acquired from the Master and Fellows of Michaelhouse (31 August 1467) and the properties secured from John Rason and from St Clement's chantry, Woodlark acquired at his own cost; so too the 'houses' or large frames which he bought and got his carpenter to alter and convey back to Cambridge, so as to make the Hall of his college. The tenements he kept in his own hands until 22 November 1475, the year of the college charter, when by a deed, written in his own hand, and sealed with his own signet of a woodlark, he made them over to Richard Roche, second Master of St Catharine's. A comparison of the autograph portions of the *Memoriale* with this document sets the authorship beyond dispute. It is Woodlark's authentic grant.

If Woodlark's first acquisitions for St Catharine's dated from 1459, it was sixteen years, then, before he could hand over the group to his corporation. Only one contribution came from out-

[1] *Documents relating to St Catharine's College*, collected by H. Philpott (1861), pp. 2–4.

side, the £100 given by Lady Joan Barnardiston on condition that one Fellow in priest's orders should hereafter pray for her soul.[1] The tenements in Stoke-by-Clare and Babraham came in during the fourteen-eighties. At the opening of the young society only two Fellows entered commons while the royal charter[2] and Woodlark's statutes[3] allowed for 'three or more'.

Woodlark's statutes show that he did not want lawyers in his college. They were expressly excluded, in contrast to the design of Henry Chichele whose proportion for All Souls was twenty-four artists and sixteen jurists, making ample provision for the latter in the books which he and Henry VI sent down from London. The splendid law incunabula still in the possession of the Codrington Library shows the tradition carried on to the end of the century. Nearly eighty years later Bishop Fox, in his original design for Corpus Christi College, was equally theological in intention: but— and this is the interesting thing about the first project for Corpus —the plan was modified. Originally the college was to consist partly of monks and partly of secular scholars. Within the space of three years the founder was persuaded to change his mind about the composition and make it an entirely secular college, adding the humanist element in the shape of the public lecturer in Greek and the Reader and Professor of Humanity or Latin, clearly pointing the way to the new learning. The accepted story of how this happened is that Fox was prevailed upon by Hugh Oldham who pointed out the inadequacy of a monastic personnel for the university in its then condition.[4] But it is not impossible that it was some-body else—and a man who had great influence in the making of early Corpus—who helped the bishop to his decision.

[1] W. H. S. Jones, *St Catharine's College*, p. 205.

[2] *Documents relating to St Catherine's College*, p. 8.

[3] Ibid., p. 16.

[4] E.g. J. G. Milne, *The Early History of Corpus Christi College, Oxford* (1946), pp. 2, 3. 'In other words, Oldham advised the foundation of a college which should serve as a training school for all forms of public life, religious and secular, and one which should be a training school only, not, as some monasteries had tended to become, a home for meditation: and he backed up his advice by the substantial argument of a gift of £4,000.' The latter sum is mentioned by Claymond in a note prefixed to the *Carta Fundationis* (cf. T. Fowler, *The History of Corpus Christi College* (Oxf. Hist. Soc., 1893), pp. 60–1). The opposition between a 'training school only' and a 'home for meditation' does not, however, adequately express the difference between a secular and a religious establishment at the university.

Fox's preparations had started early. On 31 October 1512 Merton College resolved to hand over the deeds of Corner Hall and Nevill's Inn to their warden, Richard Rawlyns, who was to make them over to Fox;[1] but about a third plot for which Fox had asked, the Bachelor's Garden, they were uncertain. Eventually, on 21 November 1512, they gave way.[2] By the beginning of 1413 they had already accepted the first of the annual payments (£4 6s. 8d.) for the not inconsiderable area of ground conceded to the founder of Corpus. This acceptance, made final in a deed of 1515, was to lead to serious trouble later: in 1701 it was stated to have been one of the reasons for the deposition of their warden Richard Rawlyns by Archbishop Warham.[3] He had let the land go at far too small a quit rent. In the Oxford negotiations Fox was not using feoffees but the services of the president of Magdalen, John Claymond, whom he had persuaded to be the president of his new college. Claymond, a skilful negotiator, must have got round Rawlyns, and evidence points to this being done in November 1511, when the Fellows of Merton were arranging 'pro quodam quieto redditu nobis soluendo in perpetuum'.[4] By January 1513 Claymond had bought out the Principal of Corner Hall, Walter Morwen, Fellow of Merton.[5] All this means that before the type of college to be created had been decided, the essential plots of land had been secured.

Fox's other agent was Thomas Barker who was buying land for him in Berkshire at the end of 1516 and early in 1517, and corresponding with him about it.[6] The landed endowment of Corpus was a progressive matter. Now it was Claymond rather than Fox who 'drew up the Foundation', and with the bishop's approval admitted the first Fellows, Claymond, who had bought from the prior of St Frideswide's Urban Hall and garden and Bekes Inn to add to the original properties acquired on perpetual lease from Merton. About the appointment of the original Fellows he had great difficulty, because people were writing to the bishop and pestering him to get entry for their children. Various reasons had

[1] *Reg. Annalium Coll. Merton.*, ed. H. E. Salter (Oxf. Hist. Soc.), p. 431.
[2] Ibid., p. 432.
[3] G. C. Brodrick, *Memorials of Merton College* (Oxf. Hist. Soc., 1885), pp. 311–12.
[4] *Reg. Annalium Coll. Merton.*, p. 419.
[5] Cf. Brodrick, p. 246.
[6] *Letters of Richard Fox*, pp. 84–6.

to be found to keep them out.[1] Only Claymond's co-operation could have succeeded in launching the college, and Fox was more reliant upon him than Chichele or Waynflete upon the first heads of their societies. It should be considered whether Claymond, who was in with the founding process from the beginning, was not something more than Fox's agent in the new orientation of the college.

With figures like Wykeham or Waynflete in mind we tend to think of this impulse towards foundation or the creation of self-governing bodies as an ecclesiastical, almost an episcopal movement. The layman, however, plays an important part in creating communities of clerks and laity for prayer and commemoration, and in certain cases in providing for his dependants and retainers. To establish a body of priests in the neighbourhood of their residences and build accommodation for them was the aim of the first and second earls of Westmorland and of Lord Cromwell in Lincolnshire some thirty years later. At Staindrop close by Raby Castle the first Neville earl established in the parish church, with Bishop Hatfield's leave,[2] a college 'of a master or warden its chaplain, and certain other chaplains, continually resident and of certain poor men of gentle birth (*generosis*) and other poor persons' who were to be, as the bishop put it 'unum corpus per se et collegium incorporatum'. There seems nothing to indicate that the college came into being then, but in 1408 the second earl took up the scheme and secured Bishop Langley's licence to found the college on 1 November, with confirmation by Henry IV on 28 November.[3] Hatfield had already received the appropriation of Staindrop church, and this was now repeated by Langley, on 18 April 1412, with an ordinance for the vicarage. The personnel of the college was now defined as a warden, eight chaplains, four secular clerks, six esquires (*armigeri*), six yeomen (*valetti*) and six other poor persons;[4] and a building was erected for them on the north side of the collegiate church by Joan Beaufort, Ralph Neville's second wife. *Armigeri* and *valetti* are interesting: 'it is most probable', Hutchinson observed, 'the Earl intended this house for the

<hr/>

[1] Ibid., p. 90.

[2] 1378: see W. Hutchinson, *The History and Antiquities of the County Palatine of Durham* (3 vols., Carlisle, 1785–94), iii. 258 n.

[3] See R. L. Storey's note in *The Register of Thomas Langley* (Surtees Soc., 1956–61), ii. 12.

[4] Ibid, ii. 12.

M

reception of his military retainers or those servants most immediately about his person'.[1]

To create an ensemble of buildings on the Windsor model so as
to house his college was the object of Ralph Lord Cromwell's
reconstruction of Tattershall castle, Lincolnshire, the building
accounts of which have lately been published.[2] The foundation was
of a warden, seven chantry priests or chaplains, six secular clerks
and six choristers with a bede house for almsmen and almswomen,
thirteen of either sex, 'to pray for King Henry VI, Lord Cromwell
and Maud Cromwell, late lady of Tattershall, and all the faithful
departed'; and exequies were to be held for Lord Cromwell on the
last day of each month.[3] The plan at Tattershall shows a grouping
of buildings that portray a fifteenth-century nobleman's world:
the hall with its double moat, the pleasaunce or garden to the
south, and on the east side, beyond the outer moat, the collegiate
church, the college and the bedehouse. Cromwell pulled down the
old parish church and replaced it by one whose chapel, and hence
whose dimensions, could more properly house the college.[4]

The bedehouse, a timber structure erected more than thirty
years after Cromwell's death, was adapted by the carpenter from a
'grete hous late bought and brought frome saint Mary Tidde
(Tydd)', a hundred and seventy-two feet long by nineteen feet
wide.[5] It had not only chambers for the bedesmen, but a hall, a
chapel and rooms for the parish priest.[6] Among the Cromwell
papers at Penshurst is an interesting series upon the organization
and financing of the college, as these duties bore upon the executors. They begin with a list of questions put to the founder in 1450
in order to clarify his intentions about appointments to office. Will
the founder present the master or should this be done 'by election
of the six priests?' 'He will present during his lifetime.' 'Should
any beneficed man with cure be taken in?' 'My lord will not that
any be taken in'; but the master or any priest might receive a
living with cure in Lincolnshire, as long as he was resident. The

---

[1] Hutchinson, iii. 259.

[2] *The Building Accounts of Tattershall Castle, 1434–72*, ed. W. Douglas
Simpson (Lincoln Rec. Soc., 1960).

[3] The statutes (of 1460) are in Hist. MSS. Comm., *Report on the MSS.
of Lord de I'Isle and Dudley* (4 vols., 1925–42), i. 179–85.

[4] Dr Simpson calls it a church of 'exquisite beauty'; *Building Accounts*,
p. xiii.

[5] Hist. MSS. Comm. *De L'Isle and Dudley MSS.*, i. 175–6.

[6] Ibid., p. xx.

scale of battels and the amount of fees and salaries were laid down on the result of the inquiry.[1] In the statutes themselves (1460) two provisions were made for education in the community, of a practical and a liturgical kind:

22   The Master shall hire a clerk or priest to teach grammar to the choristers and to all sons of tenants of the lordship of Tattershall and of the College without charge, receiving commons (if a priest 1s. 6d., if a secular clerk 1s. 2d.), clothing and four marks from the revenues of the College as his stipend each year.

23   The Master and Precentor are to hire four chaplains or clerks, or two chaplains and two clerks, skilled in song and reading, to assist the other chaplains and clerks in divine service; each of whom is to have commons in the college, clothing and stipend of ten marks a year, if the revenues of the College permit. The Master is to receive into the College four poor boys, teachable in song and reading, to help the ministry, each of whom is to have commons and clothing and all else that the choristers do, if the revenues of the College permit.[2]

'If the revenues of the college permit.' After its foundation in 1440 the college did not run a smooth course. A memorandum of *c.* 1456 drawn up for the executors refers first of all to the 'lands to be given to the college in lieu of those given by Ralph Lord Cromwell and since by authority of parliament altogether taken from the college'. This probably indicates those lands affected by the resumption of 1455. More significant, perhaps, because relating to the difficulties experienced by the executors when dealing with the earl of Warwick (the Kingmaker), is the memorandum drawn up *c*, 1480 by John Leynton, Cromwell's local executor, which deals with the earl's purchase from the executors and feoffees of the manor of Colyweston. The executors were given bonds or obligations, sixteen in all, each of a hundred marks, of which the first was paid in ready money

and never more in redy money, for which the seid executours sued longe and many day to the seid late Erle for payment of the residue of the seid revenue, shewyng unto hym the perill that was to kepe a dede mannys goode, by which the execucion of his wille was letted.

After much solicitation, the executors were assigned some of the earl's woods at Bourn in Lincolnshire, but derived little profit

[1] Ibid., p. 179.
[2] Ibid., p. 182.

from them: the prices they got were very disappointing. They were
in fact forced 'to take the seid woodes against their wills, every
acre for vii marks whereof somme were skant worth xiiis iiiid an
acre'.[1] To keep the college going as well as to satisfy Cromwell's
creditors must have been a difficult task. The problem of maintaining a foundation once launched was in any case a complicated
one in the middle of the fifteenth century.

The pattern of many such communities is half chapel, half almshouse. Physically, as at Higham Ferrers, the quarters of the
priests, clerks or canons and the almsmen or women are separate.
The former are in the college proper; the latter have their own
house without. It is a mixed community however aristocratic a
foundation, the joining of the 'gentle' with the *homines communes*
is an essential characteristic. It occurs, for example, in St Cross at
Winchester. Serving the chapel, the boys, if *choristi* or 'queristers',
provide the basis of the educational side of the foundation. For the
boys must be taught first of all in music, but also in grammar.
The proper performances of the services stood first in the founder's
intentions and for that purpose a Fellow of New College, John
Tucke, could resign his fellowship and undertake music teaching
at Higham Ferrers where he wrote the treatise still surviving.[2]

All these institutions were governed by statutes, documents of
solemn dignity and often of inordinate length, containing the
recommendation that they be read entire or by instalments in the
presence of the whole body each year. Statutes did not spring
armed from the founder's head, but were often the result of discussions and drafts made over a considerable period, sometimes as
much as six years from the inception of the college or community.
For example, Henry Chichele's statutes for his *Collegium Ani-
marum* are in a vellum book with a special seal, the pendant seal of
the martyrdom of St Thomas. They represent, in their extremely
careful dating clause, the final view of the archbishop and his
administrators about a society founded five years previously. On
certain points the college had evidently asked for further consideration to be given and the state of the text of this final copy is most
interesting, since there are erasures written over with great care,
and gaps have been deliberately left which had to be filled in with
decisions which had taken some time to reach.[3]

[1] Hist. MSS. Comm. *De L'Isle and Dudley MSS.*, i. p. 189.
[2] *Tractatus de art musica*, Brit. Mus., Add. MS. 10336.
[3] A close examination of this text shows that it differed from its two

Marked features of early foundation statutes are the historical preambles and the great fullness of detail with which the founder provided for contingencies. The college must understand its origins, and must provide against the contentions and difficulties that inevitably arose over interpretation. Where interpretation was not immediately possible, or where the statutes enjoined it, the practice was to use the services of the Visitor, who might or might not be the founder himself, for definition and elucidation.

There are many instances of historical *exordium*. One of the more attractive is in the statutes made by Archbishop Rotherham, and dated 1 February 1483, for his grammar school in Yorkshire. He looks back upon his early days in Rotherham:

We stood there in that time, without letters, we should have stood there untaught, illiterate and rough for many years, had it not been that by God's grace a man learned in grammar arrived, from whom, as from a primal font we were, by God's will, instructed, and, under God's leadership, came to the state in which we now are, and others arrived at great positions. In order that there might always be such a fountain we establish a teacher of Grammar there for ever, and because many parishioners and a number of dwellers in the hills come there the better to love the Christian religion and visit its church, we have thought to establish another Master learned in chant and 6 choristers or boys of the Chapel that Divine Service may be celebrated with greater honour, and thirdly, because that country produces many young men of great sharpness and ability and not all wish to take Holy Orders, that such people may be prepared for technical and mundane work, we have ordained a third Fellow, skilled in the art of writing and computing.[1]

Over these three, grammar, music, science and technology, 'because they are subordinated to the Divine Law and Gospel', the archbishop set a fourth, a theologian, who should at least be a Bachelor in Theology, whose business was 'to govern the community, and within the province to preach the shortest and most

---

contemporaries, the Bodleian MS. Rawlinson Statutes 53 and Brit. Mus., MS. Arundel 147. Arundel has 37 chapters to the Bodleian's 34, and this Arundel text has one clause on what is to be done when the warden and Fellows fall ill, which is not found in the final version. The University Commissioners all the same were prepared to print, in their edition of the founder's statutes, from the Bodleian version which is unsealed and is inferior both to the Arundel text and the Warden's version. E. F. Jacob, 'The Warden's text of the foundation statutes of All Souls', *Antiq. Jour.*, xv (1935), 420–31.

[1] *Early Yorkshire Schools*, ed. A. F. Leach (Yorks. Archaeol. Soc. Record Ser., xxvii, xxxiii, 1899–1903), ii. 110.

certain way to Heaven'. And in addition to this, there were to be commoners, chantry priests 'who previously have been pernoctating in different parts of the town, to the scandal of them and of the Church, men given up to leisure and idleness'. They were to be given rooms in the college, if they would work.

As a master of detail in statute-making Wykeham had few rivals. Naturally the two closely co-ordinated societies (the two St Mary Winton Colleges), demanded both length and exactitude especially over elections, particularly those during the autumn when representatives of New College travelled to Winchester to choose scholars according to the very detailed provision about who might be elected and their qualifications. Rubric 13 of the Winchester statutes on the weekly allowance for commons was a fundamental one for most college societies:

This (the weekly allowance) is to be 12d rising to 14d or even 16d in time of dearth for every Fellow and Chaplain and for the Schoolmaster and Usher; 10d for every lay clerk and 8d for every scholar. Scholars under 16 years of age may have breakfast (*jantaculum*); other members are to have two meals only, *prandium* and *cena* (lunch and supper). The Bursars are to keep a weekly account of the commons and balance it at the end of the quarter.[1]

At New College when the bushel of corn was sold for more than two shillings, commons were to be advanced. Wykeham's arrangements for the meals in the hall of Winchester are interesting and sensible. Scholars when they come in must not push to the top, but sit at side tables, 'without affectation of seniority or scrambling for places' (Rubric 14). There is to be no lingering in Hall after meals because 'men when they have eaten and drunk often indulge in scurrilities and saying of things which are not befitting, or worse, in backbiting and quarrels':

Nevertheless after supper on festivals, after drink has been served in Hall, they need not retire until curfew. On festivals in winter when a fire is on the hearth, the company present, may, for recreations sake, spend a moderate time in singing or other honest amusement such as reciting lays, reading chronicles or talking of the wonders of the universe and other subjects befitting the gravity of churchmen.[2]

Those were days before a distinction was drawn between statute and by-law.

[1] T. F. Kirby, *Annals of Winchester College* (1892), p. 80.
[2] Kirby, p. 81, modifying his rendering of 'post potacionem in Aula'.

Chapter IX
John of Roquetaillade

I hope that the subject of this paper given in the series commemorating Dr Walter Seton's devotion to Franciscan history, is not too far remote from those that normally take place here. It is, none the less, a temerarious incursion into a field not usually trodden save by a handful of specialists. Yet medieval history cannot omit the study of *mirabilia*, a comprehensive word covering not only miracle but also many types of scientific discovery. Chemistry in the thirteenth and fourteenth centuries almost invariably represented itself as revealing marvels and secrets. Alchemical writers say 'Lo, now I show you a great marvel' and proceed to describe what we should regard as an ordinary piece of distillation. Prophesying is similarly a revelation of things hidden. Both chemistry and prophecy may have dangerous consequences, but equally they may be completely respectable. Indeed, prognostication of various kinds was a universal pursuit during the early and later Middle Ages. Beginning with the Sibylline books which had their influence not only with the Greeks and Romans but with early Jews and Christians (especially the fifth Sibylline book), a large and varied body of vaticination descended to the high Middle Age, and was consulted very much as people consulted the stars. From the near and middle East came a number of prognostication books with titles and place names of Arabic origin which were eagerly seized upon and copied in the monasteries, giving an answer (if you used the tables right) to many day-to-day problems that occurred. 'Shall I go out of doors (*extra domum*) today?' 'Is this a favourable day to make a business agreement?' 'Is it right to go out against my enemy (*exire super hostem*) today?' 'Will it be a boy or a girl?' and so forth. Even Matthew Paris copied and illustrated one such book[1] for the monastery of St Albans.

The habit of divination was almost like the crossword habit: there was nothing particularly reprehensible about it in an age of astrological medicine, a period when people believed in the inherent qualities or virtues of objects and in the possibility of transmuting one substance into another if the right means were applied. There was a large and legitimate field for conjecture, and

[1] Bodleian Library, MS. Ashmole 304.

if topical day-to-day questions were asked of the prophetic
literature, the result might be diverting, at any rate harmless.
There was also, as Nicholas of Oresme was careful to point out,[1]
an illegitimate field which was the concern of the Inquisition,
particularly in the course of the thirteenth century, and it is one
from which the clergy had not been entirely exempt. Walter
Langton, bishop of Coventry and Lichfield and Keeper of the
Wardrobe, then Treasurer, under Edward I, had been accused of
consulting demons as well as of murder, adultery and simony.[2]
Against Boniface VIII and the Templars of France charges of
magic had been employed by Philip IV. The bishop of Troyes,
whose real offence seems to have been that he had dared to support
Boniface VIII, was accused of poisoning and trying to bewitch
members of the French royal family, also of having practised alchemy. The number of such charges at the court of Pope John
XXII may be a sign of the prevalence of magical practices and sus-
picions in society and thought at large. In 1318 John XXII
directed the bishop of Fréjus and two other commissioners to
investigate and punish the magical activities at the papal court of
several clerics, including a physician and the barber of the archbishop of Lille. They were reputed to have engaged in necromancy,
geomancy and other magic arts of which they possessed books, and
to have employed images, mirrors, rings and incantations to invoke
evil spirits to learn the future and to benefit or injure or even kill
other men. John pronounced all such practices as they were
charged with as diabolical. He was not unusually credulous about
magic, but so many stories of criminal sorcery were in circulation
that it was impossible for him to do nothing. At any rate the
famous writer of the *Practica Inquisitionis*, Bernard Guy, had no
doubt about the prevalence of such arts, since he included in his
book a formula for the abjuration of sorcery, divination and the
invocation of demons. The person charged who had admitted his
crime and is prepared to do penance is to abjure all baptizing of
images, all sorcery performed with the use of the Eucharist, with
chrism or sacred oil, all divination or invocation of demons as well
as the art of making images of lead or wax, and all condemned
sorceries. Dr Lynn Thorndike thinks it probable that members of

[1] 'Livre de Divinacions' in G. W. Coopland, *Nicole Oresme and the
Astrologers* (1952), pp. 50 f.
[2] Dr Lynn Thorndike, *A History of Magic and Experimental Science*,
vol. iii (1934), ch. 2, cites a number of instances, some quoted below.

the clergy figure so prominently in the magical practices of which John XXII took cognizance because he felt a special responsibility for, and exercised a special jurisdiction over, such cases, and not because clerical practitioners of magic were more numerous than lay offenders.[1] It may, indeed, have been because of the tendency during the struggle with the Mendicants to charge the Pope himself with heretical views and unusual practices. In 1326 or 1327 he had to issue a bull *Super illius specula* in which he grieved to note how many persons are Christians only in name, making a pact with hell, sacrificing to demons and fabricating images, rings, mirrors, phials and other magic devices to summon spirits and receive responses from them. This disease now prevails through the world more than usual and keeps infecting the flocks of Christians increasingly. To resist it the Pope decreed *ipso facto* excommunication against offenders and the legal penalties for heretics except confiscation of property. It may be that he felt that the Inquisition was not dealing effectively with such cases, for in 1330 he withdrew from the inquisitors of Toulouse and Carcassonne certain cases of magic arts which he had entrusted to them a decade before. John also had something to say to the alchemists who claimed to make artificial gold. The Pope decreed in the extravagant *De crimine falsi* that all who have been found concerned in the production of alchemical gold shall incur infamy and give to the poor in true gold as much as they have made of the false variety. The inquisitor Emeric writing against alchemists during the close of the fourteenth century states that the bull was the outcome of a conference to which John XXII had assembled as many natural scientists and alchemists as he could to determine whether the cult had any basis in nature. The alchemists answered 'Yes'. The natural scientists 'No'. Since the alchemists were unable to prove their contention the Pope issued his bull against them.

While looking through a little volume of fourteenth–fifteenth century medical treatises and receipts (e.g. for the *Prykking of the stomach*, for the *Sciatica passio*) contained in All Souls College MS. 81, I came across the drawing which is represented in the adjoining figure 1. It was not a discovery, since John of Rupescissa, the author of the treatise in which it occurs, is well known to historians of science and appears in most of the standard histories, though this particular text is, as I shall show, of consider-

[1] *A History of Magic and Experimental Science*, vol. iii (1934), ch. 2, 'John XXII and the Occult Arts'.

dicandu et sanandu. Cui sit honor et gloria
q̄p infinita seculox secula. Amen./
Et p̄o cura eiusdem spasim quere in p̄incipio
huius tractatus ad tale signu. ⊕⊕o.

¶ Expliat tractatus de qinta essenciaa.

ffigura   vasis./

ffigura   furnelli./

omeres radentes et foramina./

able interest. It was customary to regard John as a Catalan who came from Pertellada or Perelada in the Plain of Ampurdan, province of Gerona, which is today on the line from Perpignon to Barcelona. He himself, however, says that he was *oriundus de Castro Marcolesii diocesis sancti Flori in Alvernia Gallicana*.[1] This locates him as a native of Marcolés, a little place a few kilometres south of Aurillac; though if he was not born in a place called Roquetaillade (Lat. Rupescissa), why is this his name? The question has led to a good deal of speculation and theory, discussed by Mme Bignami-Odier in a noteworthy book.[2] Writing to her in December 1946 M. Delmas, the head archivist of Cantal, professed to have identified a village of Roques in the commune of Marcolés, which, given its rocky character, may be the origin of the form Roquetaillade, and the identification has been generally accepted. By his own account John was for five years (1315–20) a student of philosophy in the 'flourishing academy' of Toulouse, where in 1332 he joined the Franciscan Order, and spent, he tells us, another five years disputing *in pruritu philosophie* and lecturing in the subject, before he saw the light. He does not say if the early years were spent at Aurillac but he was certainly in the Franciscan convent there in 1340, and his revelations and prophesying may well date from that epoch. What we know of him relates almost entirely to his life in prison, and the works he composed there. In December 1344 the minister-general of Aquitaine, William Farmena, had him imprisoned at Figeac. From Figeac he was sent for to Avignon and incarcerated there in the *Carcer Soldani* by order of Clement VI in 1349. Froissart who had a high opinion of him said that he was put there because he prophesied against the Pope and against princes. He may have been let out for a time, for in the year 1351 the chronicler Henry Rebdorf says that 'the Pope caused to be imprisoned a certain brother of the Minorites, a notable clerk (*sollempnem clerum*) and one well lettered and who prophesied many things to come about the orders of the mendicants and future Roman pontiffs and emperors and many other marvels'. That he was released before this date seems possible from one of his treatises copied into Ashmole 1423, the prologue of which states that it was completed on 4 October 1350,

[1] Vatican Library, MS. Rossiano lat. 753, fo. 148v in the 'Liber Ostensor' discovered by Fr J. M. Poug Marti. *Infra*, p. 88.

[2] *Études sur Jean de Roquetaillade (Johannes de Rupescissa)* (1952), ch. ii, 'Légendes sur Jean de Roquetaillade'.

and there is no mention of his captivity. But in 1356 he was again
in prison at Avignon, not knowing whether he would be condemned to death. In his last two prophetic works he calls himself
'pauper incarceratus' and in one says that he had been in prison
for twenty years. This may be an exaggeration, though it is not far
off the truth. In one section of his *Vade mecum in tribulacione* he
says that he had been publicly foretelling the fearful things that
should happen to France at the hands of the English, more than
twenty years before the wars (the Anglo-French wars) began, but
the people thought him foolish and out of his wits. He was writing
then in 1349, but to a medieval Frenchman of that period the war
with the English would, roughly speaking, appear to have begun
with the Crécy campaign. If this is so, John must have been
preaching from about 1325 onwards.

This takes one back to the pontificate of John XXII and to the
period of acute controversy between that pontiff and the Franciscan Order over the poverty of Christ. In the Bull *Cum inter
nonnullos* of November 1323 John made it heretical to assert that
Christ and His apostles were not owners of the property which the
scriptures expressly said that they possessed. When the struggle
reached its fiercest stage and John XXII publicly broke with
Michael of Cesena, John of Roquetaillade must have sided, like
William of Ockham, with the humiliated General of the Order. In
the fourteenth section of his *Vade mecum* John says that the reason
why the tribulations which he foretold were to fall upon the
Franciscan order was 'because of the sin of the transgression of the
rule'. It was owing to this that God had permitted the scandal of
the attack on evangelical poverty by the Preachers against the
Friars Minor; and 'the Friars Minor were forced to succumb
because of the flight of Michael from the cunning of the Friars
Preachers': a reference to the events of 9 April 1328 when John
XXII publicly denounced Michael of Cesena, General of the
Order. In his last works John gives the reason why, between 1360
and 1365, the religious orders and the mendicants in particular
were to be afflicted by the heretical Emperor coming from the
East and by what he calls the beast ascending from the sea. The
Friars had transgressed the Rule, and significantly he quotes the
words which God is purported to have said to St Francis fore-
telling what would happen in that contingency. The reference
John gives is the *Liber XII sociorum eius qui legenda vetus dicitur*.
The XII is clearly a mis-copying by an inaccurate scribe of the

number III and the reference here is to the first part of the Legend of the Three Companions, which, as Bishop Moorman has shown, is probably *earlier* than the first Life of Francis by Thomas of Celano.[1] If this is so, it puts the sympathies of John of Roquetaillade beyond doubt, if, indeed, any doubt existed about a man who consistently praises the zealots of the Order. When he was interrogated on 10 August 1354 by Cardinal Guillaume Court and asked whether certain clerks who had been burnt for heresy in June 1354 were glorious martyrs or heretics condemned to eternal fire, he at first refused to reply, and then answered: 'If you have handed them over to the secular arm from hatred of evangelical poverty and of the decretal *Exiit*, the section *Porro*, then they are glorious martyrs in heaven; but if they have mixed themselves up with errors and other heresies, if they have denied the Catholic faith and Holy Scriptures, they are heretics condemned to hell fire.'[2]

John was thus a spiritual, belonging in his early days to the party of Michael of Cesena, and, in general, to those who based themselves upon the letter as well as the spirit of St Francis' instructions to the Order. There is therefore no wonder why he was imprisoned. If prophets were dangerous in the thirteenth century at the time of the abbot Joachim, when the wilder zealots of the Order were attaching themselves to the Emperor Frederick II, they were an even greater menace in the days when Louis of Bavaria was threatening the Avignonese papacy, especially if they were Franciscan zealots. As Miss Douie has pointed out, it is doubtful whether the spiritual party could have endured so valiantly the persecutions and ridicule to which they were subjected by their opponents without the certain conviction of the triumph of their ideals and the equally firm belief that they were the Order which would transform the world.[3] In this they had been sustained in the past by the revelations of Joachimism and by other prophecies: the most common subject of these collections was the character and deeds of the various popes, a visionary element being introduced after the writer had finished describing the events of his own age by speculation upon the fate of Christendom at the time of the expected coming of anti-Christ. It is easy to see the

[1] *Studies in Franciscan History and Legend* (1940), pp. 62–5.
[2] Bignami-Odier, p. 44.
[3] *The Nature and the Effect of the Heresy of the Fraticelli* (1932), ch. iii, 'Angelo da Clareno', portrays this confidence.

danger of such prognostications to the popes who supported the
non-zealots. It was not the alchemy which led John into captivity:
it was, as we shall see later, the 'prophetic interpretation' of the
Holy Scriptures at a time when prophecy might easily become
tendentious.

There is a fairly well authenticated tradition that John of
Roquetaillade died in 1362. One author of very much later date,
Nostradamus, says that he was burnt, but there is no confirmation
of this. Far from being distracted by prison life, he was not an un-
fertile author. The alchemical works that have survived are two:
the 'Book of Light or Mastery of the making of the true Philosopher's Stone', which is also called the 'Book of Light and
Tribulation'; this seems to have preceded the work for which he
is best known, the *De consideratione quintae essentiae*. This book on
the fifth essence is also confusingly termed *De famulatu philosophie
ad theologiam*. The texts of it, as I shall show, vary considerably;
some are with, and some without, the prologue, and later versions
expand, sometimes misleadingly, the original as it was written.
The prophetic texts are (i) the *Visiones seu revelationes*, written to
Cardinal Guillaume Court, nephew of Benedict XII; (ii) the
'Commentary on the oracle of St Cyril' or alternatively 'Commentary upon the prophesy of St Cyril';[1] (iii) the *Liber secretorum
eventuum* found only in a few manuscripts but known to Jean de
Bel and Froissart. This contains very little that is not already said
in the Commentary of St Cyril, but it is shorter and more easy to
read. It was finished 11 November 1349 in the Sultan's prison at
Avignon and is also addressed to Cardinal Guillaume Court; (iv)
the *Ostensor* written after 27 December 1356, of which the single
manuscript is Vatican Library, Rossiano lat. 753; (v) the *Vade
mecum in tribulacione* of the same year or immediately afterwards,
which is found in a number of manuscripts, mostly in the Bibliothèque Nationale or in Munich. I shall omit detailed consideration
of the Commentary on the Oracle of St Cyril which I have not been
able to read. There are other works which John himself names, but
they seem irrecoverable.

Before Mme Bignami-Odier wrote, Dr Lynn Thorndike, who
considered John to be a Catalan, had listed the manuscripts of the
Liber Lucis and of the *De consideratione quinte essentie*.[2] He has
made it clear that both of these tracts are undoubtedly the work of

---

[1] Bignami-Odier, pp. 53–112.
[2] *A History of Magic and Experimental Science*, iii, ch. 4, Appendix 22.

Roquetaillade. It is refreshing, when manuscript study has robbed his great Franciscan predecessor Roger Bacon of certain of the treatises formerly ascribed to him, to find it restoring to his successor what was formerly attributed to Bacon, Arnold de Villanova and Ramon Lull. John has therefore returned to his alchemical fame. With certain medieval Catalans, as Kopp has shown, he is in the van of iatro-chemical study: more than a forerunner of Paracelsus, and one of those who used his chemical experiments for a curative purpose.

In the Bibliothèque Nationale MS. 7151[1] of his tract on the fifth essence he excuses himself from revealing all his medical secrets:

because according to Catholic philosophers I would say in the words of Holy Scripture that to obey is better than sacrifice. Out of reverence for the statutes of our Order I will not reveal the marvellous medicines so highly desired by the world which would not only heal our bodies miraculously from all diseases, but would transmute imperfect metals into gold and silver in the flash of an eye. The truth of which mastery was by God's will revealed to me in the tribulations of prison.

The Paris Manuscript continued:

No one can reach the highest points of art unless his mind is deified by contemplation and holy living, so that he not only knows all the interior things of nature but can transmute whatever nature is capable of being transmuted.

This sanctimonious utterance is not in the shorter version of the treatise on Quintessence, as represented by the All Souls College MS. 81, and throughout the treatise on Quintessence it is advisable to go back to the more primitive text which I believe this to represent. Thus in the Paris manuscript John withholds his information about medicines not only because of reverence for the statutes of his Order, but also out of obedience to ecclesiastical prelates. This last phrase is not in the All Souls text and its ommission is much more in keeping with the author's independent character.

John's main concern is the creation of a transmuting agent and universal medicine. This is achieved not by dividing the atom, but by separating the elements. Like all alchemists, John starts from the theory of the four elements, earth, air, fire and water.

[1] Dr Thorndike thinks Bibl. Nat. MS. 7151 '14th rather than 15th century'.

By their association in varied proportions these elements give rise
to the various kinds of matter.[1] Earth, water and air typify the
solid, liquid and gaseous states of aggregated matter; fire typifies
energy. The fire-water opposites are particularly important: for
it was assumed that to reconcile them would furnish the Philosopher's Stone. From fire and water sprang the medieval idea of
the composition of metals, in which the names sulphur and mercury were abstractions standing for combustibility and fusibility.
According to this theory, conjunction of the impure principals,
sulphur and mercury, led to the formation of base metals: when of
ordinary purity, the principle produced gold and the superfine or
quintessentialized principle furnished the Philosopher's Stone,
for the stone was of gold of highly exalted purity. Now to procure
this highly purified gold it was necessary to make a sublimate of
mercury, and the *Liber Lucis* gives the instructions for this. John
advises the use of Roman vitriol or sulphuric acid, but the sulphur
which is to be used is not common sulphur, but an invisible spirit
to be found in sulphuric acid, which has the property of tincturing
things red, yet coagulates mercury in sublimation to the whiteness
of snow. John uses it with saltpetre, sometimes also with sal
ammoniac. The book shows how to separate and then to fix the
elements in a state of high purity by means of certain chemical
substances.

John does not claim originality for this part of his chemical
work. He writes it 'to help the great need and want of God's
saints, particularly at the future coming of anti-Christ, and after
all what is there so secret about these things? The philosophers
keep them entirely dark and will not reveal them even to their
children.' But why should not he?

The treatise on Quintessence does not describe how to transmute base metals into gold, but concentrates on the finding of an
elixir of life. It is in two books. The first consists of canons; the
second of remedies. The first gives instructions how to extract
quinta essentia from all sorts of substances. Quintessence is what
cures the distress of old age and can restore the lost vigour of
life, and bring back the former powers of the body, but not, he
says, in the same degree as of old. It would be absurd to think
that these remedies could induce immortality. They can only
keep our bodies fit and hale, give us good digestions and healthy

[1] I have followed here Dr Thorndike's exposition in *A History of Magic
and Experimental Science*, iii. 34 f.

complexions.[1] The secret is not an *element* nor composed of elements; it is a thing that stands in relation to the four qualities as does heaven to the four elements. And just as the heavens are regarded as the fifth essence, superior to the four elements, so it is called *quinta essentia*. It is made from *aqua ardens* (alcohol) through distillation in the alembic shown. The *aqua ardens* is poured in at the top, heated, goes up and comes down through the arms, and this has to happen several times both day and night to get real quintessence. You know it by opening a small sealed up hole and sniffing; if there is 'a marvellous smell that draws all that enter by an invisible bond' then it is *quinta essentia*.[2] If the smell is not so attractive, then the distillation must go on. There are various alternative methods of making it: by putting the alcohol in an amphora and burying in a hot-bed. You can also make *quinta essentia* from human blood, flesh and eggs, and so forth, and instructions are given.

The fourth canon is of a frankly magical kind. 'On the secret of the mastery of fixing the sun in our sky so that it shows therein and sheds life and the principle of life on our bodies.' But all that is recommended is that we should heat a gold piece or two (if you have not gold, borrow two silver florins), and quench it or them in alcohol or in good white wine. The fifth canon 'on fixing all the stars in our sky so that they may exercise their properties there' is a metaphorical way of recommending that all herbs, simples, aromatics and laxatives be stewed for three hours in alcohol, when their effect will be immeasurably improved. Then John turns to the methods of extracting the fifth essence from minerals, especially gold, and discovers that from the concept of alcohol as the fifth essence we have passed to a notion of a fifth essence in each thing. So the fifth essence can be extracted from antimony. A passage that occurs in the All Souls text alone describes the process and the result:

Which blessed liquor keep by itself in a strong glass bottle tightly sealed, because it is a treasure which the whole world cannot equal. Behold a miracle! forsooth the great sweetness of antimony so that it surpasses

---

[1] All Souls College MS. 81, fo. 100: sed quia constitutum est omnibus semel mori, fantasticum esset laborare querere in hac vita rem que posset nostrum corpus reddere immortale. Restat ergo querere que circa terminum vite nostre a deo prefixum posset corpus nostrum sine corruptione servare et infirmum curare, deperditum quoque restaurare.

[2] Ibid., fo. 102.

N

the sweetness of honey. And I declare by God's love that the human intellect can scarcely believe the virtue and worth of this water of fifth essence of antimony. And Aristotle in the book, *Secret of Secrets*, says that it is its lead. Believe me that never in nature was there a greater secret. For all men have toiled to sublimate the spirits of minerals and never had the fifth essence of the aforesaid antimony. In short I never would be able to express the half of this discovery. For it takes away pain from wounds and heals marvellously. Its virtue is incorruptible, miraculous, and useful beyond measure. Forty days it needs to putrefy in mud in a sealed bottle, and then it works marvels.[1]

I cannot agree with one writer who calls the second book of the Quintessence less interesting. This discusses the application of the new liquid (it can be in powdered form also) to particular ailments, e.g. leprosy, skin diseases and lesions, paralysis, consumption, fantastic possession by demons, fevers—tertian, cotidian or pestilential—spasms, etc. It is clear that John was a doctor as well as a chemist, and some of the things he says reflect interestingly upon the medical practice of the day, e.g. upon purgatives. Two essential points about them are, first, that they must not kill you and, second, that they should penetrate to the most remote parts and elicit the evil humours. He had great belief in strawberry water. 'I will tell you a great secret in the cure of leprosy,' he says. 'Take water made of strawberries and that water has, in the cure of leprosy, a supercelestial virtue, and know that this, along with the quintessence I have named, cures leprosy in a remarkable way.' Or it can be cured, if you have not got the fifth essence, by strawberry water in conjunction with alcohol, and he gives particulars how to prepare the water from ripe strawberries: and so forth. In the Bodleian Library MS. Canonici Misc. 37 (fifteenth century) of the *De consideratione quintae essentiae*, John is made to declare, in the second book, that there is no remedy against pestilential fevers since the disease is incurable and sent to destroy the people by divine command, against which there is no remedy save through God's goodness. I cannot discover this pessimistic passage in All Souls College MS. 81, the shorter text, and believe that this may be a later insertion. John of Roquetaillade had greater faith in his quintessence than that.

An interesting point is that in some versions of the second book John is made to pay testimony to the kindness of his jailors, through whose help he was able to obtain alcohol from a certain

[1] All Souls College MS. 81, fos. 115, 115v.

holy man, a friend of God. Again, this is missing from All Souls
College MS. 81. This may be another case of the later manipulation of the text; but the care and precision of John's writing
suggests that he was able to do certain experiments and at least
to have his notes with him in the Sultan's prison. He seems to
have had no difficulty in communicating his predictions to those
who asked him. While he was in prison he was consulted in an
amicable manner by cardinals and dignitaries, treated perfectly
well and allowed books, one of which seems to have been largely
responsible for the form taken by his prognostications. He was
also kept fairly well briefed about current events and it is evident
that he had friends to visit him. All that was necessary was to
keep him from preaching in public, or broadcasting his predictions, and to do that confinement was the only way. He was asked
very topical questions. One cardinal consulted him, shortly after
the battle of Poitiers, about the course of the Anglo-French war,
and about the future of church revenues. He got a reply that
cannot have been consoling to a dignitary of the Holy See. In
answering him John reproved him for the definiteness of his
questions. The list of queries the cardinal sent seemed presump-
tuous (he called it *maxima blasphemia dei*): the cardinal was asking
for particulars which only God could infallibly provide; but
those seeking the interpretation of scriptural passages and how
they applied to the evils of the time were more to John's thinking.
He regarded himself as having the spirit of interpretation. One
work of his to which he alludes of which no specimen survives is
the *De Interpretationibus arcanorum scripture*. He regarded himself as an expositor and the texts he mainly took were from Ezekiel
and from the Revelations.

In the *Ostensor* preserved in the unique Vatican MS. (Rossiano
lat. 753),[1] John says that he had read in prison (1356) the 'book of
the monk Sergius'. He also speaks of having a 'liber Agap'. Latin
MS. 21597 of the Bibliothèque Nationale contains the double
commentary of the pseudo-Joachim and of Sergius Bahira on the
celebrated and mysterious oracle of St Cyril. Bahira was the teacher
of Mahomet. In the earliest Islamic biographies of Mahomet
there is mention of a Christian monk, sometimes anonymous,
sometimes called Sergius, Nestorius, Bahira, whom the Arab
prophet met before his mission and in the course of one of his

---

[1] Described by Bignami-Odier, *Études sur Jean de Roquetaillade*, pp.
243–4, who attributes it to the second half of the fourteenth century.

travels from Mecca to Syria: a monk who, following certain
indications, recognized in Mahomet the prophet sent by God,
whose coming had been announced to him in a revelation. This
was, of course, good Arab propaganda. Byzantine sources that
give the same story allege that the monk was a heretic and was
bribed for making the pronouncement. Later we find the story in
this form: a monk, whom Syriac versions call Ishoyahb and Arab
versions Murhib or Murhab, having gone to the Arabian desert,
meets there an old monk Sergius Bahira, who tells him that having
had various encounters with his co-religionaries on the subject
of the cult of the Cross, he had gone to Sinai. There an angel had
appeared to him who showed him the events which were to come
about since the beginning of the kingdom of the Israelites until
the last judgement. After Bahira's death one of his disciples
named Hakim recounted to the monk Ishoyahb how his master
received the command to betake himself to the Arabian desert
near Medina where he received his revelation. A version of the
Syrio-Arab apocalypse of Bahira was current in the West during
the Middle Ages. It was a product of the apocalyptic literature
which was continually cultivated among the Christians of the
East subjected to Muslim domination until a late epoch. It is of the
same kind as the apocalypses of Enoch, Esdras, Methodius and
several of those which were composed in Egypt since the invasion
of the seventh century.[1]

John of Roquetaillade reproduces in his *Ostensor* and his
other prophecies (the *Visiones* and the *Vade mecum in tribulacione*) features characteristic of this oriental literature: notably the
Eastern anti-Christ who is due to come after the Turkish invasions
to break the Turkish power. Certain of these features he got from
the text of the Erithrean Sibyl[2] and from the prophecies of Robert
d'Uzes. The king coming from the East clothed in green, is a
Christian king. This is the great king of the Tartars (Cambalech).
The glittering car denotes the chariot of Ezekiel which is the
Roman Church. Most significant is the traditional notion of the
coming, after the death of anti-Christ, of a poor king, who will
be one of the blessed race of Pepin, King of the West: a king who

---

[1] J. Bignami-Odier and G. Levi della Vida, 'La version latine de
l'Apocalypse Syro-Arabe de Serge-Bahira', *Mélanges d'Archéologie et
d'Histoire* (École Française de Rome), t. lxii (1950), 125 f.

[2] Cf. E. Sackur, *Sibyllinische Texte und Forschungen* (Halle, 1898), pp.
117–18, 125.

will reign over the whole world for seven and a half years, who will refuse to be crowned with a golden crown and will give general peace for a thousand years. But after the millennium Gog and Magog will be unchained, the Angel of Wrath will wreak his will upon the human race and a general extermination will follow in which God will gather together his own for salvation in Jerusalem. In all John's works there is anti-Christ (or anti-Christs), there is the Toynbean Redeemer who will establish peace, and there is the final extermination of all but the saved. These are the common themes upon which he elaborates. Two points seem very important. In all cases the beneficent king is a western king. In one prophecy he is sprung from a Frankish race; in another he is of French stock, which takes the reader back to the *De recuperatione terrae sanctae* of Pierre Dubois, a treatise that looked forward to the dominance of a pacific French monarch in Europe: a sort of predecessor of Dante's *Monarchia*. The second point is the increasing particularism of the time structure. In the first treatise the time indication is vague; in the second it is clearly in the fourteenth century and in the third it is all between 1360 and 1372. John has increasingly blended with his Eastern sources detailed information about the state of Europe which he received from visitors and correspondents. It is in the last of these treatises, the *Vade mecum in tribulacione*, that he appears as a prophet of contemporary or near-contemporary events.

In the *Visiones* (another description of the *Liber secretorum eventuum*),[1] addressed to William, archbishop of Arles, the nephew of Benedict XII, one anti-Christ is Louis of Sicily, son of Peter II of Aragon, who succeeded to the kingdom in 1342. There are several others: before him there had been Frederick II of Hohenstaufen, and after Peter will come a horde of cruel tyrants rising against Charles, king elect of the Roman Empire, and this horde will be made up of various tyrants, especially from the dregs of Bavaria and from the malice of the Ghibelline people. The fifth anti-Christ is a false prophet, a pseudo-religious; the sixth a powerful tyrant in the East who will subdue the whole of Asia. But to return to nearer times: as soon as schism between a true and a false prophet breaks out, Louis of Sicily will be chosen Roman Emperor and a part of the Franciscan Order will group themselves at his side. 'Whereupon there will arise preaching monks heretically asserting that our Lord Pope John condemned as heretical

[1] As in Paris, Bibl. Nat., Lat. 3598, fo. 1. Cf. Bignami-Odier, p. 239.

the decretal of Nicholas III upon angelic poverty [the *Exiit qui seminat*, declaring that the Friars Minor by their renunciation of property were following the example of Christ and His Apostles]. But the general church and the Roman curia will hold firm in these schismatic days, the true Pope among these waves of trouble saying that the Lord Nicholas determined in a catholic fashion about evangelical poverty and that the determining by decretal of the Lord Pope John is true and catholic, for Holy Church asserts that his determination is not repugnant to the determination of Nicholas.' This interesting passage quoted *verbatim* is much in the spirit of the conciliatory Bonagratia of Bergamo, who had written to show that John XXII's pronouncements were not a radical attack upon the doctrine of evangelical poverty and that the Pope had at best recognized the especial sanctity of the Franciscan life, as for example by his canonization of St Louis of Toulouse. John of Roquetaillade is therefore careful not to criticize John XXII. But now when these false assertions by the preachers are being made, John continues, the scandal will reach the ear of the Sicilian emperor, whereupon Augustus Siculus will gather together the princes of the world and with their agreement will expel for good all the clergy. Where they are to go and how this is to be done is left entirely uncertain. The Jews will be told that their new Messiah has arisen, but in France a new family of Maccabees *ex sanguine principum Gallicorum* will arise to hammer the Sicilian. The Christian people thus led will fight the king who will fall in a pitched battle, and will be borne alive to the lower regions; conquered by Holy Church, he will be confounded before the whole age. Before Louis is chosen Emperor, John adds, he will overthrow the Saracens and when opposed by the nobility of Rome will destroy the eternal city for all time. After the death of Louis, whom he identifies with anti-Christ, the Papacy and the Empire will be transferred to Jerusalem where the sabbath of the world will be realized and celebrated. It will be noted that the expulsion of the clergy and the sack of Rome do not seem very permanent events, at any rate in the light of John's later prophecies; but strict consistency cannot be expected from this particular prophet.

Dr Kampers suggested that John's treatise upon the oracle of St Cyril of Jerusalem was written before the deaths of Louis of Bavaria and Louis of Sicily: between 1348 and 1355.[1] In this

[1] F. Kampers, *Die deutsche Kaiseridee in Prophetie und Sage* (Munich, 1896), p. 117.

treatise the Sicilian will be fought by a lion of French blood;
the lion is not precisly identified, but John suggests that it may
represent either the second son of Philip VI (whose name was
also Philip) or the Dauphin John, or, more likely, Charles of
Bohemia, 'who had been elected Emperor by the Pope and Cardinals, who is the brother of the wife of Lord John the eldest
son of the King of France'. John's ideas upon imperial election
are certainly strange. Now in each of these tracts, the *Vision*
and the *Oracle*, the Aragonese Sicilian is fought and conquered
by a hero of French origin. This may be a reference to the ambi-
tions of the house of Anjou in the Mediterranean, a sort of come-
back after the Sicilian vespers: more important perhaps is the
fact that in the treatise on the Oracle, the lion who fights the
Sicilian and imposes peace, will, in the Dubois tradition, be
ultimately elected Emperor, however that election comes about.
Forgetting that he has in the other treatise destroyed Rome, John
of Roquetaillade says that the election of the new king-emperor
will be carried out publicly there by the Roman senators, who
will ask the princes of this world to nominate an emperor from
among themselves, that peace may be imposed upon the tumults
of the present age. Another possibility, John says, would be for
the usual electors to act, but he seems to prefer the election by
compromise through 'the princes of this world'. In any case what
they elect is a *Gallus*, either a true Frenchman or one with French
blood in him. In his consistorial speech which Clement VI made
upon hearing of the Emperor Charles IV's election in 1347, the
Pope said, 'and observe that he is a Catholic, so devoted and so
munificent to the Church that he ought not only to have the
Empire by succession, as descended from sacred parents and so
forth, but the Empire is due to him by his very name, since he is
Charles and history shows that no man more devoted and munificent towards the Church than was Charles the Great'.

John's best-known work is the *Vade mecum in tribulacione*, so
called, he says, because a man who has the spirit (i.e. can understand the prophetic scriptures) will, if he is found worthy, be
able to shield himself in the day of destruction; and this book
shows him their meaning. In the Prologue he claims to have
foretold the battle of Poitiers, to have predicted the troubles
arising in Spain and, nearer home, to have informed his nephew
Anselm, who consulted him on the point, that he would be
successful in obtaining the church of the Blessed Mary of Aurillac.

He is conscious therefore of a good record in prophesying. His guide is made up of twenty intentions, intentions meaning the things that are intended or destined to happen, and the whole period is confined to thirteen years following the date of writing 1356. Within these years a great persecution against the clergy is predicted and the conclusion is expressed that only through fierce probation can the prelates of the Church be converted from their present way of living. Many of them will die by the sword, others will be burnt or destroyed by hunger, plague and various evils; and before 1362 the cardinals will leave their pleasant retreat (*requies*), Avignon. Their flight will take place within the next five and a half years and is the beginning of the stupendous events that John is about to relate. Between 1360 and 1365 there will be terrible novelties in the world. First the worms of the earth shall assume such fortitude and hostility that they shall cruelly devour almost all lions, bears, leopards and wolves. The birds of the air, not merely rapacious falcons but songbirds, blackbirds and linnets, shall tear one another. This is all necessary if the prophecy of Isaiah xxxiii is to be fulfilled. There shall arise in those five years what John calls *justitia popularis*, which means mob justice, to devour tyrants, traitors and nobles. Popular justice shall consume the riches of the nobility and those who rob the poor people shall themselves be plundered. Before 1365 is reached there will publicly appear an oriental anti-Christ whose discipline will preach around Jerusalem with false signs. John lays stress on the importance of understanding the 'marrow' of future events, i.e. 1356-9, since it is during these years that the princes of the Church are preparing to fly from Avignon. The power of the French king will not be able to protect churchmen. This period will be one of conflict: there will be an aggression of the Moslem power against the Christians, but a Spanish king will be able to wipe out the Mohammedan power, especially in Africa. When the 'sixties are reached, the world will rise in indignation against rich clerks: they will be destroyed and stripped and murdered by secular peoples (*per populos seculares*) and after the princes of the Church have seen that they can no longer raise their heads their affliction shall give them intelligence, so that they may return to apostolic poverty.

A western anti-Christ is now to arise and persecute the Church. He will publicly appear in the Roman Empire between 1362 and 1370, but his flagellations will not extend for more than three and

a half years. His régime will be followed by the rule of a supreme
pontiff, the *reparator* of the world. He is the man represented
in Ezekiel ix, clothed in linen, signing his elect with the sign
TAU on their foreheads. He is also the angel who has the golden
censer and presents upon the altar which is before the eyes of
God the prayers of the saints. He is the angel of chapter xx of the
Revelations, having a great chain for binding Satan. With him is
the mystical Elias of whom Christ said in Matthew 'that he would
come to restore all things'; of whom, says John, I have made
many treatises with abundant material in several books. These
two figures first take temporal form before 1365 in the persons of
two prophets of salvation, *duos cordelarios abjectos fratres minores.*

The first of these Minorites will be the restorer-pope we have
mentioned, the other is to be the person of Elias, the fore-runner,
and the signs of their coming is an invasion of the infidels from
the East and the flight of the curia from Avignon. The poor
friar destined to be the reparator-pope will have a hard battle
against infidels and enemies who will rise up and stone him and
'there would be great risk were Christ not to provide for his
desolate Church and to send two cranes of the redheaded kind to
take him up and bear him on their wings and save him from the
hands of the enemy'. What contemporary work of art had John
in mind? Clement VI had employed Sienese artists to redecorate
the papal palace: are these rescuing birds some which John had
seen in the papal wardrobe or on other murals?

The Reparator or Redeemer will restore all things. He is to
expel the corrupt priests from the temples, depose simoniacs,
and restore to episcopal sees the liberty of electing their prelates
(highly tendentious predictions). He is to write the 'Book of the
Reparation of the world' by Christ's art, whose virtue will endure to the end of the age. The king of France who is to come to
Rome at the beginning of his pontificate, the Pope will, contrary to
the normal Germanic method of election, make Roman emperor,
and to him God will subject the whole world. This emperor will
be of such sanctity that no emperor nor king shall be like him from
the beginning of the world save only the King of Kings and Lord
of Lords. This Gallic emperor will refuse to be crowned with the
golden crown, in honour of the crown of thorns that Jesus wore:
like Godfrey de Bouillon.

After destroying the power of Mahomet and freeing the Greeks
from the Turks, the Pope—and this is an interesting statement—

will decide that as long as the world lasts the cardinals shall be drawn from the Greek Church. This Pope will live for nine and a half years, the Emperor for about ten. The said Pope will establish in the kingdom of Sicily a king, who with powerful hand and stretched out arm will acquire the kingdom of Jerusalem, after whose acquisition the Emperor (like St Louis of Toulouse) will leave the present world and assume the habit and life of a friar minor. He will leave a son who will be king of Lombardy and will die within fifteen years.

Within this strange rigmarole, which some might consider the ravings of a demented prisoner, are certain interesting features that call for notice. John sticks closely to the text of the Apocalypse and most of his intentions bear some reference to the Patmos vision. The *cordelier* pope who becomes the divine *reparator*, redeemer and restorer, has good precedent in earlier medieval prophecy, but the colleague Elias I have not been able to trace. Once more the king of France appears as Emperor, defying the normal means of election and, it will be noted, appointed by the Redeemer-pope. In this treatise he is nearer than ever to the monarch of Dante's vision. Lastly, the assumption of the cardinals from the Greek Church seems without precedent in western apocalyptic literature. It displays the influence of the eastern Mediterranean upon prophetic writing as well as the notion of an οἰκουμένη, it is John's way of predicting the unification of the two churches. Most interesting of all is the foretelling of popular revolts, which did, in fact, take place throughout Europe in the thirteen seventies and eighties and were primarily revolts of work-people in the towns or agricultural labourers. There is a mixture of contemporary theory and observation that runs through the allegories which he presents and, to those who consulted him, must have been an alarming and fascinating feature of his work.

It must be obvious, in fine, that John of Roquetaillade is too bizarre a figure to have much influence upon fourteenth-century history or upon the annals of his order; but significant he certainly is, indicative of certain currents in the political and scientific speculation of contemporary Europe, of the break-up of the ordered medieval world and of the changing and divided state of the Franciscans in the middle of that period.

Chapter X
The Book of St Albans

It is appropriate that among the lectures which the John Rylands Library arranges season by season some at least should be concerned with its own treasures. For the student of the later Middle Ages, or early Renaissance, its incunabula afford rich possibilities: not least as illustrating the lives and activities of the early printers of this country, and the importance of the stationers and booksellers who disseminated their products. The further one advances into the literary history of the later fifteenth century, the more significant appears the function both of the early printer-editors and of the distributors and middlemen who commissioned and disposed of the works they printed; for the demand for books was undoubted. In a striking little paper published in 1943, Mr H. S. Bennett, who had been listing the fifteenth-century manuscripts of English vernacular works in the Cambridge University Library, drew attention to the strength and variety of the demand for reading matter which Caxton found existing in England. 'He found a considerable reading public available, and secondly, he found that this public had been accustomed for half a century at least to read matter of all kinds.'[1] There was a market for books, whatever their source, and little control over the conditions of their sale; for, as Mr Gordon Duff once observed, in the early days of English printing, at all events between 1483 and 1533, there was no protecting wall against the undenizened alien selling books where he could.[2] In the course of the sixteenth century such an import system came to be felt unfair upon the English, or the resident alien, bookseller, as the wording of the Act of 1533, which curtailed the liberty given to the non-resident alien pedlars of books, suggests.[3] But in the fifteenth, the demand for books was met along competitive lines, both in London and without. A provincial press in this country at work in those early days must therefore be of considerable interest, especially when it prints in the vernacular.

[1] 'Caxton and his Public', *Review of English Studies*, vol. xix, no. 74 (April 1943), p. 119.

[2] *A Century of the English Book Trade* (1905), p. xv.

[3] *Stat. Realm*, iii. 456, repealing, owing to the growth in the number of native printers, the Act of 1 Richard III.

Among its early *flores* the Rylands possesses three books from
a notable provincial, the printer of St Albans. In re-printing the
St Albans *Chronicles of England* (1497) Wynkyn de Worde called
him 'one somtyme scole mayster of Saynt Albons', and as such he is
usually known. One of the three is the Book of Hawking, Hunting
and the Blasing of Arms, commonly called the *Boke of St Albans*,[1]
printed in 1486. Another is the St Albans version of the Chronicles
of England printed perhaps three years previously.[2] These are the
only surviving English works of the St Albans printer, whose first
book was the humanistic treatise, Agostino Dati's *Libellus super
Tullianis elegantiis* (1479), followed by the thoroughly orthodox
medieval Albertus, *Liber methodorum significandi* (1480). That year
he printed another well-known work of literary eloquence, the
Rhetorica nova of the Minorite Lorenzo Traversari of Savona, a
copy of which the Rylands possesses. Lorenzo, who had been a
pupil of Sixtus IV, gave it the alternative title of *Margarita elo-
qentiæ*, and the colophon says that it was written in the University
of Cambridge. Like Dati's treatise, it is a very Ciceronian pearl.
Thus two of the earliest productions from the St Albans press are
works upon composition, introductions to the correct—the new—
style, and it was not till the end of the schoolmaster's time that
he came to his own native tongue. In the middle period are good
medieval works on Aristotle, but with these we are not concerned.

Most of this printer's works state that they were printed
Apud villam sancti Albani. There is no direct evidence that his
press was within the abbey precincts, nor indeed that there was
any connexion between it and the library of the great house,
though the proto-humanism of the abbey under John of Whethamstede is well known, and Thomas Walsingham shows clear signs
of it, before the abbot's great days.[3] It is indeed possible that the
printer may have drawn certain of his texts from the monastic
library, if it was allowed to lend; but when Blades, the editor
of the facsimile edition of the *Boke of St Albans* speaks of 'the
St Albans Chronicle' as issuing from the schoolmaster, it is well

---

[1] Copies listed in Duff, *Fifteenth Century English Books* (1917), no. 56.

[2] W. Blades, in his introduction to the *Boke of St Albans* (p. 17), dated
it '1483 [?]'. Mr Gordon Duff, *Fifteenth Century English Books*, p. 29,
'[1485]'. In Wynkyn de Worde's edition of 1497, the *compilation* is
definitely ascribed to 1483, but there is no indication given of the date
of publication.

[3] *The St Albans Chronicle*, ed. Galbraith, pp. xli-v of the editor's
introduction.

to be cautious. Strictly speaking, the term 'St Albans Chronicle' should be used with the meaning Mr C. L. Kingsford attached to it; as standing either for the anonymous chronicle of 1422–31, printed in the Rolls edition of Amundesham, or for the historical entries in abbot John of Whethamstede's *Register*.[1] The chronicle to which Blades refers is an extended form of the *Chronicles of England* which Caxton printed in 1480 'at the request of dyvers gentylmen', and the basis of this was the *Brut* Chronicle, with the continuations of 1333–77, 1377–1419, 1419–61. The schoolmaster made the *Brut* the nucleus of his volume of general history, which he divided into seven parts corresponding with the seven periods of history. The *Brut*, here presented in the translation attributed to John Maundevile, takes up the story from Part IV, and fills the remainder of the book; the earlier parts were drawn, he says from [in this order] Geoffrey of Monmouth, Bede, Gildas, William of Malmesbury, Cassiodorus, St Augustine, Titus Livius, Martin of Troppau and Theobaldus Cartusiensis. Now to assume that the schoolmaster was himself the compiler—or anthologist—of the earlier part of his *Chronicles*, borrowing from, or working amid, the books of the abbey, would, I think, be hazardous. It is more likely that he took (for this was his method) an existing compilation—he refers to the 'new translation' used by him—to combine with the *Brut*, and this view may find support in his title: 'the Chronicles of England with the fruit of time'. What is the 'fruit of time'? May it not be the translation of a Latin *Fructus temporum* or popular work on the chronology of history,[2] which he found, ready-made, for his use? If this suggestion is correct, there will not be very much to connect the *Chronicles of England* with the great abbey near which it was printed; and it should be emphasized that the *Brut*, at any rate in its continuations, belongs to a non-monastic cycle: the cycle of history written by laymen for the laity, drawn upon and copied by historians of the City of London, as the editors of the *Great Chronicle* have recently shown.

It is evident that both the Chronicles and the *Boke of St Albans* were destined for the well-to-do laity, the 'dyverse gentylmen' of

[1] *English Historical Literature in the Fifteenth Century* (1913), pp. 150–1.
[2] He expressly mentions Bede's chronological work, the scheme of which clearly determines the chronology of the book. On Bede's doctrine of the *aetates*, cf. W. Levison, 'Bede as Historian', in *Bede, his Life, Times and Writings*, ed. A. Hamilton Thompson, pp. 112–23.

whom Caxton speaks; and perhaps for the literate lady, for she certainly existed generations before the *Boke* was published. One such was the writer who has given her very problematical name to the *Boke*, wherein she is alleged to have been the compiler of the treatise only—certainly not of the treatise on fishing which angling books, excluding Mr Eric Taverner's, still mother upon her. There is nothing to certify that Mistress Juliana Bernes or Barnes, whose name occurs in the *explicit* to the treatise on hunting, the second item in the *Boke*, belonged to the proud family of the Bourchiers, the first lords Berners; or that she became a nun of Sopwell, or was a religious of any brand. The name Bernes, adopted in the *Short Title Catalogue*, was borne by a prominent member of the Mercer's company in the later days of Edward III. John de Bernes, mayor of London in 1370-1, bequeathed to the City a large sum of money to found a chest for relief work: by his will, enrolled in the Court of Hustings in 1375, he directed his property to be sold and the proceeds to be kept in a chest under four keys for the purpose of loans to needy persons, the keys to be kept by the several misteries of the Grocers, Mercers, Drapers, and by the City Chamberlain respectively.[1] (The City did not scruple to borrow £500 from it for defence purposes in 1399.) In the first half of the fifteenth century Berneys (William) is the name borne by a well-known solicitor—if I may so term him— a man who acted as a 'feoffee to use' after the deccase of his clients, some of them notable people like Sir Thomas Colepeper of Sussex.[2] But there is no reason why Berners should be ruled out: in the fifteenth century the names Berners, Bernhus, Bernes, Berneys differ very little, and the indexers of the Close Rolls find it difficult to distinguish between them. There is nothing to rule out Juliana being a Berners, which was also the name of a respectable armigerous family of Ikelingham in Suffolk;[3] at any rate, she appears to have been very much at home with 'gentle' pursuits.

Her identity apart, the attack upon her as an author has been severe. 'The Book of St Albans', Professor Skeat remarked, 'is a mere hash-up of something much older. Most of the hawking and hunting is a translation of the Venerie de Twety of the time

---

[1] *Calendar of Wills proved and enrolled in the Court of Hustings, London,* ed. R. R. Sharpe (1889-90), ii. 180-1.

[2] *Reg. Chichele,* ii. 50, 276, 383-5.

[3] *Cal. Close Rolls, Henry V,* ii (1419-22), 240. Their manor bore that name.

of Edward II.' In view of this rather depressing statement from a classic authority, we might well spend a little time upon the contents and derivation of the *Boke of St Albans*.

It is a compilation devoted to the pursuits and interests of a gentleman, a *generosus* ('country gentleman', for all that the *Boke* contains about dogs and birds, unnecessarily narrows the scope). The first treatise, covering quires *a–d* inclusive—the quires are of eight leaves—is on hawking and the diseases of hawks. 'In so much that gentill men and honest persones have grete delite in hawking and desire to have the maner to take hawkys; and also how and in waat wyse they shulde gyde theym ordynateli: and to know the gentill termys in communyng of theyr hawkys: and to understonde theyr sekeneses and enfirmities. . . . Therfore thys boke fowlowyng in a dew forme shewys veri knawlege of such plesure to gentill men and personys desposed to se itt.' To know the correct terms when you talk falconry, and not be guilty of the infelicities of the ignorant *nouveau riche* sportsman, the type of persons castigated in the cartoons of the Cruickshanks, Leech, and, in much later days, G. D. Armour: this, as in the subsequent treatises, is of supreme importance. The hawking section, whatever its remote derivations—in this country they run from Adelard of Bath and the thirteenth-century treatise in Cambridge University Library, MS. F.F. vi, 13, into a fine crop of later variants—is an elaboration of the work on hawking in Harleian MS. 2340, described as 'the Boke of Hawking after Prince Edward, King of England'. This is written in a hand of the middle fifteenth century, but is certainly earlier than that, and dates from late Edward II or early Edward III. In the Harleian MS. the medical items are largely identical with those of the St Albans *Boke*,[1] but the *Boke* is much more than a veterinary surgeon's guide or a dietary: it gives instructions upon the aviary and how to make it ('how ye shall dispose and ordayn your mewe'): and it concludes with a glossary of technical terms used in hawking. I remember, when a boy at school, one of my fellows explaining to me that the hawker's vocabulary is the most technical and complicated in all the literature of sport. That boy, a passionate falconer, became in time Marshal of the Royal Air Force.

At the end of the section on hawking there is an attractive list of *accipitres*, showing that the hawks had a class system corresponding

---

[1] E.g., 'How the Frounce commyth. The Frounce commyth when a man fedith his hawke withe Porke or Cattisflesh iiii days to geyder.'

with the social strata of medieval society. An Emperor's hawks
are 'an Eagle, a Bawtere, and a Melowne; the simplest of theis
iii will flee a Hynde Calfe, a Fawn, a Fox, a Kydd, an Elke, a
Crane, a Bustard, a Storke, a Swan, a Fox in the playn grownde.
And theis be not enlured ne reclaymed by cause that they be so
ponderowse to the perch portatiff. And theis iii by ther nature
belong to an Emprowre.' The king's hawks are a gerfalcon and a
gerfalcon's tercell. A prince has a 'falcon gentill and a tercell
gentill'; a duke has 'a falcon of the rock'; an earl a peregrine falcon;
a baron a bustard, 'and that is for a Baron'; a knight has a sacret;
a lady a merlin; a young man has a hoby. 'And yet there be more
kinds of hawkys.' There is a goshawk, 'and that hawke is for a
yeoman'; a tercell, 'and that is for a powere man'. Even the clergy
have their hawks: 'there is a Spare hawke' (Sparrow hawk), 'and
he is an hawke for a priest. Ther is a Maskyte, and he is for a
holiwater clerk.'

The treatise on hunting, with which Dame Juliana is specially
associated, is a metricized version of the British translation of
Le Art de Venerie, by Guillaume Twici or Twiti, huntsman to
Edward II. The translation from the Anglo-Norman text, written
before 1328, is found in three manuscripts, Phillipps 8336;
Gonville and Caius College, Cambridge, 424 (described as by
'William Owich'); and Cotton, Vespasian B. XII. In the Cottonian
manuscript, the *Art de Venerie* is followed by a treatise known as
'Master of Game', which in 31 out of its 36 chapters is a translation, with illustrations, of the *Livre de Chasse*, by Gaston de Foix,
begun in May 1387. The 'Master of Game' was compiled by
Edward, second duke of York, Edward III's grandson. It was
printed by Mr Baillie-Grohman in 1904. What Dame Juliana—
if it is she—has done is to take the English translation of Twici,
versify it, and add material from the 'Master of Game'; and it
seems possible that she used the Vespasian text itself, though, of
course, the two treatises may have been found in conjunction
elsewhere. The preface is the schoolmaster's: 'Lyke wise as in the
booke of hawkyng aforesayd are writyn and noted the termys of
plesure belongyng to gentill men havyng delite therin; in thessame
maner thys boke folowyng shewith to sych gentil personys the
maner of huntyng for all maner of beestys, wether thay be beestys
of venery, or of chase, or rascall (vermin). And also it shewith all
the termys convenient as well to the howndys as to the beestys a
forsaid.'

Dame Juliana puts the lore of hunting into the form of an address
to her pupil, giving as her source of information 'Tristram', that
is, Sir Tristram of the Round Table, a mighty hunter and authority
on the chase. Tristram was supposed to have invented the technical terms of hunting, and readers of the *Morte d'Arthur* will
recollect that in youth, after his return from France, whither he
had been sent with Governale 'to lerne the language, and norture
and deeds of arms', he took to music and sport: 'he laboured ever
in huntynge and hawkynge soo that we never rede of no gentylman more that soo used hym therin. And as the book sayth, he
began good mesures of blowynge of beestes of venery and beestes
of chace, and all maner of vermayns; and all these terms we have
got of hawkynge and huntynge is called the book of Syr Trystram.
Wherfore as me semeth, all gentylmen that beren olde armes ough-
ten of ryght to ponder Sir Tristram for the goodly terms that
gentilmen have and are, and shal till the day of dome, that therby
in a maner all men of worship may dyssever a gentylman fro a
yoman, and from a yoman a vylayne. For he that is gentyl wyll
draw hym unto gentyll tatches and to folowe the custome of noble
gentylmen.'[1] No passage could more revealingly portray the
social sentiments of the fifteenth century. These, then, are Dame
Juliana's assumptions, and she begins:

My dere childe take hede how Tristram dooth you tell
How many maner beestys of venery ther were:
Lysten to youre dame and she shall yow lere.

At the outset nomenclature is of great importance. Each beast
'of venery', hart, hare, boar and wolf, has its own special collective
term: deer—that is, hart, hind, buck and doe—go in *herds;*
roes are in *bevies;* pigs in *sounders*, and wolves in *routs*, and she
goes on to define a 'little', a 'middle' and a 'greet' (great) herd
(20, 40 and 80). Of all beasts hunted, the hare is chief:

Now for to speke of the hare my sonnys secureli
That beest kyng shall be calde of all venery

.   .   .   .

For my leif chylder I take it on honde
He is the mervellest beest that is in ony londe.

It is upon the hunting of the hare that Dame Juliana's most

[1] I quote from the Rylands copy of the *Morte d'Arthur*, printed by
Wynkyn de Worde.

o

characteristic lines are found. In the *Venery de Twici* the author
is most of all concerned with horn-blowing—what blast to blow
on what occasions—and, like its author, Juliana deals with the
calls made to the hounds: both writers insist that the calls must
be made in French:

> Now to speke of the haare how all shall be wrought
> When she shall with honndes be foundyn and foght,
> The first word to the houndis that the hunt shall owt pit
> Is at the kenell doore when he openys it.
> That all may hym here: he shall say *'arere!'* ('Back!')
> For his howndes wolde cum to hastely
> That is the first worde my sonne of venery.
> And when he hath couplyd his houndes ychoon (*everyone*),
> And is forth with hem to the felde goon,
> And when he has of cast his cowples at will,
> Then shall he speke and say his howndes till
> *'Hors de couple, avaunt se avant!'*

Then 'so ho! so ho!' thrice; and then 'sa sa, cy avant!' And so
forth. If you want them to go more slowly and quietly, you say
'Sweff, mon amy, sweff!' There is much good observation in the
stanzas which explain why the hunted deer makes for water. From
this point onwards the dependence of the text on the *Master of
Game* is evident, for the teaching the dame gives to her child is
replaced by a dialogue between master and man. The man speaks:

> (*Man*)   Yit wolde I witt maister whi theys houndes all
>   Bayen and cryen when thay hym (the hare) cache shall.

> (*Master*) For thay wolde have helpe that is thayr skylle
>   For to flee the beest that thay reune tyll.

>   Tell me mayster, quod the man, what is the skyll
>   Why the haare woolde so faynne renne ayenest the hill?

>   Quod the mayster: 'for his leggys be shorter befoore
>   Then behynde: that is the skyll of yoore'.

But the dame and her child return in the last stanzas, where we
are reminded of the more utilitarian aspect of hunting in the
elaborate instructions for dismembering and trussing the boar
or deer when killed. While hunting was essentially a 'gentle'
(i.e. a non-mercenary) pursuit, it aimed also at stocking the larder,
and according to Dame Juliana's receipts, no part of the deer

should be wasted. The culinary instructions 'to my childe' are minute and certainly outdo Mrs Beeton. Possibly the 'child' might find this the most valuable part of the treatise: perhaps a better reason than the hawking and hunting patter for acquiring the Boke.

Our fifteenth-century literature abounds in proverbs, adages, comparisons.[1] Immediately after Dame Juliana's *explicit* the schoolmaster has filled up the remaining leaves of the quire with amusing trifles.: Beasts of the chase that are 'sweet and stinking': the properties of a good greyhound—'headed like a snake, necked like a drake, footed like a cat, tailed like a rat, sided like a teme,[2] chined like a beam'. The properties of a good horse, which are worth quoting:

> A goode hors shulde have xv propertees and condicions.
> It is to wit, iii of a man, ii of a woman, iii of a fox,
> iii of an haare and iii of an asse.
> Off a man, boolde, prowde, and hardy.
> Off a woman, fayre brestid, faire of here, and esy to lip upon.
> Off a fox, a faire tayle, short eris with a good trot.
> Off an haare a grete eyghe, a dry hede and well rennyng.
> Off an asse a bigge chyne, a flatte leg and good houe (hock).

And various maxims:

> Arise erly, serve God devouteli, and the world besily: doo thy werke wiseli; Yeue thyn almese secretly. Go by the way sadly. Answere the peple demurely. Go to thi mete appetideli. Sit ther at descretely. Of thi tonge be not to liberalli. Arrise therfrom temperatly. Goo to thi soper soborly, and to thy bedde merely. Be in thyn Inne jocundely, plese thy love duly, and slepe surely.[3]

After these diversions, the printer's method of filling space,[4] the longest treatise of the Boke of St Albans is reached—the *Liber Armorum*, divided into two parts: the heraldic definition of a gentleman, both by descent and by coat armour; and the main principles observed in the blazing of arms, a brief explanation

---

[1] For such proverbs and precepts, before 1400, cf. J. E. Wells, *A Manual of the Writings in Middle English, 1050–1400*, ch. vii and supplements.

[2] The (taut) main chain of the plough.

[3] For earlier sets, cf. Wells, op. cit., p. 379.

[4] Another example is his insertion of a list of collective terms: e.g., a pride of lions; a litter of whelps; a superfluity of nuns; a blush of boys; an 'uncredibility' of cuckolds, etc.

of heraldic terms, illustrated by examples. For this *Liber* there are two distinct sources: the *De officio militari* of Nicholas Upton, canon of Salisbury, from which the schoolmaster copied Book IV; and the English 'Book of the Lineage of Coat Armour', a fifteenth-century compilation.

There is no need to expatiate upon the importance of heraldry as a subject of polite study and speculation in the later Middle Ages. In the fifteenth century it aroused absorbing interest. If to the minds of Malory and Caxton (who printed a translation of the *Ordeyne*) chivalry had a moral value for its inculcation of the free and knightly qualities, heraldry was the formal way of displaying the gentle lineage which to contemporary minds disposed a man towards such virtue.[1] Here it is only worth noting that the organization of the Office of Arms dates from the late fourteenth to early fifteenth century: that great cases in the Court of Chivalry when arms were in dispute, like the Grey-Hastings suit, evoked widespread comment; and that the revival of the French war by Henry V invited heraldic interest in the captains and their retinues of well-born retainers. Fifty years later Edward IV's expedition to France was to have its personnel portrayed in a College of Arms manuscript which gives each leader his badge, and is as much a heraldic document as a muster roll.[2] But to return to Henry V: on the Close Roll under 2 June 1417, stands a royal letter addressed to the sheriffs of Hampshire, Wiltshire, Sussex and Dorset. In recent expeditions abroad, it stated, many persons had taken to themselves arms and tunics of arms called 'coat armours' (a reference to the tabard, the descendant of the military jupon), when neither they nor their ancestors had used such armour in the past. The sheriffs were accordingly to proclaim that nobody must assume or bear arms unless they had a right to the same, either by descent or by the grant of some person with sufficient authority: and that all, save only those who fought at Agincourt[3] should, under pain of exclusion from the expedition (Henry was preparing for the second Norman campaign), show on a certain day warrant for the arms they bore.[4] The writ instituted a little

[1] Thus Richard Ullerston, in his 'De officio militari', dedicated to Henry V, maintains the connexion between noble birth and virtue.
[2] Ed. F. P. Barnard (Oxford, 1925).
[3] 'This day shall gentle his condition', as Shakespeare makes Henry V (most historically) say.
[4] *Cal. Close Rolls, Henry V*, i (1413–19), 433.

inquiry into the arms borne by the newcomers in his expeditionary force.

It betrays the hand of the Duke of Clarence who, between 1417 and 1421—i.e. during the second campaign which ended in the conquest of Normandy and the Treaty of Troyes—made for the Kings of Arms and the Heralds a group of ordinances that defined their duties in a most interesting way. The first chapter of the Office of Arms actually took place in the field before Rouen, while the siege was still in progress, on 5 January 1420. The three kings of Arms and four heralds were present.[1] The ordinances direct that Garter King of Arms and the other kings in their own provinces, shall get knowledge of all noblemen and gentlemen, and especially of those who ought to bear coats in the service of the king, his lieutenant, and their commissaries, and register their names, arms and issues with proper differences. The herald is not to make a grant of arms without the licence of the first King of Arms: officers of arms are to frequent good company and to apply themselves to the study of books of good manners and eloquence, of chronicles and accounts of honourable deeds of arms and of the properties of colours, herbs and stones, so that they may be able, justly and suitably, to assign to each person, the arms that belong to him.[2] The granting of arms is therefore essentially the reception of a man 'en l'estat de gentil homme'. Clarence's instructions bore fruit later in the *Libellus de Militari Officio*, by Nicholas Upton, canon of Salisbury, written some time before 1434–40, and dedicated to Clarence's brother, Humphrey, Duke of Gloucester. Upton, in his salad days, had fought with Thomas Montague, Suffolk and Talbot in France, and when Humphrey encouraged him to take Orders after 1430, his mind went back to the pennons flown in the great expedition, and how it was necessary for a good herald to recognize each banner and coat of arms and to make personal note of all who were in 'l'estat de gentil homme'. (In 1389 Richard II, by grant of arms, had received John of Kingston into the estate of gentleman, and had made him an *armiger*, in order that he might challenge and be challenged by a French opponent.[3]) After the ordinances were issued, the heralds could confer the status of

---

[1] A. R. Wagner, *Heralds and Heraldry in the Middle Ages* (1956), p. 64.

[2] Ibid., p. 60 f.

[3] *C.P.R., 1388–1392*, p. 72.

gentleman, if their chief authority permitted; thus it was an authoritative guide on the nature of knighthood and gentility, on war-like exercise, on the 'noble' colours, and on the details of the shield and coat, that the canon of Salisbury penned with an astonishing list of citations, not least from the Canon Law. The *Boke of St Albans* is not so well arranged nor so scientific; for the colours it substitutes precious stones; for the discourse on nobility it inserts a little mythology from the Trojan wars which, in Lydgate's other English version, might be said to form the 'chronicles and accounts of honourable deeds of arms'; for the Trojan legend, equally with the Arthurian cycle, provided the historical background, so to speak, for the profession of arms and the exercise of the chivalric virtues.[1] They were the source of the 'joyous and pleysaunt historyes' which were written 'for our doctrine'; whereas, as Mallory said, 'to give faythe and byleve that all is true that is contained therin, ye be at your liberty'. We shall never understand the historian in the Middle Ages if we forget that his work was written as much to entertain and divert, as to constitute an objective record.

The *Liber Armorum* in the Boke first sets out to distinguish gentleness from ungentleness. All gentleness comes of God in Heaven. There were originally in Heaven ten orders of Angels bearing coat armour, but there are now only nine. For Lucifer with 'mylionys of Angels' has fallen out of Heaven into 'other places'. Just as a gentleman might say that all men come from Adam, so also might Lucifer say that he and all his Angels came from Heaven. Adam himself was, so to speak, neutral: 'a stock unsprayed and unflourished'. In the earlier stages gentleness was not quite hereditary: in the sons of Adam and Eve were to be found both gentleman and churl.

How then shall gentlemen be known from churls? There is, first of all, ancestry. Cain, for his evil conduct, was the first churl, and all his descendants were churls because of his unfraternal behaviour. On the other hand, Adam's son Seth was made a gentleman through the person of his father and mother. Noah was a gentleman 'of kynde', but of his three sons, 'Sem, Cham and Jafeth', Cham became a churl because 'ungentleness was found to his own father'. On account of his regrettable and unfilial

---

[1] For the significance of the Trojan legend in England, and its connexion with the Arthurian, cf. A. E. Parsons, 'The Trojan Legend in England', *Modern Language Review*, vol. 24, pp. 253 f., 394 f.

behaviour Noah cursed him and gave him the north part of the
world for his habitation. He was to dwell where there was sorrow
and care, cold and mischief, in the third part of the world, which
should be called Europe, that is to say, the country of churls.
Jafeth, on the other hand, was given the best part of the world,
the part where wealth and grace should be, in other words,
Asia, that is to say, the country of gentlemen. Addressing 'Sem'
Noah promised that he should be a gentleman, and take the
Orient, 'that other part of the world which is called Africa, that
is to say, the country of tempurness': by which it will be clear that
the Flood must have somewhat confounded Noah's sense of
geography. At all events, of the offspring of the gentleman
Jafeth came Abraham, Moses and Aaron, and the prophets, and
also the King of the right line of Mary, of whom that gentleman
Jesus was born, very God and man; 'after his manhood, king of the
land of Judah and of Jews, a gentleman by his mother Mary, and
Prince of Coat Armour'.

The origins of coat armour was then sought. It was made and
figured at the siege of Troy, where 'in *Gestis Troianorum*, it telleth
that the first begynnyng of the Law of Arms was'. This existed
before any law in the world save the Law of Nature, and before
the ten commandments of God. Now this Law of Arms was granted
upon the nine Orders of Angels in Heaven each Order 'encrowned'
with precious stones and divers virtues: and so follows a little
lapidary or account of the virtues of precious stones, a favourite
form of Anglo-Norman literature. Topaz stands for truth, emerald
for hardiness, amethyst for chivalry. Each of these stones, with
their virtues, represents the hierarchy of gentleness: Gentleman,
Squire, Knight, Baron, Lord, Earl, Marquis, Duke and Prince.
Everthing now proceeds in nines: the nine articles of gentleness,
and the nine vices that make against gentleness. The articles of
gentleness are divided into five 'amorous' and four 'sovereign'.
The five 'amorous' attributes are to be lordly of countenance,
'treteable' in language, wise in answer, perfect in governance and
'cheerful to faithfulness' (doing tasks cheerfully). The four
sovereign gentlenesses are these—few oaths in swearing; 'buxom
to God's bidding'; 'knowing his own birth in bearing' (in his
bearing), and 'to dread to offend his sovereign'. The vices are
divided into determinable and indeterminable. Determinable are
predicates of action at a particular crisis or occasion. Indeterminable are: 'to be full of sloath in war, to be full of boost in his man-

hood, to be full of cowardice to his enemy, to be full of lechery in his body'; the fifth to be 'full of drinking and drunkenly'. The four determinable vices: 'to revoke his own challenge, to slay his prisoners with his own hand, to void from his sovereign's banner in the field, and fifthly, to tell his sovereign false tales'.

Though coat armour can be traced back to the siege of Troy, the source of so many institutions, knighthood existed before then and a greater institution before that. 'Know ye that these two orders were, first, wedlock, and then knighthood', and knighthood was made before coat armour was ordained. The first knight was Olibion, son of Afteryall, whom Afteryall 'smote flattyng' with his son's sword nine times in token of the nine virtues. But knights can be made not only with the sword, but with the bath—and the bath is 'worthiest by cause of 4 royalties'— that means because the bath is used on four occasions in the ceremonial life of a king—when as a young man he is knighted: when a king or emperor is crowned or when a queen or empress is crowned; and at a meeting of sovereigns. But gentleness *can* be acquired: it is not entirely inherited. A man may receive a grant of armour by one of the Heralds: he may have a lordship conferred upon him 'by seal of patent to him and his heirs for ever': or he may wear the coat armour of a Saracen whom he has slain on Crusade. There may also be a gentleman spiritual—a churl may so be 'a gentleman to God and not of blood'. But of course an ecclesiastic may also be a gentleman by birth. If a gentleman's son be made priest, he is a gentleman both spiritual and temporal. Christ was a gentleman of his mother by value, and bore coat armour of ancestors; the four evangelists had gentle ancestry, sprung as they were from Judas Maccabaeus; but after his death his kin 'fell to labours and were called no gentlemen'. The four doctors of Holy Church, however, were 'gentlemen of blood and coat armour'.

Then follows the second part of the treatise on the actual blazing of arms, which, as I said, is simply translated from Nicholas Upton. Yet it would be an error to undervalue its utility. For the herald of an important noble (and the Wars of the Roses had by no means killed off the nobility and gentry of England, as is sometimes thought), the recognition of arms was an essential matter. The rolls of arms exhibited at the Birmingham Exhibition of Heraldry (1936), many preserved at the College of Arms, display the sixteenth century as, perhaps, an even more heraldic century than the fifteenth; and when we recollect that the first twenty-five years saw the hey-day of the memorial brass in which coats of arms figure predominantly, and consider the number of sepulchral monuments bearing the shields of deceased justice, baron of the Exchequer, or shire knight, and the heraldic glass that filled the windows of so many collegiate and parish churches, we shall think of the early Tudor age as no pallid aftermath of the Middle Ages, but their fruition, in an atmosphere of greater order and security.

In Wynkyn de Worde's edition of the *Boke of St Albans*, 1496, the explicit of the Treatise of Coat Armour runs thus:

Here we shall make an end of the moost specyll things of the boke of the lyngage of cote armurys: and how gentlemen shall be known from ungentlemen. And consequently shall followe a compendyous treatyse of fysshyng with an angle which is right necessary to be had in this present volume: because it sheweth afore the manere of hawking and hunting with other divers matters right necessary to be knowen of noble men,[1] and also for it is one of the disportes that gentylmen use. And also it is not soo laborious ne soo dishonest to fysshe in this wyse as it is with nettes and other engynes which crafty men do use for theyr daily increase of goods.

Why did Mr Gordon Duff, in transcribing this explicit, insert the little word *sic* after laborious? Surely the whole point of the insertion of the treatise in the Book is its 'gentle' character. The 'gentle art' does not mean that fishing is a mild and recreational sort of pastime: it means that it is the pastime of 'gentil' men, that is, of people who do not swink and sweat, or have to get their living by the gross methods of the net and the 'otter': 'laborious' and 'dishonest' are the terms used of 'craftymen', i.e., craftsmen and mechanics, who employ various engines and devices to extract fish out of the rivers for a living.

The treatise therefore has no connexion with Dame Juliana Berners, Bernes, Barnes, or Bernhus. But it is prior to the *Boke of St Albans*. In its earliest surviving form it—or the greater part of it—is contained in a privately owned manuscript[2] written on five sheets of paper folded in quarto form; and the paper has the watermark of a gloved hand, which, along with the character of the script, points to the first half of the fifteenth century as the

---

[1] I.e., in the sections which precede the part devoted to fishing.

[2] Formerly in the Denison Collection: later sold to America, where it is [or was], the late Mr Murgatroyd told me, in the possession of Mr David Walker, Tuxedo Park, New York State.

P

period of writing. The original extends as far as the instructions
on trout fishing, and finishes with the section on the bait to be
used in September. When compared with the Treatise as printed
in the *Boke of St Albans*, there is, as the editor of the edition of the
Boke published in 1810 observed, the customary difference of
orthography, and there are three instances of variations in the
introductory matter: there are also, as the more recent editor of
the early fragment has pointed out, various gaps which the Treatyse fills:[1] thus suggesting that what we have called the 'earliest
surviving form' is not the original, but a copy from a more complete text, from which Wynkyn de Worde printed:

Treatise (before 1420).

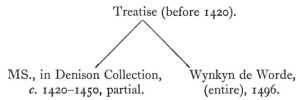

MS., in Denison Collection,   Wynkyn de Worde,
   c. 1420–1450, partial.   (entire), 1496.

It is a delightful treatise in the true English style: that is, it
begins with an appreciation of the scenes and the country which
fishermen writers from Izaak Walton to Lord Grey have so
enjoyed: but in a way which contrasts fishing with noisier and
more breathless pastimes: and a nice vein of humour it shows:

> For huntyng as to myne entent is to gret labur. The hunter must all
> day renne and folow hys houndes, travelyng and swetyng fal soyr he
> blowythe tyl hys lyppys blyster, and wen he wenyt [*thinks*] hyt be a
> hare, ful often hit ys a heyghoge. Thus he chaset, and wen he cummet
> home at even, reyn beton, seyr prykud with thornes and hys clothes
> tornes, wet schod fulwy som of hys howndes some surbatted [*footsore*],
> suche grevys and meny oþer to the hunter hapeth wiche for displesous
> of hem þat loueth hyt I dare not report all.[2]

Now it will be recalled that in the *Complete Angler*, Part I,
Chapter 1, Piscator (that is, Walton), as he goes along, meets a
hunter and a hawker and argues with them. Each makes a speech
extolling his own sport, the hawker praising the beauty and
significance of the flight of birds, circling in the upper regions so
that they are 'lost in the sight of men, and attend upon and con-
verse with the gods'; the hunter, eulogizing hunting as a game for

[1] *An Older Form of the 'Treatyse of Fysshynge wyth an angle'*, ed. T.
Satchell (1883), pp. ii–iv.
[2] *Treatyse*, p. 2.

Salamon in his parablys sayth that a good spyryte makyth a flourynge aege: that is a fayre aege & a longe. And syth it is soo: I aske this questyon:. Whiche ben the meanes & the causes that enduce a man in to a mery spyryte.: Truly to my beste dyscrecõn it semeth good dysportes & honest gamys in whom a man Joyeth wythout ony repentannce after. Thenne folowyth it ꝑ go ꝛ de dysportes & honest games ben cause of mannys fayr aege & longe life. And therfore now woll I chose of foure good dyspoꝛ tes & honeste gamys: that is to wyte:of huntynge:hawkynge: fysshynge:& foulynge. The beste to my symple dyscrecõn why che is fysshynge : callyd Anglynge wyth a rodde : and a lyne

The Book of St Albans, woodcut of an angler

princes ('Hunting trains up the younger nobility to the use of manly exercise in their riper age'), and for the excellence of the dogs employed. Then Piscator, who hopes that he will not perpetrate a watery discourse, praises water as the eldest daughter of Creation, the element upon which the spirit of God did first move: and as the source of 'daily traffic and adventure'. But Piscator also claims angling is an art. 'Is it not an art to deceive a trout with an artificial fly? A trout that is more sharp sighted than any hawk you have named, and more watchful and timorous than your high mettled Merlin is bold? And yet I doubt not to catch a brace or two to-morrow, for a friend's breakfast: doubt not therefore, sir, but that Angling is an art, and an art worth your learning: the question is rather, whether you be capable of learning it? For Angling is somewhat like poetry, men are to be born so.'

Our fifteenth-century treatise does not, as Walton did, speak of the antiquity of fishing, which some (Mr Radcliffe among them) say is as ancient as Deucalion's flood. It goes straight to the practical question of how to make your tackle (for the fisherman had no Hardy or Farlow to rely upon, and all tackle had to be made at home): the rod, in two pieces, of hazel, willow or ash; the line, which must be coloured to suit the nature of the water (as we to-day camouflage casts), and—'the moost hardyste craft in making of your harnays'—the hooks; the line of plaited horse hair, one strand for the roach, the bleak and the gudgeon; nine strands (too thick!) for the trout, grayling and the barbel—this shows that in the fifteenth century trout ran larger than to-day— fifteen hairs plaited for the salmon. The treatise gives some valuable practical advice on concealment:

And for the principall poynt of anglyng kepe you ever from þe watur and from the syzt of fyche fer [far] on the londe or els be hynde a busche or a tre þat þe fysche see you not, for yf he do he wyl not bytte, and loke ye shadow not the watur as moche as ye may for hyt ys a thynhe [thing] wyche wyl a fray þe fyche and yf he be a frayd he wyl not byt a good while aftur.[1]

The *dubbed hook* is the fly; the treatise enumerates twelve methods of dressing the artificial fly; and if these be compared with Walton's *Complete Angler*, Part I, Chapter V, it will be seen that Walton's twelve patterns are the same, for they are taken,

[1] *Treatyse*, p. 17.

body, wings and all, from the Treatise, with occasional obscurities left out. Thus:

The Treatise: *June:* The mauve fly, the body of dusk wool and the wings of the blackest mail of the wild drake. The tandy fly at Saint Wyllyam's day. The body of tandy wull and wynges contrary eyther ayenst another of the whitest mayle of the wilde drake.

Walton: *June:* The eighth is the Moorish fly: made with the body of darkish wool, and the wings make of the blackish mail of the drake. The ninth is the tawny fly, good until the middle of June: the body made of tawny wool, the wings made contrary one against the other, made of the whitish mail of the wild drake.

Walton has therefore copied and made more intelligible the instructions in the Treatise, embodied in the Book of St Albans: but he has got St William of York wrong: his day is 8 June. Perhaps, however, he got a good fish on the tawny fly (evidently one of the sedges) about the 15th of that month. The fact of this copying and adaptation, to which both Mr R. B. Marston and Mr Eric Taverner have called attention, should not diminish our delight in the charming author of the best nature book of the seventeenth century.

This, then, is the *Boke of St Albans,* and its later addendum with which Dame Juliana Berners is by a sort of historico-poetic licence connected. Let it be so. Whoever she was, she must have been admirably attuned to country sights and sounds: the *too-root* of the horn, the music of the deep-voiced and long-eared hounds, the fluttering of hawks into the dappled sky. The Middle Ages shall yet remain for us a time of glamour and joyfulness, even if the overworked archdeacon or the laborious crofter did not always find them so. This does not prevent our tracing the derivation of things, and learning that our medieval ancestors had no literary copyright, took what suited their purpose, and published it for the service of those who could use it best.

Index